As the world wakes up to the need for more natural and environmentally friendly living, so, too, are we pursuing new and more holistic ways to care for our animals. Today's options range from natural foods and products that are free of byproducts and chemicals to a myriad of holistic healing modalities. This groundbreaking, holistic dog-care book tells you about:

- ACUPUNCTURE FOR ARTHRITIS AND HIP DYSPLASIA
- REAL BONES AND HOMEMADE BISCUITS THAT ARE GOOD FOR YOUR DOG
- WHAT IS WRONG WITH RAWHIDE
- RAW FOODS YOU COULD FEED YOUR DOG
- THE BEST FLEA-REPELLING RINSE AFTER A BATH
- HOW *YOUR* STRESS CAN MAKE YOUR DOG SICK
- NOSODES AS AN ALTERNATIVE TO VACCINATIONS
- TREATING ALLERGIES WITHOUT CORTISONE
- HOW GARLIC CAN BENEFIT YOUR DOG
- THE WORST DOG FOOD YOU CAN BUY—AND THE BEST
- THE WAYS TO HELP YOUR DOG RECOVER FROM SURGERY
- THE SYMPTOMS OF A SICK DOG . . . AND MUCH MORE

Mary L. Brennan, D.V.M., runs a holistic veterinary practice in Georgia specializing in small animals and horses. She is a member of the American Veterinarian Association and lives in Atlanta. **Norma Eckroate** coauthored *The New Natural Cat* with Anitra Frazier. She lives in Los Angeles.

THE NATURAL DOG

A *Complete Guide for Caring Owners*

MARY L. BRENNAN, D.V.M.
with Norma Eckroate

Illustrated by Glenna Hartwell

A PLUME BOOK

PUBLISHER'S NOTE

The information in this book is not intended as a substitute for consulting your veterinarian. Any attempt to diagnose and treat an illness should be done under the direction of a veterinarian, preferably one who is holistically oriented. Neither the publisher nor the authors are responsible for any adverse effects or consequences resulting from the use of any of the suggestions, preparations, procedures, or recipes in this book.

PLUME
Published by the Penguin Group
Penguin Books USA Inc., 375 Hudson Street, New York, New York 10014, U.S.A.
Penguin Books Ltd, 27 Wrights Lane, London W8 5TZ, England
Penguin Books Australia Ltd, Ringwood, Victoria, Australia
Penguin Books Canada Ltd, 10 Alcorn Avenue, Toronto, Ontario, Canada M4V 3B2
Penguin Books (N.Z.) Ltd, 182–190 Wairau Road, Auckland 10, New Zealand

Penguin Books Ltd, Registered Offices: Harmondsworth, Middlesex, England

First published by Plume, an imprint of Dutton Signet,
a division of Penguin Books USA Inc.

First Printing, January, 1994
10 9 8 7 6 5 4

EXCERPTS REPRINTED FROM:

Free Radicals, Stress and Antioxidant Enzymes—A Guide to Cellular Health by Peter R. Rothschild, M.D., Ph.D., and Zane Baranowski, C.N., published by University Labs Press. Second revised edition copyright 1990, Peter Rothschild and Zane Baranowski. Reprinted by arrangement with Zane Baranowski.
Los Angeles Times article, "No Pests, No Poisons" by Karen Dardick. Copyright 1992 by Karen Dardick. Reprinted by arrangement with Karen Dardick.
The No Barking at the Table Cookbook by Wendy Boyd-Smith. Copyright 1991 by Wendy Boyd-Smith. Reprinted by arrangement with Lip Smackers, Inc., P.O. Box 5385, Culver City, CA 90231-5385.
The Puppy Report by Larry Shook. Copyright 1992 by Larry Shook. Reprinted by arrangement with Lyons & Burford, Publishers, 31 West 21st Street, New York, NY 10010.

REGISTERED TRADEMARK—MARCA REGISTRADA

LIBRARY OF CONGRESS CATALOGING-IN-PUBLICATION DATA:
Brennan, Mary L.
The natural dog : a complete guide for caring owners / Mary L. Brennan, with Norma Eckroate ; illustrated by Glenna Hartwell.
p. cm.
Includes bibliographical references and index.
ISBN 0-452-27019-7
1. Dogs. 2. Dogs—Health. I. Eckroate, Norma, 1951– II. Title.
SF427.B75 1993
636.7'0887—dc20 93-3938
CIP

Printed in the United States of America
Set in Palatino

This book is dedicated to all of my dog friends
who have so generously taught me over the years.

Acknowledgments

The authors give heartfelt thanks to:

Kelly and Lily, constant supervisors and advisors, who stamped their paw of approval on every page in the process of writing this book

Carol and David Stenstrom, who introduced us, certain we would make a great team to write this book

Michelle Tilghman, D.V.M., a colleague and a friend, whose help on this book was invaluable

John Ottaviano, O.M.D., a wonderful teacher

Sandra Martin and Stephany Evans, agents extraordinaire

Rosemary Ahern, our supportive editor

Matt Sartwell, whose encouragement made this book a reality

Glenna Hartwell, whose art makes our book come alive

Alfred J. Plechner, D.V.M., Brian Moore, D.V.M., Susan Thorpe-Vargas, Sharon Sherman, Andi Brown, Jeff Bennett, Jim Gidlow, and the hundreds of experts dedicated to natural care of dogs to whom we are indebted

Contents

Introduction

As the world wakes up to the need for more natural and environmentally friendly living, so, too, are we pursuing new and more holistic ways to care for our animals. Today's options range from natural foods and products that are free of byproducts and chemicals to a myriad of holistic healing modalities.

I find that people often get sidetracked by the word *natural*. Many health-conscious people don't realize that just because something is "100 percent natural" does not mean that it is always perfectly safe to use. For example, pyrethrum powder, an insecticide used to combat fleas, is derived from chrysanthemums. You could certainly say that it is totally natural; in small amounts it is also fairly safe. However, concentrated doses of pyrethrum powder are toxic. Many dog groomers who use the powder daily become sick from exposure to this "natural" product. Digitalis, the heart medication that is isolated from foxglove (an herb) is also natural. However, digitalis must be carefully administered; an overdose could kill a dog or a person.

There's an old saying that a little bit of knowledge can be dangerous. While there are many natural foods and products that are totally safe, it's important that we educate ourselves before using any product.

Natural care goes beyond foods and products. Holistic veterinarians offer valuable choices in health care. We have all of the tools of allopathic medicine (traditional Western medicine) as well as numerous other healing modalities such as acupuncture, homeopathy, herbal medicine, and such. Although allopathic medicine relies to a great extent on pharmaceutical drugs, with their many negative side effects, most holistic healing modalities have only positive side effects. However, the main difference in efficacy is that holistic modalities usually treat the *cause* of health problems whereas allopathic medicine treats the *symptoms.* When you treat the symptoms rather than the cause, you can be assured that further health problems will, in all likelihood, arise in the future.

There is a time and a place for allopathic medicine, and I am grateful that the options of surgery and pharmaceutical drugs are right there when I need them. In emergency situations drugs can literally save a life. Additionally, I find that some natural treatments are not yet perfected to the point where they are 100 percent effective. I live in the South where parasite and skin problems are rampant and can be life-threatening. Some drugs and vaccinations are necessary to combat these diseases and health problems. I will be grateful when more natural products are perfected for problems such as heartworm, rabies, and intestinal parasites, but at present I must use some of the pharmaceutical alternatives.

We have taken on the responsibility of caring for the animals we have domesticated so they can share our lives. That is no small responsibility. It is one that we take on willingly and happily, however, grateful for what the animals give us. Some of the habits and bodily requirements of dogs are still very close to what Mother Nature intended, and we must honor these traits.

My holistic veterinary practice extends to both small and large animals—primarily dogs, cats, and horses. You probably won't be surprised that my own household currently includes two dogs, Kelly and Lily; two cats, Cris and Twisty; and one horse, Charlie. However, because this is a book on dog care, I'll tell you mainly about Kelly and Lily in the pages that follow.

It is my heartfelt desire that you and your dog will benefit from the information in this book. May it serve you and bring both quality and longevity to the life of your beloved canine friend.

PART ONE

The Natural Approach

1

The Right Dog for You

As many of us have experienced, the bond with an animal companion can be very special. From snuggling up to your feet on a cold night to protecting a home, dogs have a special place in millions of lives. When a dog with the right personality and temperament is combined with the individual or family able to meet that dog's needs, the result is often a marriage made in heaven. But not every dog is right for every home. Among the many breeds and mixed-breed dogs available, it's important to find the one that's right for you.

Before adopting it's imperative that you understand the commitment you are making. Feeding, training, grooming, and trips to the veterinarian are all commitments of both time and money. Also, when you bring a dog into your home, that dog makes a lifelong commitment to you. Are you ready, willing, and able to return that commitment? It's unfortunate that so many people adopt dogs in haste. When that happens, sadly, the dogs often wind up at the animal shelter when the novelty wears off and the demands of dog owning become apparent.

Are you ready to make these commitments? If so, let's start from the beginning in considering the type of dog that's suitable for you. If you don't already have a dog, why do you want one? Do you want a pet and companion to share your life? Does this dog need to be a watchdog as well? Do you have children? Do you have a yard or live in an apartment?

Choosing the Right Breed or Mixed Breed

Often a person's favorite breed of dog is not suitable for his or her circumstances. I advise writing down all the expectations you have for the dog in your life and then considering which breeds, or mixes of breeds, will best meet your requirements. Some basic criteria to consider include the level of exercise and grooming care needed and the breed's suitability to urban settings such as apartment life. If you have children, you'll want a dog who interacts well with them. For example, one of my favorite breeds, the wire-haired fox terrier, would not fit well into my life. While I adore their energy, perky attitude, and terrier feistiness, I don't have enough time to properly exercise a terrier.

My two poodles, Kelly, a miniature, and Lily, a toy, are perfect companions, great travelers, and socialize well with other dogs. They seem to have infinite patience, waiting in my office or car long hours while I work, tolerating the shortest of exercise periods, and acting as great watchdogs. Well, at least Kelly is a great watchdog. Kelly and Lily go everywhere with me, taking their jobs as veterinary assistants seriously.

Recently, while I was the veterinarian on call at a horse show, I was sitting in my truck with the two dogs. Right in front of us a horse had a terrible accident. I instinctively leapt out of the truck and rushed to care for the horse. I returned 30 minutes later to find that in my hurry I had left the truck door open. There sat the two girls, patiently waiting for my return—they had been told earlier that they could not get out of the truck. They had also barked and growled at anyone trying to shut the door, so it remained open. I would not deliberately test a dog in this manner, but I was very relieved that after years of training Kelly and Lily had reacted in such a responsible manner.

Breeds can only be considered for their general characteristics, since there are exceptions or exceptional individuals in all breeds. It is even possible that there might be a terrier somewhere that could fit into my lifestyle, but it would not be a terrier who is typical of the breed.

Before looking for that perfect dog, it's a good idea to get a clear idea of your expectations, both physically and psychologically. Everyone has a different personal relationship with his or her dog and each dog has a different capacity to fulfill an owner's expectations. For instance, don't expect a poodle to react the same as a Great Dane in a given situation.

Even if you plan to get a mixed-breed dog from an animal shelter (which I heartily endorse), a basic knowledge of the type of breeds that would work for you will help to narrow your focus. In most cases, even with puppies, the mixed-breed dogs will be described by the two or three breeds that predominate. Falling for the first set of beautiful eyes or bundle of cuteness won't serve either you or the dog if you aren't able to provide the right environment. It's not a service to take the wrong dog home if you just won't be able to give it what it needs.

What about getting a mutt? Mixed-breed dogs are readily available for adoption, usually at a very low cost. They make wonderful pets and have interesting, less predictable appearances. How should you go about selecting a mixed-breed dog? Some mixed breeds have one breed that stands out. For instance, collie or shepherd or terrier may clearly predominate. Others are the result of many generations of mixed breeds and are truly mutts. With a mixed breed, the dog's characteristics and instinct are unknown factors. Since you will have no breed criteria to guide you, you'll have to use your common sense. Here are some criteria to look for:

- Bright, clear eyes
- Walking and running without difficulty
- Healthy skin and hair
- A friendly personality; not aggressive or growling
- A size that's right for you and your lifestyle

If you're looking at a mixed-breed puppy, check it as you would a purebred—looking for normal eyes, legs, toes, tail, and so on. In general, select one that matches the size and basic type you have in mind. Remember, though, unless you have the advantage of meeting both the mother and father of the puppy, it may be difficult to determine how large the puppy will be as an adult. If at all possible, take the dog you are considering to your veterinarian before finalizing the adoption.

There are many books available on different breeds. Study the breeds to better understand the characteristics of the breeds you are most interested in. You might also want to attend dog shows, talk to breeders, and discuss your questions with a veterinarian to help you decide. If you already own a dog, a study of the breed might help you better understand your dog.

One of my clients could not understand why her male husky roamed away from home. I explained to her that huskies, particularly males, have a tendency to roam and will usually do so if given the opportunity. After this discussion, she was more aware of her dog's basic instincts and was able to work out ways to deal with him more effectively.

Another common complaint I hear is: "Why won't my dog stay out of the pool?" This problem is most often encountered by the owners of hunting dogs, specifically those bred to retrieve in the water. Labradors and golden retrievers are especially attracted to pools, but many breeds love the water.

Different breeds respond and interact differently with people. I am accustomed to the quick response and large vocabulary of words that my poodles understand in day-to-day interaction. Some of my friends do not feel comfortable with this, preferring instead a dog who is content with playing ball and needing little personal interaction.

If you want a dog who is a good protector for your home, consider a breed that is respected on sight such as the Doberman or German shepherd, and one that is easy to train.

When dealing with the working breeds, such as herding dogs, the focus of intelligence is different, because they are usually quick, responsive dogs that were bred to be in control of situations, such as herding sheep. But this instinctual ability to herd other animals can become an undesirable trait if your dog starts to chase other dogs, people, or cars. In trying to herd people, these dogs often nip at the heels in the process. Do not misinterpret this as overaggressive behavior. It's instinctual with them. When well trained, this innate intelligence can be put to other uses. Most of the herding breeds make excellent obedience dogs, but if their intelligence is not challenged, they will often use it in whatever way they can, frequently in managing the household (whether the owner realizes it or not).

Shelties are particularly good at running households. While giving a talk a short time ago to a shelty club, I made the comment that shelties train their owners well. The club members laughed and all agreed that this is true. They went on to relate numerous stories of how their shelties took over in various domestic situations.

After you have decided on the personal characteristics that are important to you, it is time to consider the finer details. What breed would best fit into your lifestyle? How much time will you be able to spend with this dog? Where will the dog stay? Do you have a safe fenced yard or will your dog be confined to an apartment most of the time? Are you able to devote daily grooming time to your dog or do you need a dog whose grooming needs are minimal? What are your expectations of the dog? The answer to each of these questions is highly individualized.

Another factor to consider is how much time you plan to spend with your dog. If you work during the day, you will have to allow time in your schedule for the dog. Some people take a morning walk with their dog, combining their own exercise time with the dog's. Large or very active dogs may require walks twice a day, plus some running. Even within the same breed each dog's exercise needs are somewhat different. Try to be fair to the dog, because under-exercised dogs may not be happy, leading to less interaction with the owner and sometimes to destructive behavior. And, of course, proper exercise is vital for health.

One puppy I owned, Pete, a Jack Russell terrier, was extremely active and required an enormous amount of exercise and training time on a daily basis. I finally decided that I just didn't have enough time to devote to this puppy, so I found a 25-acre horse ranch for him to live on. At the ranch he had plenty of exercise but little human interaction or training. Eventually, Pete was given to Jerry, a local horseshoer, who proved to be the perfect owner for him. Jerry made sure he had plenty of exercise as well as training and attention. But, because of his lack of training in the past, Pete would bite if he didn't get his way. It was a long, slow process, but Jerry finally taught him how to socialize with people. Now Pete proudly accompanies him whenever he is shoeing horses. Pete deserves the happy life he got but it's a shame it took so long.

Some of the saddest dogs I have met in practice are those that are unknowingly neglected. This usually involves grooming problems and is commonly seen in breeds requiring special care such as those with long hair. Many long-haired dogs or thick-coated dogs can mat or develop very tangled hair under the surface of their outer coat. If you are considering a long-haired dog or one of the thick-coated breeds, remember that grooming is a top priority—often a daily requirement. Depending on the breed, daily grooming may take only a couple of minutes, but you must make the commitment to do it.

Climate is another factor to take into consideration. If you live in a cold climate, a short-haired breed may not do well. Similarly, long-haired breeds that are native to cold climates may have trouble adapting to hot climates. At the very least additional clipping may be required to help them cope with the weather.

Chows are an example of a breed that needs constant attention. Though they are not necessarily long haired, their hair is so thick that it does not shed out easily. Instead, the shed hair catches in the surrounding hair and can become badly tangled. Poodle hair behaves in the same manner—the tight curl in the hair traps the shed hair and it must be combed out. (See chapter 5, "Grooming.")

You may have to prioritize your requirements for "the perfect dog," because it might be necessary to compromise on some of these points.

Adopting a Puppy Versus an Adult Dog

You must also consider whether you want a puppy or an adult. To some extent this will affect where you shop for a dog. Puppies require training and more time, both with direct attention and cleanup. When you decide to raise a puppy, you are making a major commitment and will need a lot of patience. I advise prospective puppy owners to remember that an eight-week-old puppy urinates approximately once an hour and must be fed three to four times a day.

It is best to adopt a puppy who is between 8 and 10 weeks old. By eight weeks the puppy has had the time it needs with its mother to be weaned and is ready for life on its own. In any event, a puppy should be adopted before 14 weeks, because the puppy's ability to socialize or imprint with its owner is greatest before this time and decreases greatly after 14 weeks. Avoid puppies raised in kennel situations with little human interaction that are older than 14 weeks. These puppies do not relate well with people and behavioral problems often result.

Do not think a puppy will be mentally mature when it reaches its full body size. Puppies, like children, mature slowly. They do not really settle down until they're two or three years old. Also, puppies often display some destructive behavior due to teething and learning experiences. Each puppy demonstrates its own individual personality differently as it develops. They need mental stimulation through new experiences and patient instruction to develop to their fullest potential. Raising a puppy is fun and challenging, but it's not a commitment to be made lightheartedly. In her book, *The Chosen Puppy* (see "Suggested Reading," p. 331), Carol Lea Benjamin gives some helpful guidelines on adopting a puppy and focuses on the special needs of dogs who are adopted from animal shelters.

Be sure to get the health records of any puppy you adopt. Many puppies are vaccinated and wormed before being adopted; if not, take the puppy to your veterinarian immediately to initiate its health care.

An adult dog may be a better choice for many people. If you are thinking of adopting an adult dog from another individual, always inquire as to why they are getting rid of their dog. Unfortunately, people are not always honest in answering that question, so it is wise to insist on a trial period to make sure the dog gets along in your home environment. You may have problems if the adult dog is not housebroken or turns out to be a biter. While these problems can often be reversed, unless you are willing to put a lot of time into dealing with them, this is not the right dog for you.

If you have children, check with the previous owner about the dog's experience with children. Some tolerate and even seem to enjoy dealing with kids, including their noise, sudden movements, and playful tendencies, such as dressing or riding the dog. But other dogs become defensive and may even bite. Dogs raised with children may be more tolerant of their behavior. Large dogs are often less defensive and tend to be popular with families. But remember that large dogs can be boisterous and rough in their play. They might not understand that small children are not as resilient as other dogs. Small dogs are more easily injured and may be defensive in their behavior toward children.

Lily, my toy poodle whom you will hear more about in the following pages, does not tolerate children well. She views any situation that involves children as something close to torture. While visiting friends with children she remains constantly vigilant so as not to be stepped on. These visits are not restful for her and produce a stress-filled environment. We often visit Dr. Michelle Tilghman, a fellow holistic veterinarian in Stone Mountain, Georgia. Dr. Tilghman's two-year-old daughter, Rosie, loves Lily, but Lily does not appreciate Rosie in any way. No amount of tender petting on Rosie's part can make up for her unpredictable, noisy playtimes and other typical two-year-old behavior. On the other hand, Dr. Tilghman's golden retriever, Roxy, isn't even fazed by Rosie's behavior. One day I saw Rosie wearing a bicycle helmet that was "borrowed" from her mother's closet and riding Roxy around the yard! The ever patient Roxy stepped carefully as she carried her little rider, seeming to enjoy Rosie's enthusiasm.

There are many positive points about adopting an adult dog. They are often already sensitized to people's needs and trained to some extent. I have adopted puppies as well as fully grown adults and found pros and cons to each. Mostly it depends on the individual dog and the traits you are looking for. I adopted Lily as an adult. She just happened to embody the specific traits I was looking for at the time. To be very clear about them, I reviewed my situation and then made a list:

Situation: After the recent death of a 17-year-old male miniature poodle, my other dog, a 15-year-old female miniature poodle, was lonely and grieving. Because I was moving my household in a few weeks, the new dog must be adaptable to quick changes.

Traits Needed:

1. Nonthreatening small dog for companion to 15-year-old dominant female poodle.
2. Must be adaptable to change and like car travel.
3. Must be trainable and able to eventually work without a leash.
4. Must socialize well with other dogs.

These were the main traits I was looking for. But what I didn't write down is that I wasn't emotionally ready for another dog. I had been extremely close to the dog who died and I just hadn't completed the grieving process. I wasn't ready to become emotionally attached to another dog yet. On the other hand, Kelly, my 15-year-old, needed the camaraderie of a companion and I was concerned that her health would deteriorate quickly if I didn't find her one.

Because of my conflicting feelings I didn't make a major effort to find another dog; I was fortunate that one found me. Two weeks before moving across the country, I visited a friend and met Lily, a three-year-old white toy poodle. My friend was desperate to find a home for Lily but had not had any luck. She had rescued Lily from a breeding and dog-showing kennel a month earlier. Lily had finished her show career and was retired to be bred. Unfortunately, after being bred repeatedly for a year and a half, Lily did not get pregnant, so the kennel decided to euthanize her. No care had been given to Lily during that time, and both her skin and teeth were severely infected. My friend interceded, offering to clean her up and find a home for her.

When I met Lily, she had been shorn of her hair and her teeth had been cleaned. She looked like a miniature lamb. Having experienced only a show ring, a grooming table, and a cage, at three years old, Lily was not housebroken or socialized. Lily met my requirements, however, so I decided to try and see how she would fit into my life. Despite the problems she presented, I had a feeling that Lily belonged with us.

Kelly was very accepting of this small new friend and her outgoing disposition. After three years of dog shows, car travel was second nature to Lily, and her quick mind and attentive attitude gave me hope that she was trainable. Socialization was an entirely different issue that only time could answer.

Socialization is a learned process of positive interaction with humans. This was the process that was most questionable with Lily; it is a very important consideration when adopting any puppy or adult dog. When you say something to your dog, the dog must care about and react to what you are saying. When Lily first came to live with us and I reprimanded her for incorrect behavior, she didn't care if I was angry with her or not. She would simply look at me and act as if my being upset with her behavior was not her problem. It took six months to get Lily's attention to the point that she began to care about right and wrong behavior. Since her behavior was already set as an adult, I had to be with her constantly to reinforce her new training. She came to work with me every day, traveling everywhere. Finally by the end of a year she was fairly well trained. The consistent environment she received from the people in her life was one component of her rehabilitation. Kelly was the other. Kelly patiently taught Lily all the dog behavior she had not learned as a show dog, including self-defense and how to protect the house. Lily is now five and has become a very reliable, self-assured little dog. The years of reinforcement have been worth it.

Providing a consistent, nurturing environment for Lily was the key to training her and teaching her trust. She is now a thoroughly adjusted, trained, and socialized dog, who has found her niche as "office manager" at my clinic. Lily even has an entire set of human friends now!

Teaching an adult dog to care about how you feel about their behavior can be difficult. The part of the brain in which socialization skills are learned and remembered diminishes in development after 14 weeks of age. If human interaction has not occurred by that age, the odds of the puppy developing these social skills diminishes greatly. I was grateful that Lily was slowly able to be socialized into our lives.

Where to Find Your Dog

Now that you've narrowed the choice to one or several breeds that would be appropriate for your situation, the next step is to find out where to get your ideal dog. There are a variety of places to choose from, each with its positive points and potential problems.

We'll take a look at some of the possibilities and discuss the pros and cons. Dog purchases are usually carried out through breeders, pet shops, private individuals, veterinary clinics, or at flea markets. And, of course, adoptions from animal shelters are fairly inexpensive. Socialization is one of the factors I considered when reviewing the different places to adopt a dog.

I do not recommend puppies procured from the "puppy mill"–type kennels. Most of these operations are an embarrassment to the dog world. The parent dogs are often poorly cared for and indiscriminately bred, resulting in puppies with numerous health problems. According to estimates compiled by the Humane Society and the American Society for the Prevention of Cruelty to Animals (ASPCA), up to 90 percent of puppies sold in pet stores come from puppy mills, even though store owners will deny that *their* puppies come from these disease-infested breeding factories. Conditions at puppy mills have been well-documented in recent years. In his book *The Puppy Report,* Larry Shook describes the "often barbaric" puppy mills: "Puppy-mill dogs are found being raised on wire, like chickens, or in cramped quarters, like veal. Dams and sires live their entire lives in cages and are bred nonstop from the time they are six months old until five or six years of age. When females have mothered themselves to exhaustion and their litter sizes drop, they are often killed. ASPCA reports that the mothers' bodies are sometimes fed to the surviving puppy-mill dogs."[1]

Puppy-mill dogs are often inbred, resulting in immune system problems or congenital problems such as umbilical or inguinal hernias. (I'll talk more about genetic problems later in this chapter.) Also, poor care of the parents often results in puppies who are improperly nourished, infected with parasites, and/or have a host of other health problems. Hernias or other surgically correctable problems are usually repaired before you see the puppies, thus you may not be able to determine if a puppy had a problem that could be passed on to future generations.

In addition to hereditary health problems, research has shown that aggressive tendencies are also genetically triggered. Even dogs who are usually mild-mannered can "turn" on their owners or, worse, an infant or small child, attacking with a vicious and even deadly force. Often the result of inbreeding, these temperament problems may show in subtle ways until one day your dog takes an aggressive turn. If your dog injures someone you could wind up being sued and paying substantial penalties. That's why meeting the mother of a puppy can be extremely helpful. If she is docile and sweet, you'll know that at least half of your puppy's parentage has a good temperament. If the mother growls or barks at you, there is reason for concern.

1. Larry Shook, *The Puppy Report,* Lyons & Burford, Publishers, 1992, p. 57.

A good breeder will allow you to take the puppy to your own veterinarian for an exam before the sale is final. A bill of sale should provide certain safeguards for you as a buyer. *Dog Law,* written by attorney Mary Randolph, provides a good sample contract. Also, insist on a written guarantee against genetic diseases, such as hip dysplasia and progressive forms of blindness. Because these problems are so rampant today, many top breeders also provide certification that the parents both have healthy hips and eyes. The Orthopedic Foundation for Animals (OFA) will certify healthy hips based on X rays after a dog is at least 24 months old. Certification from the Canine Eye Registration Foundation (CERF) will indicate that the parents are unlikely to pass along genetic eye problems. OFA and CERF certificates for the parents do not guarantee that a puppy will not develop these problems, but they do indicate that it is less likely.

More and more ethical breeders are trying to eliminate genetic diseases that occur through inappropriate breeding. One way to do this involves a restricted transfer, which is

> . . . a contract between the new owner and the breeder stipulating that the dog will not be bred until it is old enough to be tested for inherited disease and has been certified disease free. Some restricted transfers require that the animal be spayed or neutered at six months of age, with AKC papers not passing to the purchaser until this is done. You may not be interested in acquiring a pet under such conditions, but you can be sure that breeders imposing them are deeply committed to improving the quality of their breed.[2]

When answering an ad to buy a puppy you may be able to learn quite a bit about the breeding conditions by the attitudes and concerns of the breeder. A compassionate breeder who really cares about dogs will be as concerned about the suitability of a potential home as you are about the dog. Questions about your interest in the breed and its special needs indicate a breeder who wants only the best for the pups. When you visit the litter be alert to the conditions in which the puppies and mother are kept. Is the area clean and sanitary? Is

2. Ibid., p. 93.

the room warm enough for the puppies? Are water and food bowls clean? Is the mother available for you to see? If the breeder doesn't want you to see the mother, beware. She might be sick, dirty, or exhibit aggressive tendencies that could be passed along to the pups.[3]

Here are some further guidelines on where to get a puppy or dog:

Adopting from a Dog Breeder or Kennel

PROS	CONS
Known bloodlines and character traits. Usually good health care; worming and vaccinations. You can look at the parents and get an idea of how the puppy will turn out. Sometimes buyers are given written guarantees and OFA and CERF certification.	Puppy may not socialize if kennel is large and puppy is sold after 14 weeks of age.

Adopting from a Pet Shop

PROS	CONS
Large selection of different dogs. Health care is usually up to date. However, not recommended because of numerous potential problems.	Very stressful environment. These puppies often come from "puppy mills" and have infectious or congenital health problems when you take them home. Also prone to illness after they

3. Ibid., pp. 91–98.

are sold due to stress and high exposure to other puppies. Often puppies are more than 14 weeks old when sold and not socialized. Breeding and source of puppies may be difficult to determine or questionable. Unable to tell how puppy will turn out because parents are not available.

Adopting from a Private Individual

PROS	CONS
Socialization may be better, more individual contact. Might see at least one parent. May learn more about personality traits.	Health care may not be up to date. Probably little or no information on hereditary problems. Unlikely to have OFA or CERF registration papers on parents.

Adopting from a Veterinary Clinic

PROS	CONS
Health care up to date. Health and behavior problems are usually known.	Usually have only adults available.

Adopting at Flea Markets

PROS	CONS
Usually inexpensive.	Extremely stressful environment. Dogs are often ill or become ill shortly after purchase. Poor health care and/or health records. No guarantee about claimed breed.

Adopting at an Animal Shelter

PROS	CONS
You are giving a home to an animal who would probably be euthanized. Can often find purebreds that you might not be able to afford otherwise.	Exposure to many diseases. Unknown background and potential training problems. Questionable hereditary problems; questionable health history.

Before you decide on a dog, check several sources. Remember, after you take a puppy or adult dog home, it may be hard to return him even if you have a money-back guarantee. Once you have opened your heart to an animal it is difficult to let common sense prevail. You may wind up with a sick animal who requires expensive veterinary care.

If you are adopting an adult dog, always do so on a trial basis. If you find that you are unable to cope with the dog's needs or behavioral problems that develop, it may be best to return the dog.

When You Take Your New Dog Home

If you have any other animals at home, it is essential that you take your new puppy or dog to the veterinarian before bringing her into your home. Even dogs who seem healthy might have fleas or mites or suffer from intestinal parasites or a bacterial or viral disease. Any of these problems are best treated immediately so they aren't passed on to your other animals. If you suspect a problem or disease, it is often wise to isolate the newcomer from other animals in your household for five to seven days.

Also, be prepared when you bring your dog home. If you already have the proper food and necessary supplements, collar and leash, food and water dishes, and special place to sleep, your new dog will be well on her way to a stress-free introduction to your household.

Rehabilitating a Stray

Every now and then an animal chooses us. Sometimes we're willing to put up with problem behavior because a dog decides we're the right human for them. In addition to an immediate veterinary exam, you may need to consult a dog trainer to help with socialization or discipline problems. Bach flower remedies (see p. 160) can alleviate some emotional problems, including dogs who are insecure, withdrawn, aggressive, or even those with incontinence problems.

Genetic Problems

Genetic problems are commonplace today because for years breeders have practiced inbreeding or linebreeding to refine certain desired traits within the breed. As an example, German shepherds were bred for a long, sloping profile from their shoulders to their tails. Breeding for this "look" resulted in hip dysplasia, a now firmly entrenched genetic trait of this breed, which develops into a painful, debilitating condition that worsens with age. It is so sad to see this problem in this athletic breed. Golden retrievers, Irish setters, and rottweilers are also known for a high predominance of hip dysplasia. (See the "Health Problems" section for complete description.) Dogs can be certified free of hip dysplasia by verification through X rays.

Because acupuncture has become known as an effective treatment for hip dysplasia, and I am one of the few veterinary acupuncturists in my area, I see many affected dogs and know the agony they live with on a daily basis. Buying a dog from a responsible breeder is the best way to avoid this crippling deformity.

When breeding is done to highlight these desirable traits, certain genes may increase in frequency, causing an increase in the odds that trait will occur. The tragedy is that this also increases the odds that undesirable traits will occur. In other words, in order to get a certain desirable body type or look, the health problems that often accompany it are accepted as a part of the process. The breeders who perpetuate this practice have little concern for the pain and suffering that genetic health problems cause to our animal companions.

Dr. Alfred J. Plechner, who wrote the book *Pet Allergies: Remedies for an Epidemic,* is a leading researcher on the problems that result from this type of genetic manipulation. Dr. Plechner is currently writing a book on this subject, which he finds heart wrenching for both the dogs and their owners. He says, "Our dogs were created for certain functions. When man restructured the genes for his own purposes, the gene pool became too close for the dogs to maintain a normal lifestyle. Now we are seeing the medical effects which are often painful and tragic."

It is helpful to know up front which breeds are prone to these problems. While it is difficult to tell which individual within a specific breed may be affected with a genetic abnormality, certain guidelines can be followed to help educate you on traits to avoid. Some of the breeds that are especially prone to these problems include German shepherds, Irish setters, golden retrievers, rottweilers, Doberman pinschers, boxers, English bulldogs, poodles, Akitas, West Highland white terriers, Scotties, collies, and cocker spaniels.

English bulldogs make good family pets. Their boisterous nature and loyalty endear them to their owners. These dogs have long been favorites of mine, but you must beware if you are unfamiliar with the breed and its problems. They have been bred to have large heads and narrow hips. This combination has made giving birth naturally difficult, resulting in many cesarean sections to deliver puppies. Also, their short noses make it difficult for bulldogs to breathe properly in hot weather, particularly when the humidity is high.

Another common genetic problem is hemophilia, or excessive bleeding. There are several different types of this illness in dogs. The most common breeds affected are Dobermans, golden retrievers, and

Scotties. Many times this condition will remain undetected until the dog suffers an injury or requires surgery. Hemophilia is an unpleasant surprise during an emergency, because it can make a condition that would otherwise be fairly simple into one that is life-threatening.

Hemophilia is a more difficult condition to avoid. If a dog has papers, however, you can check for father-daughter crosses or brother-sister crosses to avoid an inbred dog with a higher predisposition for the condition. I have seen hemophilia in one mixed-breed dog of unknown parentage, though it is uncommon in mixed breeds.

Boxers are a wonderful breed of dog with strong character traits and a regal bearing. It's unfortunate that this breed has become so predisposed to tumors, which are relatively common. Again, I would advise checking the health records of the parents carefully and examining registration papers to avoid an inbred.

Some breeds have been selectively bred for specific traits such as color or size. Unfortunately, some of these traits also carry other, less desirable genes with them. An example would be poodles. An intelligent breed originally used for hunting, poodles have been selectively bred for so long that many now have neurotic personalities or a too-fine coat. This is unfortunate in a breed that is known for its intelligence and good disposition. I have owned both normal and neurotic poodles and know what a joy a well-adjusted poodle can be as a companion.

One way to avoid genetic problems due to inbreeding is to be sure that the puppy you adopt is not the product of a mother-son, sister-brother, or other closely related cross. If you are buying a purebred puppy, check both the mother's and father's papers for this type of breeding in their backgrounds. If the puppy doesn't have papers, get all of the background you can on the parentage.

The bottom line is to carefully check out any dog you are considering adopting. What may seem like a bargain for a "purebred" at the flea market could turn into a nightmare when health problems arise. If you are buying a dog with papers, it's best to look carefully at the parents and registration records before making your selection.

2
Behavior and Training

I think of my dogs as friends and I treat them in a way that respects that special friendship. As with any human friend, it is important that the expectations of both owner and dog are met to have a truly rewarding relationship. When you adopt a new dog, whether it is a puppy or an adult, you must be willing to spend time training her. Dogs don't train themselves. Most dogs want to please a new owner, but often they just don't understand what it is you want them to do. And they can't predict what will upset you.

Think about it this way: If the dog has never been housebroken, he won't understand why you get upset when he urinates on the carpet. It will take time and patience to get the message across. From the dog's perspective, an owner must be consistent and predictable. When training a dog, you must make a conscious effort to be consistent with your methods if you want him to retain what he's learned. Don't expect a dog to learn a new behavior pattern right away. He may seem to comprehend what you are asking, but it usually takes many sessions and continual repetition before a dog is reliably trained.

As an owner you want your dog to behave in a way that suits your particular lifestyle. But people rarely think about what a dog wants. Dogs also have preferences. In fact, most dogs are definite about what they like and dislike. It's true that they can't always have their way, but understanding these preferences will assist you in training your dog to the behavior you desire.

If an owner's behavior is predictable, the dog is comfortable and feels secure; when your behavior patterns become less predictable, your dog is confused. While your lifestyle may bring erratic and chaotic days from time to time, keep in mind how this affects your dog. Perhaps just a little conversation about your problems with him may be all that's needed to calm an otherwise traumatic experience and help him to understand what's going on.

Because each dog has its own intelligence capability, each individual dog will train at a different rate and in a different way. It may take only a week or two to housebreak one dog, whereas another may take a month.

The basis of any good human relationship is communication and this is equally true of your relationship with your dog. When you establish a relationship with your dog you are making a commitment to look out for its well-being. Like any relationship, there are some basic understandings about the needs and requirements of each side. The communication you develop with your dog will help both of you to understand these basic needs.

As an example, here are the basic requirements I expect of my dogs:

- They must be leash trained and obedient when walking.
- They must be able to follow commands when they are not on a leash and obedient without a leash in an open area.
- They must be able to ride in a car for long periods and not leave the car unless told to do so.
- They must be housebroken (including my house, hotels, and other people's homes).
- They must be sociable and affectionate and also get along well with other dogs.

Make a list of your own like the one above. Then put yourself in your dog's position and think about what is expected of you. Here's what my dogs expect of me:

- I must provide food and water on a regular basis.
- I must provide a clean, pleasant living environment.

- I must provide regular grooming (including painting Lily's nails) and health care with continual upkeep in checking for parasites or other health problems.
- I must interact with the dogs on a regular basis, and provide lots of affection.
- I must provide sufficient exercise on a daily basis.

Depending on your individual situation, your dog's requirements may vary from Kelly' and Lily's.

By looking at the requirements of both the owner and the dog, each individual's perspective can be appreciated and it will help you avoid disappointing one another. When you look at his requirements, it's really very little considering all that he gives back.

The Training Process

There are two basic schools of thought on dog training. One is punitive training where physical force is used to teach a dog. The other is reward-oriented, positive training. Larry Shook explains the difference in his book *The Puppy Report:*

> "Punishment training"—Dr. Ian Dunbar's phrase—really doesn't teach a dog what not to do. It just teaches what not to do when the owner's around, says veterinarian and trainer Dunbar. The owner, in the dog's eyes, becomes "The Punisher." For dogs punished into obedience, the moment of truth is the moment of discipline. They do what they're told because they fear the consequences if they don't. When dogs are rewarded into obedience, socialized into canine good citizenship, the moment of truth is all the time. They do as they're bid because they want to. There's no mistaking a dog trained with punishment for one trained with affection, just as there's no mistaking a person reared with a rod for one reared with love.[1]

Later in this chapter I'll discuss professional trainers. If you decide to take your dog to a professional obedience class, talk with the instructor to determine what school of thought dominates his or her

1. Larry Shook, *The Puppy Report*, Lyons & Burford, Publishers, 1992, p. 115.

teaching style. If you don't like the instructor's methods after the first class or two, find another instructor.

In reward-based training the reward you give is your dog's indication that she has pleased you with an appropriate response. It's helpful if you use the same reward whenever you train your dog. But food treats are only one option. Think about what she likes best: is it dog treats, a lot of affection, or playing with a favorite toy? This reward will become associated with correct responses.

Lily, my toy white poodle, was unsocialized and untrained when she came to live with me at three years of age. Since she was unsocialized, training her with affection as a reward did not work. She loved jerky dog treats, so that was the reward I used in training sessions.

Expecting too much of a puppy can create lifelong problems. It always surprises me to see how much some owners expect of their dogs—often a lot more than they expect from their children. Many times I've been confronted with angry owners who just don't understand why their puppy hasn't been housebroken in three days. I always explain that it's difficult to housebreak young puppies who urinate an average of once an hour. You have to be with them constantly so they understand what's going on and make the proper associations. If you can't be with them all the time, it will take longer and you'll either have to keep the puppy outside when you're not home or paper-train him.

During training sessions, you need to consider all the facets of your dog's learning capabilities. Humans usually communicate through the spoken word, whereas dogs will utilize speech as well as hearing, body language, and (sometimes) smell, and integrate all of them when communicating with you. An example would be when your dog misbehaves. Let's say Rusty chewed on your new couch, making a sizable hole. First he would hear your voice, probably screaming at him. The pitch and loudness of your voice indicate anger. Then you make quick body movements as you attempt to grab him, also indicating anger. In this case, these indicators speak "louder" than the words you choose. You could say, "Wonderful dog," in this scenario and your dog would interpret it as "Bad dog."

Knowing some of the body language of dogs can be very useful in understanding them and helping with the training process. In the wild, they use body language to demonstrate their order in the pack.

Also, most owners are familiar with the "submissive pose" that dogs often take, lying on their backs when encountering their acknowledged leader, whether it is a dog or a human. Just remember that your dog interprets more than your words when interacting with you.

Dealing with Behavior Problems

Sometimes dogs do things that cause us concern, especially if we don't know if it is normal or not. Many times when adopting an adult dog, the new owner encounters annoying behavioral characteristics such as extreme shyness, aggression, or inappropriate urination. There may be a pattern to these problems, such as urination when the dog gets excited because company has arrived. Often the new owners assume these "problem" behavior traits are set in stone and cannot be changed.

It's important to talk with your veterinarian about these behavioral problems, because they could actually be symptoms of a health problem. If a medical condition is not the cause, your veterinarian may be able to prescribe natural remedies or suggest training to eliminate or lessen the problem. Homeopathic medication is often very effective in dealing with these problems. Because of the delicate nature and highly individualized cases of behavior problems, however, I am not going to discuss any specific remedies here. Take your pet to someone who specializes in homeopathy. (See "Homeopathy" on page 165.)

Bach flower remedies are also very effective in helping to deal with behavioral problems. You may want to read up on Bach flowers and decide to try them on your own, or have your holistic veterinarian suggest one. (See "Bach Flower Remedies" on page 160.)

In some cases, training can work miracles by correcting behavioral problems. If there are special problems that have not responded to training, you must alter your training methods or consult a professional. There is often a simple solution for exasperating behavior problems, if you take the time to find it. For example, my poodle, Lily, would get very upset when I went out without her, even if I was just going out to lunch. Lily let me know that my behavior was unacceptable to her by urinating in the office doorway as soon as I walked out the door. Obviously this was not a problem I could correct, because she only did it after I had left. To stop the urinating, one of the technicians in my clinic started following her around the minute I left, catching her in the act, and disciplining her with a stern voice reprimand. They also reinforced her training by taking her outside immediately. Within one week she was broken of this pattern.

Not all problems are this easy to solve. Try to understand why your dog is exhibiting the problem behavior, so you can determine if the behavior can be altered. Consulting a professional dog trainer is often helpful; he or she should be able to give you a method that's appropriate to your circumstances.

If your dog is an adult and new to your household, then it's best to allow time for the dog to settle in. Remember that it will take time for her to forget the training she got from her previous owners. She will also need time with you to bond and gain confidence so training can be instituted. This "settling-in" period may be only a few weeks for some dogs; others may need several months for trust to develop.

Each one of us influences our dog with our own personality. Whether we realize it or not, over long periods of time our dogs react to our behavior and adjust theirs accordingly. Years ago I adopted Coco, a two-year-old poodle who was very nervous. In fact, Coco's behavior actually bordered on the neurotic; he overreacted to everything and was not responsive to training.

I adopted Coco from a friend who was very nervous and constantly busy. Coco's behavior definitely needed improvements but, when I considered the previous owner's personality, I decided to give him some time to calm down and adjust to a quieter environment. Over six months' time he gradually changed his behavior, becoming easier to train and quieter in nature. Although never losing his love of activity, Coco became more sensible and was a joy to be around.

Years later, my energetic little Coco even assisted in retraining a puppy who had destructive tendencies. The puppy calmed down and stopped destroying things within five days of coming to live with Coco and me. Coco, with his very active nature, kept the puppy thoroughly entertained. Coco even provided clandestine instructions on how to jump onto the dining room table for a better view of the yard. (They did this while I was away from home, of course.)

Coco had another behavior trait that I was never able to change completely. He loved women, but didn't care for men. After years of working with him to accept men, he became more tolerant but never quite trusted them completely. This worked in my favor one day when two men tried to attack me in an empty parking lot. The door to my car was open and I jumped for the front seat. As I made it to the seat Coco landed in my lap, biting the first hand that reached in, while snapping and snarling. The commotion woke up my other poodle who joined in the attack. Because of the distraction they created, I was able to slam the door shut, lock it, and drive off. That was one day that Coco's aggressive tendencies toward men saved me from potential harm.

Like Coco, many dogs have a preference for humans of one sex. It's common for male dogs to bond strongly with female owners and female dogs with male owners. But there is no hard or fast rule concerning this. When you are introducing a dog into your household, the dog will usually select the person it wants to be closest to if there is a large family. If at all possible, that person is the best one to train the dog.

Animal Communicators

There is a growing group of animal behaviorists who call themselves "animal communicators." They actually "talk to the animals" through a mental form of communication. Although many people are skeptical about such things, I have seen very positive and occasionally revealing results when animal communicators are consulted.

Animal communicators are consulted for various reasons. Some owners just want to understand their dogs better, but most of the time an animal communicator is called upon to deal with a specific behavior problem after repeated attempts to correct it through more orthodox methods. For others it's just entertainment to hear what their dog has to say. I have also seen numerous positive results including success in solving undiagnosed health problems as well as finding lost pets. There may be a lot of phonies in this field, but there are also many successful and genuinely gifted people who call themselves animal communicators.

For the most part I have found animal communicators to be reliable and have enjoyed my interactions with them. When Lily (my toy white poodle) first came to stay with me she did not jump on anything, including the couch, chairs, or bed. Because of this she would not learn to get into the car, always having to be lifted. I consulted an animal communicator who asked Lily if she had any problems. We learned that she had poor vision and was unable to focus on any close-up objects. I had noticed that she squinted when held by someone and just assumed it was an odd habit of hers. This explained why she was unwilling to jump up onto furniture or the car seat—she had trouble seeing where she was going.

I know it's difficult for many people to imagine that this type of mental communication can be effective, but I have seen many instances where the findings were accurate. When consulting with an animal communicator remember that this is an animal they're talking to, not a person. Look at things from your dog's perspective and expect to hear about things that are important to your dog, such as food, play toys, or illness.

Through my work with animal communicators I have noticed that dogs have a keen memory of negative experiences in their past. Sometimes we can understand problem behavior by learning about the bad experience that started the behavior.

Of the many amazing experiences I've had in consulting animal communicators, one situation involving a cat stands out. Tabitha was brought into the clinic because of inappropriate behavior. She was urinating or defecating on the bed—common behavior for an angry cat—but only on Sundays! The lady who owned the cat was beside herself because Tabitha had been doing this for some time and her husband had threatened to throw the cat out unless it stopped.

My friend, Beatrice Lydecker, was at the clinic that day seeing clients. Beatrice is a well-known animal communicator and author of a classic book on the subject, *What the Animals Tell Me* (Harper & Row, 1979). I found no medical problems so I referred the case to her. Beatrice "talked" to Tabitha, asking why she was making the mess on the bed. The cat explained that she always took a morning nap on the bed. However, her Sunday naps were being interrupted of late. After her owner went to church, another lady was coming over to the house. The other lady didn't like the cat and threw her out of the bedroom when she and the owner's husband went into the bedroom. Tabitha was angry and would make a mess on the bed after the lady left to let them know her displeasure. So the cat "spilled the beans" and the husband's affair was revealed.

As with any professional, you must be discerning in choosing an animal communicator. For the most part I have enjoyed working with them, finding that a true "animal's perspective" can be enlightening and sometimes amusing. Many good animal communicators even work over long-distance telephone, tuning in to your animal with the same astonishing results.

Obedience Classes

Obedience classes encompass a wide scope of training besides the "sit, heel, stay" stuff. I believe this type of training is highly underrated. It is a valuable tool that can help immensely with your dog's learning process. In an obedience class your dog learns to interact with you and cope with a situation in which distracting stimuli and other dogs are present. Each dog responds in a different way to these experiences and you learn what your dog's response will be when a given situation occurs.

The obedience training on the leash works wonders for your dog. It teaches the dog to be under control on the leash and hence to have responsibility for his actions. The dog learns that the owner expects certain responses from him and that a reward comes when the proper response occurs. Usually the reward is praise, so you're also teaching the dog to respond to positive feedback.

Each breed responds to obedience training in different ways. Some are challenged by it and absolutely love it. Most of the herding breeds enjoy obedience work, because they have been bred to take direction and act in a responsible manner. Shelties, in particular, often excel and many go on to do advanced obedience training with hurdles and retrieving exercises. But not all dogs can be trained to this extent—don't expect a Saint Bernard to respond like a shelty!

One of my clients owned several different breeds of dogs and showed them on a regular basis. Since they were all large, energetic dogs, they went through obedience training to help with handling and coping with the show ring. Comparing the responses of the different breeds was interesting. The owner had used the same training methods for a number of years and thought that the breeds were fairly predictable in his hands. His standard poodles were quick learners, eager to please. They usually finished the course in record time and did well in long-term retention of their lessons. The chows were not necessarily slow learners, but were more resistant to training. They eventually learned the obedience work but required more reinforcement after the course was completed. On the other hand, the mastiffs were slow learners; they were much more interested in the other dogs than in the training.

Any good book that describes your dog's breed (or mix of breeds) will give you some general guidelines on that breed's abilities in terms of training. But remember, each dog is an individual, so don't limit your dog either.

Training Halters, Collars, and Leashes

When doing obedience training it's important to use the correct restraint. Consult the trainer about his or her preferences. One of my favorite methods of restraint for large, boisterous dogs like golden retrievers and Labradors is a dog halter. This wonderful invention is made of strong elasticlike straps that fit on a dog much like a horse halter. When pulled, the halter tightens on the dog's head, getting its attention and directing it to you. In the correct hands, this training tool can be quite effective with very little strength required by the handler.

The choke chain is the most common collar used for obedience work and most dogs respond well to it. Check with your trainer for correct fit and size of the links. Most trainers prefer leather leashes, because it's easier to grip leather and the leash is strong. Choke chains are not for abuse but restraint. In the wrong hands, however, a choke chain can cause injury to a dog if an owner gets overzealous about it.

My own poodles are very obedient on the leash and don't require choke collars. Since we socialize a lot they have colored nylon collars—with matching leashes, of course. Since my ladies are fashion-conscious, they have several changes of outfits to suit the occasion. Lily also has several hats (which match her collars and leashes) that she wears to horse shows and parties. I thought this was all rather silly at first, but did it just for the fun of it. However, when beautifully outfitted the "girls" definitely show off and get a lot of attention. This is an association-type behavior they learned early on in their lives and it gives them a great deal of pleasure.

FIGURE 1. To best control a dog on a leash, choose from (1) a halter made of strong, elastic like straps, or (2) a choke-chain that has large links.

Choosing a Dog Trainer

It's best to interview a dog trainer before signing up for classes so you can make sure you've found one that both you and your dog are comfortable with. The best places to check for referrals are pet stores, veterinary clinics, friends, or, if necessary, the Yellow Pages.

Before interviewing a potential trainer, write down your goals for training your dog. Then you can compile a list of questions to ask.

The most common training requirements are:

- Basic obedience—sit, heel, stay, etc.
- Off-leash work
- Advanced obedience work, such as hurdles, competitions, etc.
- Guard dog training

In addition to this list, specialized dog training is done for hearing-impaired or sight-impaired owners or for hunting dogs.

After you've looked over this list and decided what kind of training you want your dog to have, you can formulate specific questions, such as:

1. What methods do you use to train the dogs?
2. How long will the training take?
3. Will my dog have to come back for more training at a later date?
4. What if my dog doesn't respond to the training?

Good trainers will be able to answer all of these questions without hesitation and give you confidence in their abilities.

Many basic obedience classes are offered in a group format. You get some individual training time as well as group interaction. Having attended group classes with various dogs over the years, I have had many positive experiences.

Coco (the miniature poodle I mentioned earlier) was a frustration to train. He was very intelligent and felt he knew the appropriate time to sit or stay or lay down. His attitude was "Who do you think you are to tell me what to do?" He eventually learned obedience with leash work and off-leash work, but was never consistent in sitting or lying down.

Despite these shortcomings, Coco saved the day with his exceptional off-leash work when he became a last-minute substitute for a movie role. Kelly, who performed excellent obedience work and many tricks, was hired to do the role. Unfortunately she became very shy when put in front of cameras, lights, and lots of people. Thank goodness, Coco had accompanied us. I only brought him along because he threw such a fit about being left behind. So, when Kelly didn't perform, I decided to try Coco in the role. His true show-off nature surfaced and he performed well. His only problem arose when he had to detour through a door on the stage for a particular scene. His intelligent, logical poodle mind couldn't understand why he should take this long way around when it was so much quicker to walk straight across the set. But eventually he did the scene and performed magnificently, obeying my hand signals as he walked off-leash through the door. I was relieved he had accompanied us and worked so well as a last-minute movie star.

Hand signals are taught in obedience training, and I have found them to be a valuable tool to accompany voice commands. I often take my dogs along when I go horseback riding and give them commands at a distance. My oldest dog, Kelly, now 17, has lost her hearing and relies solely on hand signals to figure out what I want. She even learned a new one—be quiet—when she couldn't hear me tell her that anymore. Kelly has always been a good watchdog and barks when she suspects a problem. She even learned to look at me occasionally to check and see if she should stop barking. She learned this new hand signal at age 14, so it's never too late to train a dog.

3

Your Dog's Living Arrangements

Safety and comfort are important considerations for the dog you love. Most owners are aware of the basic comfort needs of their pets, but many are uninformed about the hazards that threaten their dogs' safety. In this chapter we'll review some of the basic concerns the astute owner must address, ranging from proper ventilation in a doghouse to poisonous plants in the yard.

Is your dog in the house most of the time, does he live outdoors, or does he divide his time between the house and the yard? If you haven't gotten your dog yet or are a new owner, this question must be addressed. Each dog has a preference and each owner has his or her own opinion. The objective is to find a living arrangement that makes both dog and owner happy. It may require a bit of give-and-take from both parties.

Your dog needs at least one space or area that belongs to him alone. It may be a section of the floor, a dog bed, a place on the furniture, or a corner of the patio that he chooses as preferable to all other locations. Some dogs spread out and claim several locations throughout the house or yard that are particularly appealing. Try to respect your dog's choice—if it is within reason—because only he knows what is most comfortable.

My dog Kelly loves to sleep on marble floors. I don't know if it's her sophisticated good taste that draws her to marble or if its hard cool surface gives her better dreams, but marble is definitely one of her favorite sleeping surfaces. Recently, when Kelly accompanied me on a visit to a friend, she wandered into a formal living room that is off-limits to dogs. After some searching I found her asleep in the room's marble entryway.

Often when an owner chooses where the dog should sleep or stay most of the time, the dog is not in agreement. I have heard many complaints from owners about their ungrateful dog who doesn't appreciate the new doghouse or dog bed that they have spent a fortune on. Sometimes it can be just a matter of adjusting to something new and other times you can make a new item more appealing to your dog so she will accept it.

Living Outdoors

It's a joy to see an active dog frolic in the outdoors. One of my friends has a young German shepherd who loves to run around her horse farm. In hot, humid weather the dog, Paws, has learned to dive into the swimming pool, swim a lap to cool off, and then she's ready to go again. Dogs on farms often use ponds the same way. Paws always shows visiting dogs this practical and exciting way to beat the heat, but most of them decline her invitation for a dip in the pool.

If you are going to leave your dog outside in the heat during the summer, be sure that he is also kept outside during the spring as the weather conditions gradually grow warmer. This gradual adaptation is preferable; it is less stressful on the body than allowing the dog to remain in air-conditioning for long periods and then expecting him to tolerate the heat outside.

If your dog is living outdoors all the time, he will need a shelter that is easily accessible and protected from the weather. A covered porch, garage, or doghouse will work as long as it provides protection from excessive sunlight as well as rain and cold. Excessive sunlight combined with heat can cause a dog to have a heatstroke. Since some dogs don't have much common sense about curtailing their activity in high heat, it's very important to provide a place that's out of the sun.

An outside kennel shouldn't be the only shaded area available to your dog, because many are unventilated. Especially in high humidity it's very helpful to cool off the dog by keeping the air moving inside the kennel. Even a small fan can help to create a breeze that will make a difference. In big kennels, large fans or ceiling fans are often used to keep the air circulating. I advise caution if you are considering air-conditioning your dog's kennel. Health problems can result from the constant temperature change as the dog goes in and out on extremely hot days. For hunting and performance dogs, air-conditioning is definitely not recommended, because the dogs lose their tolerance for heat and are then more prone to heatstroke. The same is true for cold conditions. If you expect your dog to tolerate cold for long periods, it's best not to heat the kennel. Or, if you live in an extremely cold climate, you can heat it a little, so the kennel is warm enough to protect the dog from excessive cold but doesn't keep him overly hot.

If your dog lives outside in cold winter weather, it is important that she remain in that environment from early fall on into winter so she can adapt gradually to the weather and, depending on her breed, grow the proper winter coat. Many things influence a dog's ability to grow a winter coat: the length of the day, the temperature change, and the constant exposure to the climate. So to develop the best coat possible to protect the dog from the cold, leave your dog outside beginning in September or October, depending on your area, and on through the winter months. If you get a new dog in the winter or if you move during the winter from an area of the country with warm winters to an area with cold winters, your dog may be unable to withstand the cold. In that case, other arrangements such as modestly heating the kennel or bringing the dog indoors will be necessary.

Living Indoors

The indoor dog has different requirements. Always have an idea of where you want your dog to sleep, then try to work out the best arrangement with her. Some people are okay with the dog sleeping on the bed with them; others are not comfortable with this. Of course, the smaller the dog the better this arrangement works out. But I've found that just as many large dogs like to sleep on beds as small ones. It always amazes me when the owners of really huge dogs admit that they allow their dogs to share (or maybe take over) their beds. If you don't want your dog on the bed, you must be very firm. Disciplining a dog for trying to join you may be easier said than done. It seems that dogs are extremely talented at tiptoeing into the bedroom when you're asleep and sneaking into the bed with you. Impossible, you say—you would notice a Great Dane climbing into bed? Don't bet on it. The successful ones seem to know when their victims are sound asleep and then move in. One miniature poodle I owned would curl up innocently at the foot of the bed when I first got in, but once I was asleep she took over whatever area she pleased. She also learned that I would move over if she kicked me a few times and took advantage of that strategy to get the best position on the bed.

One friend told me about the sleeping habits of Oliver, his miniature schnauzer who naps at the foot of the sofa during the day. When he's ready for serious sleep at nighttime, however, he wanders into his master's closet and curls up under the dirty clothes. Then, when morning approaches, he shifts to the bed, with his head resting on his master's shoulder.

One concern I caution people about is the possibility of contracting parasites from the dog when you are in extremely close proximity—such as sharing a bed with him. Tapeworms, ticks, fleas, and sarcoptic mange mites are among the parasites that can potentially be passed from dogs to humans. (See more on these parasites on page 295.) During a house call one day a client questioned me about sleeping arrangements. Was it bad to allow a pet to sleep with her? I reminded her that checking for parasites is important and also stressed keeping the dogs especially clean if they are going to sleep with her. But she continued to query me, asking about possible disease problems, odors, and stains. Since she had owned dogs for years I thought her concerns were a bit overly cautious. She finally admitted, in a barely audible whisper, that her newly acquired Vietnamese pot-bellied pig was sleeping on the water bed with her.

Your dog may choose a sleeping area that you do not approve of, such as a white couch, particularly if shedding is a problem. If your dog has chosen an area that is unacceptable to you, then you must not allow him access to that area, but should provide him with an alternative sleeping area. It helps if the alternative is appealing. Remember to reward him when he goes to the new area. If providing a new area doesn't work and your dog persists in sleeping where you don't want him to, a portable kennel can be used as a sleeping area. Many dogs enjoy these kennels for sleeping, because they are in a safe, enclosed area. If you plan to use an indoor kennel regularly, be sure there are some comfortable blankets and towels to lie on and toys or chew bones to keep him occupied.

Unless they are put in stressful circumstances, many house dogs adapt well to temperature changes as they go from air-conditioning to extreme outdoor heat. However, the heat becomes stressful if you take your dog from an air-conditioned home and expect him to go on a long run or an all-day hike. Not only does the dog's body have trouble regulating its temperature, but the dog may not be able to identify when he is overheating because he is accustomed to being able to cool down in air-conditioning.

The Dog Bed

Many types of dog beds are available in stores or you can easily make one. The new foam beds are comfortable and easy to clean. If you're thinking about a wicker bed, think again: if your dog likes to chew or if she's a youngster, the bed could become a big chew toy. If you put a pad in the bed, make sure it's washable. Most dogs like a blanket over the pad—but not just any blanket will do. I've observed that warm colors appeal more to dogs. I don't know why, because their color vision is questionable. At my house Kelly and Lily fight over which one gets the bed with the yellow blanket. In the clinic I experimented with blanket color preferences and found that yellows and oranges were favorites, pink came in next, and the cool-toned blues and greens were least liked. This is only a subjective observation and by no means applies to every dog; however, if you're having trouble getting your dog to use the dog bed, try using a warm-colored blanket.

Whatever pad and blanket arrangement you use, make sure it's large enough for your dog's comfort and easily cleaned. I recommend cleaning the dog bed at least once a month or more often if your dog has fleas, a skin condition, or odor problems. (See "Fleas," page 260.) Wash the bedding in a mild soap; harsh detergents can cause skin reactions. Because many dogs are sensitive to products such as Lysol, I recommend a bleach and water solution that you can spray on the surface of the bed for disinfection purposes. Mix one part bleach and 30 parts water in a spray bottle and keep it for this purpose. If bleach would damage the bed, get a disinfectant from your veterinarian—Nolvasan or Roccal work nicely.

Yard Safety

The first consideration for a safe yard is the fencing. Most dogs do well with chain-link fencing. I would advise that you invest in the heavy-duty chain-link fencing because it withstands a lot of wear. Another plus is that chain-link fencing requires very little maintenance and it's unlikely that your dog will get stuck in the little diamond shapes. But it's not right for everyone. The negative features of chain-link fencing are: it can give a toehold to climbing dogs, it can be dug under, and dogs may bark more because they can see through it.

Although a solid wood fence can give you and your dog more privacy, many dogs like to see what's going on beyond their own yards. My dogs have always enjoyed watching the neighborhood events—and commenting on them with barks. When we moved to a house that had a privacy fence, the dogs stopped spending time outdoors. Previously they had been outside half the time. After moving to a house with a chain-link fence, they returned to their outside activities.

I don't recommend the wire fencing made of larger squares or stock wire, because dogs can catch their heads or legs in this type of fence and become injured. You might say, "My dog would *never* do that." Don't count on it. Over the years it's been my experience that animals can do some pretty odd things, and getting stuck in stock wire fences ranks high on the list.

When you check the fencing in your yard, it's important to be thorough. You must block all escape routes. You might think your dog will never notice that little hole. But remember, all your dog has to do is walk around and check out the yard. Dogs are territorial and generally know their everyday environments very well.

Even animals with very little intelligence are pretty smart when it comes to escape routes. I learned that lesson the hard way in veterinary school when I was herding dairy cows with three other students. The cows had to be herded down an area between fences with about 20 chain gates to guide them. Being students and in a hurry we decided not to repair one of the broken chain gates and only put up the top chain. We naturally thought the cows would never notice. Well, there might as well have been a neon sign saying, "This way to escape." The first cow made a sudden turn exactly at the broken gate, ducking under it. The rest of the herd—20 in all—followed, while my classmates and I ran after them as fast as we could. What we had not considered is that these cows had traveled this way several times a day every day for years. They knew every inch of the route and had no trouble spying the easy gap that would lead to freedom. I guess it was a fun adventure for them!

If your fence is painted, check the type of paint that was used to be sure it's not toxic in case your dog chews on it. There are very few lead-based paints left around but every once in a while I come across one. Only a few months ago I treated a puppy with a severe stomachache. We weren't able to determine a reason for the illness until the owner noticed that the puppy had been chewing on a wall next to the fence. The building was old and the paint lead-based. From the looks of the wall, the puppy had been chewing on it for a while. Because the puppy was only weeks old and had ingested so much of the paint, little could be done. Despite much effort, we lost the puppy.

Toxic plants in the yard are another potential source of problems. Most of us are familiar with the most common plants that are toxic to animals, including oleander, yews, and castor-bean plants. However, there are many toxic plants and they vary in different climates. If you have a question about plants that are currently in your yard, or are planning to add new ones, check with your veterinarian or local county agent.

Pesticides that are sprayed on lawns, plants, or gardens are another potential source of harmful toxins. As we become more environmentally conscious, it is clear that many products that were used with abandon for decades are now considered unsafe by many experts. Soil and groundwater contamination are the result of the rampant use of toxic chemical pesticides. In recent studies by the Environmental Protection Agency, toxic residues of 74 different pesticides were found in wells in 34 states. Perhaps you could say it was worth the risk if our crops were safer because of the use of these pesticides. Unfortunately, that is not the case.

Today agriculture suffers a greater loss to insect damage than it did in the 1940s, when few crops were sprayed. Unfortunately, when we destroy one type of pest, we often create pests out of species that were not a problem in the past. For instance, spider mites used to be killed by other insects. But when we kill off their predators, the spider mites proliferate. Additionally, insects, weeds, and plant diseases often become resistant to the chemicals that we develop to control them. And when we spray toxic chemicals onto plants and soil, we also kill off the beneficial insects like ladybugs, spiders, lacewings, and parasitic wasps. (Also see "Stresses from Chemical Hazards in Our Yards and Cupboards," page 148.)

There are now pesticides available that are made of natural ingredients. But check the label carefully. Even many products that are labeled "safe" for pets can cause health problems. Some dogs have higher sensitivities than others. Even if your dog visits a home where toxic pesticides were used in the yard within the last few days, he could be affected. Sunlight usually breaks down the pesticides over a period of days, making the residue less toxic. If areas of the yard are not exposed to sunlight, however, the toxicity may last longer.

In congested suburbs dogs are frequently exposed to toxic pesticides through the air when neighbors spray their yards. Discuss this matter with your neighbors. Perhaps you can educate them on the problems of toxic chemical pesticides. If they are not willing to cooperate, ask them to let you know before they are going to spray so you can keep your dog indoors.

Other pesticides to be cautious with are those sprinkled on the ground. Snail bait can have very serious consequences if eaten. Many dogs die from it or suffer permanent liver damage. Rat poison is another product with potential lethal effects. Many other substances are dangerous, so if you are uncertain about any product, call your local poison control center or ask your veterinarian to check for you. If your dog ingests a toxic pesticide or other poison, fast action is necessary. The faster you are able to detect the problem, the better chance your dog has of being saved.

Another precaution necessary in your dog's environment is to be sure no antifreeze is ingested. People often work on their cars in the driveway or yard and don't realize how dangerous a small pool of antifreeze is to their pets. Antifreeze can cause irreparable damage to the dog's kidneys if ingested. For some reason dogs find the taste appealing and readily drink it if it is available. If you find that your dog has been drinking antifreeze, get her to the veterinarian as soon as possible to begin treatment. Antifreeze causes a series of chemical reactions to occur in the dog's body, resulting in crystals that block the kidneys from performing their filtering process. So the faster the treatment starts, the faster the chemical reactions can be stopped to prevent crystal formation.

Self-Sufficient Dogs

Dog doors and self-feeders are used by many owners so their dogs can access the yard at will and eat when they please. Most dogs enjoy being able to use a dog door to come and go as they choose; this door can be built into a door, a wall, or a special type of sliding-glass door. I prefer the soft pliable plastic type with a magnetic system that closes the dog door after each use. The other types of dog doors—metal, wood, and hard plastic—can cause potential harm when a dog changes its mind about going outside and tries to back up. Occasionally a dog will trap its back under the door and injure itself. My dog Kelly is very nosy, always wanting to know what's going on outside but not necessarily wanting to make the commitment to go all the way out the door. She will stand with her head poked out the dog door as she watches the world outside. Sometimes she voices her opinion with a bark.

I'm not a fan of self-feeders. I much prefer to monitor daily food consumption while providing clean, nutritious food. There are several problems with self-feeders. First, the food left in the container can become infested with insects such as roaches and ants. The roaches present a sanitation problem and ants sometimes sting. Another drawback is the possibility of mold forming or bacteria growing on the food. In high humidity mold and bacteria can grow very quickly, and these contaminants are not always visible to the naked eye. Also, if food is left exposed to sunlight and high heat for long periods of time, some of the nutrients are destroyed, particularly the vitamins. The last problem with self-feeders is overindulgence. Some dogs just don't know when to stop and become overweight when self-feeders are used.

Safety Precautions

In today's society safety precautions are paramount. You may be aware of some of these points, but let's review them as a reminder:

1. When you have a dog who is aggressive or occasionally bites, post a warning sign on your fence and next to your front door.
2. Do not allow your dog to chase the mail carrier, trash collectors, utility workers, or other service people. Many of these people are armed with repellent sprays to protect them from dog attacks. These sprays can sometimes damage a dog's eyes and may cause other health problems.
3. Think about your body language when you're around your dog. Many bites have occurred when dogs misinterpret their owner's behavior. Most dogs are protective of their owners and will be watchful if you are interacting with someone they don't know. Quick movements or playful roughhousing can seem threatening to your dog and elicit an unwanted response.

Observe your dog the next time you have visitors. Many dogs position themselves where they can be aware of what's going on. One of my dogs has the habit of watching over me when a new person is visiting. Once a group of friends came to my house with their friend, a man visiting from the Middle East. In his culture dogs are not kept as pets so he was totally unfamiliar with them and very skeptical when I explained how protective even miniature poodles can be. Later in the evening as this man walked by me, he suddenly turned and pretended to attack me. He didn't expect the dogs to react, but I did. Both of them were on him instantly. At the time Coco was 17, frail, and had only two teeth—but that didn't stop him. I was more worried about the other dog who had a hard bite and was trying to sink her teeth into the man's ankle. Fortunately I was able to intervene before much damage was done, and held off the dogs. The visitor was shocked and had learned a lesson about dogs the hard way. Both dogs were quite pleased with themselves, but frail little Coco seemed particularly gratified by the experience of coming to my rescue as he strutted about for several days with an inflated ego.

4

When You Travel

Do you travel with your dog or is it necessary to make arrangements for her care while you're away? There are many considerations to deal with in either case.

Traveling with Your Dog

Traveling with your dog is a joy for some and an ordeal for others. Understanding your dog's needs when traveling will make travel time much more enjoyable. Having traveled extensively with dogs for many years, I have learned that being prepared can make all the difference. The following safety rules concerning car travel should always be adhered to.

Rules During Travel

- Always carry a leash in your car for *each* dog.
- Your dog must remain quiet and controlled in the car.
- Don't allow your dog to leave the car in an uncontrollable manner.

- In hot weather, always carry fresh water and water bowl in your car.
- Dogs riding in the back of a truck must be leashed.

Now let's look at the reasons behind each safety rule. First, it's essential to carry a leash in the car for each dog; you never know when it will be necessary to leash the dog, especially in emergency situations. Although this is one of my strictest personal rules, I broke it one day. I had three dogs and two leashes in the car when it broke down on the interstate. It was a hot day, and all power was gone on the car so I could not get the windows down. I had to take all the dogs with me to go for help. I tried tying two of the dogs together but they couldn't get along. So I walked a half-mile leading two dogs and carrying one. I've never broken the leash rule again.

Car manners are equally as important because an unruly dog in the car could cause an accident. Choose the place where you want your dog to remain during the trip and firmly enforce that he must stay there. Allowing dogs to leap from the front seat to the back can cause disastrous results. I've patched up dogs that have gone through windshields and set legs that were broken because of seat jumping. It's especially important to control your dogs in city traffic, where you must deal with stop-and-go traffic and aggressive drivers.

When you stop the car and prepare to get out, train your dog to leave the car in an orderly manner. Be very strict about your rules and be consistent in enforcing them. A German shepherd who scrambles and scratches as she leaps out of the car could harm you. The dog is also in danger if she wanders out into the street. One of the best commands to teach your dog is "stay." When leaving the car you should use the stay command until it's safe for your dog to get out. If you travel a great deal and need to use a leash in some circumstances, it is best to apply the leash right after using the stay command. Dogs can learn all of these rules very proficiently. If you have problems, consult a dog trainer.

Bringing fresh water and a water bowl in hot weather is rather obvious, but not all owners realize how easy it is for a dog to overheat and dehydrate in a hot car. You may go into a shopping mall for just a few minutes and end up getting sidetracked. A few minutes can easily turn into an hour. In hot weather it can take as little as five minutes for a dog to overheat. Later in this chapter I'll discuss this topic further.

FIGURE 2. A specially designed no-spill water dish is great for car travel.

My own dogs use a traveling water dish designed not to spill. A lid with a deep hole in the middle allows the dogs to drink and keeps the water in the bowl. I've carried one for so long that my poodles expect it even on short trips in the car.

If your dog must ride in the back of a truck, always be sure he is securely leashed in. Many states have laws requiring restraint of dogs in trucks, because you never know when a quick stop or turn will occur. Dogs are often thrown out of the back of the truck; sometimes the owners don't even notice when this happens. The dog can be thrown into oncoming traffic and get hit or be lost.

Adaptability to Travel

Is your dog a good traveler? Some dogs love it, whereas others are less enthusiastic. Some dogs are prone to motion sickness in the car. Nervous or excitable dogs may do well in the car but not on airplanes. Air travel is more challenging for a dog than car travel. Although it's preferable to arrange for your dog to travel in the passenger section with you, this is not possible for large dogs, who must travel in the special section of the baggage compartment reserved for perishables. In that case, he is alone and must endure a strange, possibly frightening situation for a long period of time. Dogs who fly regularly seem to adapt and tolerate air travel. But dogs can suffer jet lag and may have trouble adapting to a different time zone just as people do. The book *Dog Law* has an excellent section on air-travel regulations and additional safety precautions (see "Suggested Reading," p. 333).

How Can Travel Be Made Easier?

If your dog is used to traveling in the car, taking a longer trip may just be a matter of a few adjustments. Realize that when you take a rest stop, your dog probably needs one too. Exercise and the opportunity to urinate and defecate should be provided on a regular basis. Frequent travelers know their dog's requirements. Long-distance car travel will be much easier if you have some idea of your dog's elimination schedule. For instance, one of my dogs always has a bowel movement before breakfast and one has it afterward. Then we're okay until late afternoon just before dinner. Years ago I had a dog who got very nervous when first leaving on a trip. I learned that a stop after one hour to let him do whatever was needed would settle him down; then we would all have a smooth trip.

Many owners find that by following the rules I've outlined and adding a little bit of common sense, their dog has no trouble adapting to long trips. However, if your dog is a nervous type, suffers from motion sickness, or is unruly, there are other options. Of course, natural remedies such as herbs and Bach flower remedies are preferred by holistically oriented owners. When necessary, your veterinarian can give you a prescription for a mild tranquilizer—though this should be a last-ditch choice.

Let's look at some typical responses to travel and what to do about them:

Nervous Traveler—Won't Settle Down

Holistic treatments:

- Valerian root tablets or capsules are relatively safe and effective and do not result in the loss of coordination that a prescription drug such as Acepromazine can lead to. Give one tablet or capsule for each 10 to 20 pounds of body weight. (See "Herbs," p. 163.)
- Bach Flower Rescue Remedy is a nice way to settle down the nervous dog and can be used together with valerian root. (See "Bach Flower Remedies," p. 160).

Other options:

- Acepromazine is a tranquilizer that must be prescribed by your veterinarian. It works well in the hard-core cases that can be settled down no other way. The problems with Acepromazine include loss of coordination, which lasts from 8 to 12 hours, and other occasional side effects. Twelve hours is an extremely long time to tranquilize even the most unruly dog. (See "Tranquilizers and Other Sedatives," p. 173.)

Motion Sickness

Holistic treatments:

- Nux vomica, a homeopathic remedy, can be given 30 minutes prior to leaving. I suggest a potency of *6C* or *12X*. Nux vomica works wonders with motion sickness. It may have to be redosed while en route. I have had success in using it to prevent car sickness, seasickness, and air sickness. Combining it with Rescue Remedy often works well, particularly if the dog is also a nervous type. (See "Homeopathy," p. 165.)
- Bach Flower Rescue Remedy is an all-purpose remedy for trauma and stress. It can be administered along with other medications. (See "Bach Flower Remedies," p. 160.)

Other options:

- Dramamine can be prescribed by your veterinarian, but I

have not found it to be 100 percent reliable for motion sickness.

- Acepromazine (mentioned above for nervous dogs) is also used to prevent vomiting. However, I am always concerned about the long tranquilizing effect that lasts up to 12 hours. (See "Tranquilizers and Other Sedatives," p. 173.)

The Unruly Traveler

Unruly dogs can be dangerous to drive with and must be restrained in some manner. When traveling in a car, the restraint options include a dog kennel, a leash, a harness, and a separating gate. If you have a vehicle that is large enough to accommodate a kennel, it's often the best option, because it gives a dog freedom of movement and is comfortable. Leashes can present a danger if the dog is suddenly thrown off balance while traveling. A sudden jerk could injure a dog's neck, or a dog could fall off a seat and be unable to move. *Do not* use a choke chain when using a leash for restraint in a car. A harness is safer for your dog and can be attached to a leash. Separating gates are used in station wagons and vans, creating a separate back area for the dog. If your vehicle is adaptable for a gate, they are very effective, allowing freedom of movement with normal ventilation.

Health Certificates When Traveling

Health certificates are required in certain instances as proof of a dog's health status and vaccination history. A health certificate can be obtained from your veterinarian. These certificates are required by airlines if a dog is flying with you either in the passenger or special cargo section. When traveling by car, you may be asked for a health certificate at a checkpoint when crossing a state line. However, I frequently travel across states lines and have only been asked once for a health certificate on my dogs. The state also asked for a certificate on my horse, who was traveling with us. Some states just require proof of rabies vaccination with a certificate—not just a tag.

International Travel

If you are traveling to an area where you're not sure what's required, ask your veterinarian to find out. The rules of international travel requirements for dogs vary greatly from country to country but each requires specific vaccinations within a certain number of days prior to leaving. The consulate of the country you're going to can usually provide you with the necessary paperwork and answer your questions.

Be sure to inquire about quarantines, because some countries (including England and Australia) have a mandatory quarantine period that all dogs entering the country are subject to. Hawaii also imposes a strict quarantine (currently 120 days). In addition to a long separation from your dog, quarantines can be expensive, because you must pay a large fee for the care of your dog.

Health Records

When traveling long distances be sure to take along a copy of your dog's health record. A home health record that lists vaccinations, wormings, and other pertinent data can be obtained from your veterinarian. If a rabies tag is lost or any questions arise, the health record is a handy reference.

I have often been called upon to treat dogs whose owners were simply traveling through town when a sudden illness put an abrupt halt to their journeys. I am always grateful when the owner has health records in these cases, because the record helps me to rule out certain problems and focus on others. Since most health records also list your regular veterinarian, it is relatively easy to reach him or her in an emergency without having to track down a phone number.

Once I was visited by a man traveling through town whose 18-year-old dog was very ill and needed extensive treatment. Due to the poor condition of the dog, the likelihood that she would not recover from the illness, and the high cost of the needed care, I advised him that euthanasia might be the best choice. The owner said he understood the costs and the slim chance for survival, but wanted to pursue treatment. I was glad to do this but concerned because he drove a very old, rusted, and dilapidated car and his clothes were somewhat shabby. I felt guilty having this nice man spend his last dime on a dog whose chances were so slim. A phone consultation with the regular veterinarian enabled me to discuss the case but also provided me with assurances that money was no problem to this client. It seems that the owner had strong underworld connections—hence the disguise. I was extremely grateful that the dog defied all odds and responded well to treatment. She was able to continue her travels with her owner a short time later.

Remember the Weather

Always take weather conditions into account when traveling with your dog. Keep in mind that a dog cannot adjust to temperature changes as easily as you can. Your dog cannot take off a coat to feel cooler or put one on to warm up. She must regulate temperature changes internally. A dog's main way to cool down is to pant—they do not sweat through the pores of their skin like people do. Some dogs sweat on the underside of their feet, but this allows very little body cooling. Because the dog is so limited in cooling off her body, you must control her environment as best you can.

Dogs who travel with you can be acclimated to diverse temperatures, but their ability to do so depends on the breed and its adaptability. For instance, in cold weather huskies develop dense coats with thick undercoats (a layer of soft, dense hair close to the body) suitable for freezing temperatures. However, you cannot expect a husky with a winter coat to tolerate hot weather. To adapt to hot temperatures the husky would need to be kept in the new warm climate as the weather changed from cold to warm; this would allow the coat to change gradually and become thinner. Even though the coat changes, this does not guarantee that the husky will be able to fully tolerate warm temperatures, because this breed is genetically predisposed to growing a coat for cold temperatures and this natural heavy coat can only thin out so much.

Other heavy-coated breeds such as chows have become popular pets in warm climates. These dogs require extensive clipping so they will not suffer in the heat. If you're unsure about your dog's needs, check with your veterinarian or groomer about the pros and cons of clipping your dog's coat if your travels will expose him to a change in climate.

Sometimes it is necessary to leave your dog in the car when traveling in order to take a meal break. When traveling in hot weather, shade from direct sunlight is crucial to protect your dog from overheating. If you need to leave your dog outside, even for a short time, be sure to provide shade. It can take as little as five minutes for a dog to overheat. I have treated many cases of overheating and the comment I always hear is "I thought he'd be all right; I was only gone for a minute."

Many dogs suffer heat exhaustion and dehydration from being left in cars. Because many dogs will jump out of the car if the windows are left open, owners usually leave them open a few inches—but often not enough to allow for proper ventilation. Even with the windows down all the way, a car can heat up rapidly when it is sitting in direct sunlight. In some areas of the country it may take 10 to 15 minutes for summer temperatures to become high enough to affect your dog. However, in the Deep South the temperature in a car can climb to a dangerous range in less than five minutes. If you must leave your dog in the car in hot weather, leave the windows down and park in the shade. The best policy may be to leave your dog at home in hot weather.

If your dog is panting rapidly and feels hot to the touch, she may be suffering heatstroke. Sometimes in very advanced stages of heatstroke, the panting will stop. If you are able to take the temperature and it is 104°F or higher and the dog has been exposed to excessive heat, heatstroke is the likely diagnosis. (See "Taking the Temperature," p. 197.) Heatstroke is a life-threatening condition; the dog must be cooled down immediately. If possible, take the dog to the closest veterinarian. If a veterinarian is not available immediately, the best way to cool the dog is to put her in a bath of cool water or run cool water over her body until the temperature goes down. Then take her to the veterinarian as soon as possible.

When traveling in cold weather and leaving your dog in the car, try to provide a blanket so your dog can curl up and keep warm. Don't think your dog's coat is enough to keep him warm. One of my dogs enjoys wearing a dog sweater on cold days and graduates to an insulated dog coat if she accompanies me to a horse show in cold weather. This is an option if your dog is unaccustomed to severe cold for long periods. My toy poodle, Lily, prefers another solution to the problem of cold weather—get someone to hold you inside his or her coat. She is a master at convincing people to do this and stays quite warm as a result.

Boarding in Kennels, with a Dog Sitter, or Leaving Your Dog with Friends

When you are going out of town and cannot take your dog with you, it is sometimes difficult to decide on the best care. Whoever is charged with the care of your dog is taking on a big responsibility, so be sure they are up to it. You also want to be sure your dog has a rapport with the people who will be caring for her. If this rapport does not exist, your dog will miss you even more. It is stressful enough to have you away; she also needs emotional support from her caretakers.

Whether you board your dog in a kennel, have a sitter come to your home to care for her, or ask friends to care for her in their home, it is also important that the caretakers understand the dog's feeding and watering instructions and exercise regimens. Put all of this in writing so it is clear. Make sure the dog's own diet is available, with added supplements. This is no time to cut back on nutrition.

Also leave complete health records and your veterinarian's phone number. In case of an emergency, your out-of-town number is also vital. Some people also leave a written permission letter, allowing a veterinarian to treat the dog as necessary in their absence in an emergency. Others notify the veterinarian before they leave town, preapproving any emergency care that may be required.

If you select a boarding kennel, always inspect it before leaving your dog there. In general, the criteria for selecting a groomer on page 58 relates to a kennel as well. Certainly cleanliness, safety, and friendly personnel are important aspects.

When a dog is cared for in her own home, there are fewer stresses, but the dog may get very lonely if the caretaker only comes in once or twice a day. In a kennel or in another home the unfamiliar environment can add to a sense of disorientation, so it's important that the dog be given lots of affection. Friends who care for your dog in their own home may not be aware of certain hazards in their home or yard, so alert them to any potential problem areas.

Be sure the dog's toys are available, as well as a piece of clothing you have worn, such as a pair of socks or a T-shirt. Your scent will be reassuring in your absence. Bach flower remedies (especially Rescue Remedy) can also be helpful in dealing with the emotional issues of a separation from a beloved owner (see page 160). And be sure to talk to your dog prior to the trip, giving all the details, including when you are leaving and when you are returning. Even if she doesn't understand the words, your dog will probably comprehend more than you might think.

5
Grooming

The Importance of Grooming

Owners are often confused about the specific grooming needs of their dogs. Does she need to be brushed? How often should I bathe him? Would she be more comfortable with a short clip? These and many other questions are commonly asked about grooming.

You must first consider each dog individually, according to the dog's age, breed, and living situation. Dogs with heavy undercoats have very different grooming requirements than short-haired dogs, and an outside dog may have different grooming priorities than a dog kept inside the house. Some dogs need to be brushed daily, whereas others will rarely need it. However, brushing is good for all dogs, even if their hair is short. The brushing helps to clean the coat, distributes the body oil through the hair, and removes dead hair. In addition, most dogs enjoy brushing and it helps create a caring bond between you and your dog.

Before acquiring a dog it's necessary to learn about that particular dog's grooming requirements. Most people are aware that poodles require regular grooming, but some breeds, especially those with long hair, also need considerable grooming care. It's the semi-long-haired dog that can fool you about grooming care. Dogs like Bouvier des Flandres have beautiful hair but it tends to be somewhat fine and can tangle easily, thus requiring regular brushing. Because they are large dogs it can take time to brush them out, so consider carefully when deciding to adopt a high-maintenance dog. It's not fair to bring a dog into your home unless you are able to properly care for him.

Some well-known small breeds that must be trimmed and brushed on a regular basis are: Pekingese, Lhasa apso, Shih Tzu, cocker spaniels, schnauzers, and Yorkshire terriers. Middle-size breeds that require regular grooming include springer spaniels and shelties. Large-size breeds include: Akitas, Bouvier des Flandres, golden retrievers, sheepdogs, Samoyeds, Great Pyrenees, Saint Bernards, and German shepherds. Dogs with double coats or undercoats such as chows require special grooming when they shed their undercoat.

If you have a question about the grooming needs of a specific breed, call a professional groomer, ask your veterinarian, or consult a book on grooming.

To keep your dog in optimum health and best understand its individual grooming needs, it's advisable to do a daily check using the criteria listed below before you begin brushing the coat. After all, your dog can't tell you if something is hurting, so you want to check the entire body for potential problems, including the possibility of injuries.

Grooming Checklist

Coat quality	Check hair for dryness, mats, and bald spots
Skin	Look at color; check for dryness, scaliness, hot, moist areas, and injured areas
Ears	Check for excessive wax buildup, redness, or discharge
Eyes	Check for discharge buildup under eyes and debris or hair in eyes
Paws	Look between pads for foreign objects, ingrown hairs, cuts, or signs of infection
Genital area	Look for signs of redness, enlargement, or discharge
Tail	Check for injuries

If your dog is a house dog, it may be necessary to give more frequent baths and brush more often to prevent shedding. Outside dogs also need regular grooming and should not be neglected. The old adage "out of sight, out of mind" is not appropriate when it comes to your dog's grooming needs. In fact, dogs who are kept outside may need closer attention because they are often subjected to conditions that cause matted hair or exposure to diseases.

After you have gone through this daily checklist for a couple of weeks, you will be thoroughly aware of your dog's body. Then you can then set up a schedule of regular care, which might be daily or weekly or whatever timetable best meets your dog's individual needs.

Professional Groomers

If your dog is one of the many breeds that require regular grooming (such as a poodle), you will have to have the dog groomed by a professional or learn to do it yourself. Professional groomers offer a variety of services and could save you time, but you will have to transport the dog back and forth unless you can find a groomer who will make house calls. In some large cities professional groomers come to your home and work from a well-equipped van. Ask your veterinarian and friends for recommendations.

When you're interviewing a potential groomer, don't be afraid to ask lots of questions. Be sure that you feel comfortable with this person. Here are some questions to start with:

- Do you have referrals from clients?
- What are your hours of operation?
- Do you have experience in grooming my dog's breed?
- What brands of grooming products do you use? Find out if they use natural products or products with harsh (and potentially toxic) chemicals that could dry the coat or irritate the skin.
- Do you sanitize the kennels, grooming surface, and equip-

ment between dogs? This is important as a guard against bacteria and disease.

- Do you require the dog to be vaccinated? Unless the groomer checks vaccination records, you cannot be sure that your dog will not be exposed to kennel cough and other diseases. (See more on vaccinations on page 183.)
- How do you restrain the dog during bathing and the grooming procedure? A leash attached to a stand on the grooming table or sink is the most common method. If your dog does not tolerate this, be sure to inform the groomer. Do not allow tranquilizers to be used unless absolutely necessary, and have them administered by a veterinarian; the veterinarian will evaluate your dog's health and use the correct type and dosage. Tranquilizers can be dangerous to your dog if she is older or sensitive to the drug used, and they should be avoided unless absolutely necessary.

Other factors will be more subjective. Are the premises clean and orderly? Ask to see the grooming area. Do you like the groomer? Does your dog like the groomer? How does your dog react to the groomer when first handled? You'll also want to inform the groomer of any sensitive areas or physical disabilities to be aware of when grooming your dog.

One of the advantages of doing the grooming yourself is that you become very familiar with your dog's body and can note any problems that may require attention. If you take him to a professional groomer, be sure to check his body thoroughly after it's clipped. Many times dogs have been brought into my clinic with problems such as tumors or extensive infections that had worsened before being spotted, and could have been treated if caught earlier. So don't use the groomer as an excuse to avoid examining your dog's body on a regular basis. Although many groomers do an excellent job of noticing problems, remember that only you know your dog best. You are the best judge of your dog's health status.

Doing the Grooming Yourself

Many owners prefer to groom their own dogs. If you are going to do it yourself, you'll need specific equipment for the job. I advise purchasing a grooming book that includes details about which clippers and other equipment will work best for your dog. The book will also give you some ideas about clipping patterns. The expense of the equipment alone can deter some people, but if you are truly interested in grooming your own dog, I advise you to visit a groomer's shop and observe how dogs are clipped, bathed, ear hair removed, nails cut, and so on. If you think you're up to it, then try it yourself. Don't expect to clip a dog as quickly as a professional groomer. Be patient and go slowly at first. It can take time to gain the experience to groom efficiently.

I groomed my own dogs for many years and enjoyed this special time with them on a regular basis. My aunt was a professional groomer so she taught me many details that gave my trim jobs a professional look. Eventually, though, my veterinary practice became increasingly demanding on my time. My dogs liked being groomed on the same day and I just wasn't able to set aside that block of time to groom them. So now I usually take them to a professional groomer. If you can devote the time needed, I encourage you to groom your own dog. One major plus of doing it yourself is that you can control the entire process, from the products you bathe your dog with to the size of clipper blade you use. For sensitive dogs or those requiring special handling, home grooming may be the answer.

Grooming Equipment

Remember, good quality grooming equipment is expensive, but this is an investment that will serve you for years to come.

Brushes and Combs

Many types of brushes and combs are available, and the type of coat your dog has will determine the best selection for your dog. Depending on the breed, you will need to select one or several tools from each type in the following list: a bristle brush, a wire brush, a dematting brush, a regular comb, and a flea comb. To be sure you get the correct ones, consult a professional before buying these items.

The most commonly used brush is the wire brush or slicker brush. The wires are spaced at variable intervals, enabling you to choose a brush that fits your dog's coat type. If the dog has fine hair that must be separated to prevent matting, it's best to select a brush with wires that are close together. If your dog has coarser hair, a brush with wires farther apart will work best. Bristle brushes, the type that many people use, are often used on dogs whose coats don't tend to tangle and simply need normal cleaning and stimulation.

Dog combs are usually made of metal with variable widths available. Combs with handles are easier to use. Flea combs have very close teeth and can actually separate fleas from the hair; the hair must be tangle free, however.

Scissors

Select a type of scissors that has very sharp blades and slightly rounded tips. I prefer the scissors that can be bought at a beauty supply store, used by hairstylists; they stay sharp longer and can be sharpened. Keeping your scissors sharp is important for several reasons. First, dull scissors will pull your dog's hair when you cut it, which can be irritating and even painful to your dog. Second, dull scissors make your hands tire quickly because they have to work harder.

Scissors with slightly rounded tips are safer to use so you can avoid accidental pricks. You will be amazed at how fast your dog can move when it's time to clip the nails. It's these quick unexpected moves that cause injuries; and the rounded tips will help decrease that likelihood. One of my own poodles, Coco, was a master at knowing when it was time to trim his nails. Those paws would disappear under his body as if on springs. I would have to lift him up to extricate them. At that point in our grooming regimen he would cleverly give me the signal that he had to go outside for a break, knowing that I would not refuse his request and thereby stalling the nail clipping process a little longer.

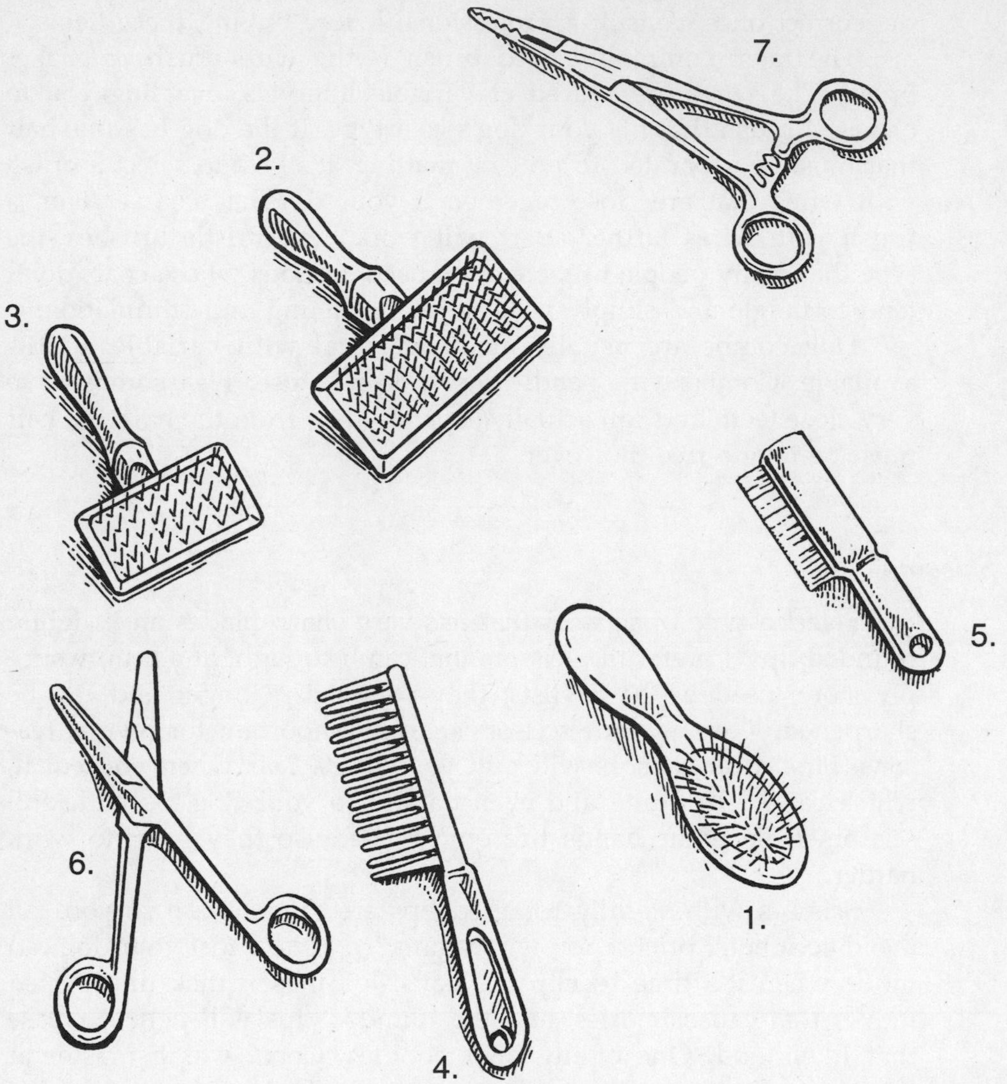

FIGURE 3. Grooming Tools:

1. bristle brush
2. wire (slicker) brush
3. dematting brush
4. regular comb
5. flea comb
6. rounded tip scissors
7. hemostats for removing ear hair

Clippers

If you have a dog that requires clipping, research your dog's specific needs before buying a clipper. For instance, if you have a dog who just needs his coat clipped down without any close, fine work, then a large, powerful electric clipper will not only do a better job, but it will also last longer. Here are the basic types of clippers that are available:

Large-Animal Clippers

Used to do body clips, particularly on thick coats. They have a powerful motor and large, wide blades.

Small-Animal Clippers

Used to do closer, more intricate clips. Special features are available such as interchangeable blades, adjustable blades, and cordless clippers.

It is wise to invest in good clippers. From personal experience, I recommend clippers with an easy changeable blade system such as a snap-on type. This will save you time and the frustration of chasing little screws around the grooming table while trying to change your blades. Despite my years of surgery, I have not become adept with a simple screwdriver, and any way to avoid using one is fine with me. The screws are very small and after many changes they tend to become stripped. Cordless clippers are a nice concept, but they also have some limitations. Usually the blades are not changeable and power is limited. Although large-animal clippers are heavier, they overheat less often on those big jobs such as body clipping a chow with a heavy tangled undercoat.

Other Grooming Equipment

Additionally, you will need the following:

- Tweezers or hemostats—used to remove ear hair
- Grooming table—the table or counter should be a height that is comfortable for you, with a nonslip surface.

- Restraining leash—a special leash that restrains the dog to the grooming table
- Clipper lubricant—check at your pet store for an oil or spray lubricant; use regularly while clipping.

Grooming Procedures

Here's a step-by-step guide to a thorough grooming:

STEP 1: Eyes and Ears

Cleaning your dog's eyes and ears should be a part of your regular grooming process. Once your dog becomes accustomed to it, you will find it takes very little time to perform the task of removing the ear hair and cleaning the debris from the corner of the eyes. Older dogs who are not accustomed to these procedures may need some time to acquire the necessary patience. Go slowly and, as always, explain what you are doing and why. Your soothing and comforting words will go a long way toward reassuring him. It's easier to teach a puppy to tolerate this part of the grooming and accept it as commonplace.

Some dogs' ears are floppy and hang down over the ear canal, thus creating a breeding ground for infections. Many breeds, including poodles, have hair in the ear canal. If left in place this ear hair tends to catch debris and ear wax, which can hold moisture, bacteria, and yeast, creating an infection. Pulling out ear hair may cause a little discomfort, so try to pull out as much as possible each time, using tweezers or hemostats. You may find that you can pull out the ear hair with your fingers; which is fine if it works for you. It may take a while for your dog to be patient as you do this, but most dogs will eventually allow and accept this procedure.

Next, check the eyes for hairs, foreign objects, and discharge that tend to accumulate at the inside corners. Many toy breeds have malfunctioning tear ducts, thus requiring constant cleaning around their eyes. To remove the brown stain under the eyes use hydrogen peroxide on a cotton swab. Be gentle; and do not get the hydrogen peroxide in the eye. Do not cut or tamper with the eyelashes—they serve as protection for the eye.

STEP 2: Nail Trimming

Many owners avoid trimming their dogs' nails, which is one of the most important parts of the grooming process. Why is nail trimming so important? Well, when nails get too long they can cause problems ranging from back pain to fractured legs. Long nails can also be deadly weapons that can cause injury to the dog himself, other dogs, and people. Dogs with protruding eyes, such as Pekingese and Boston terriers, are at special risk when nails become too long, because they can easily scratch their eyes and cause a corneal lesion.

One of my friends has a borzoi who loved to run in the house. Sadly, he caught an overlong nail in the carpet while running and fractured his front leg. Granted, such accidents are rare but they do happen. A simple nail trimming would have prevented this unfortunate accident.

When nails are left too long, the toes may start to turn sideways. This change in toe direction will cause the dog to alter the ways she uses her body, often causing pain. You may think few caring owners would let their pets get into this shape. But, unfortunately, because most people find nail trimming a challenging procedure, it's more common than you'd think. About two-thirds of the dogs I see daily in my clinic need their nails trimmed.

Like ear cleaning, it's best to train your dog to accept nail trimming at a young age. Many dogs seem to have an aversion to it, so it may be necessary to have a friend help you restrain your dog the first few times. I have seen the most even-tempered dogs react violently to nail trimming. Remember to talk to your dog throughout the procedure, explaining what you are doing and why you are doing it in a calm and soothing voice. If you have never trimmed the nails before, have your groomer or veterinarian show you how. The toenail has a vein and a nerve; you must be careful to avoid trimming too far. If you accidentaly cut into the vein or nerve, your dog will let you know, and it will be much more difficult to regain his trust. If the nails are still too sharp after trimming, use an emery board or a nail file to smooth them off.

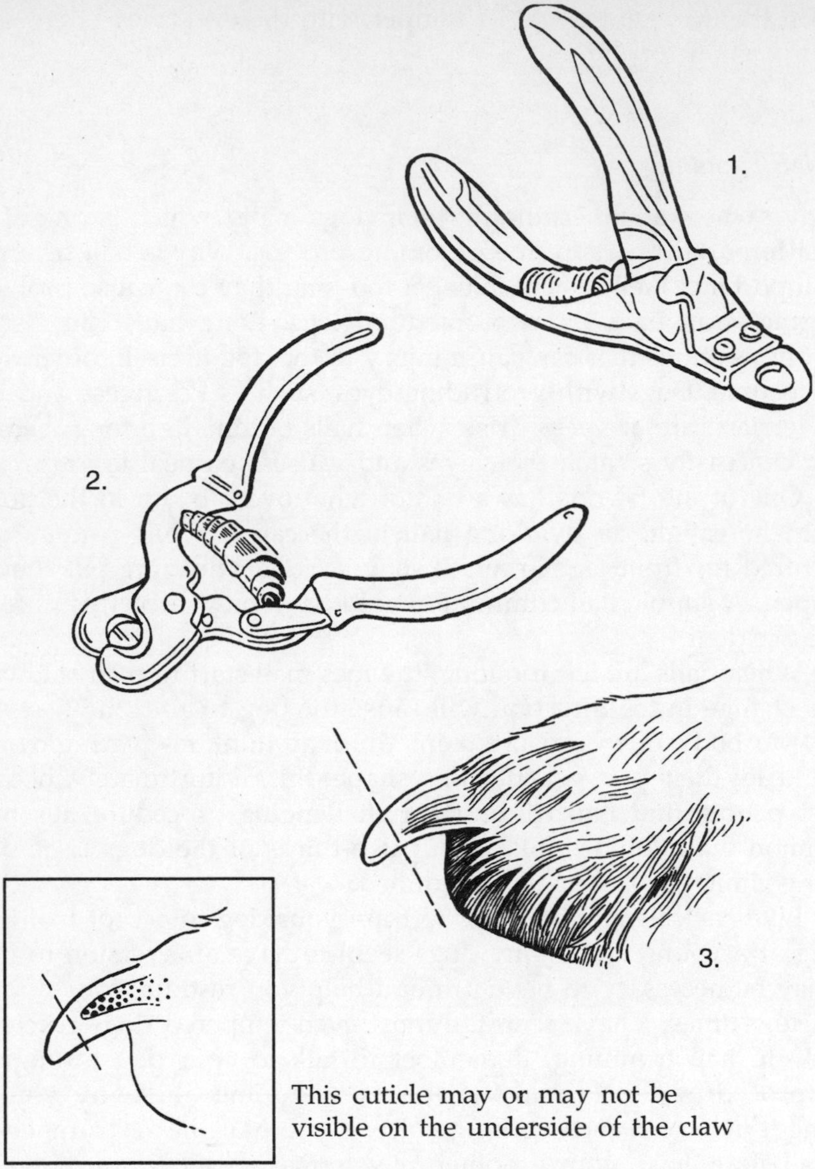
1.
2.
3.
This cuticle may or may not be visible on the underside of the claw

FIGURE 4. Nail Clipping:

1. guillotine-type nail clippers
2. White nail clippers
3. clip only the area below the broken line

STEP 3: Teeth

Note: While all dogs can benefit from regular teeth cleaning, for safety reasons do this only if your dog will allow. Training a dog to allow teeth cleaning from puppyhood is the best. If your dog will not allow teeth cleaning, do not persist. BE SURE YOUR VETERINARIAN CHECKS TEETH DURING ALL EXAMINATIONS.

Yes, your dog's teeth can be brushed, too. Tiny particles of food trapped between teeth can lead to decay and periodontal disease, just as it does for us humans. If there is a yellowish or brownish color to the teeth, particularly the molars in the back, you may need to have the veterinarian do a teeth cleaning rather than attempting it yourself. Do not put it off, because many health problems can result from decay and periodontal disease. (See "Tooth and Gum Problems" in Part II.)

A home dental kit for dogs is available from the Natural Pet Care Catalog (see p. 327). This kit includes a specially designed toothbrush and beef-flavored enzymatic toothpaste containing hydrogen peroxide to help control plaque and bad breath. This toothpaste does not have to be rinsed. Another alternative is to use a child's toothbrush and a toothpaste for dogs from a pet store. Be sure the toothpaste does not contain fluoride.

Wet the toothbrush with water and use only a very small amount of toothpaste, because you won't be able to rinse the dog's teeth as you rinse your own after brushing. To brush the teeth, simply lift the mouth and brush top and bottom teeth, including the front and back sides. Use a gentle to slightly firm stroke as you brush. Too firm a stroke could damage the gums.

STEP 4: Checking for Mats and Removing Mats

Check over your dog's body for mats. Mats occur in the dog's coat when hair that has been shed does not fall out and becomes tangled in the coat with the remaining hair. These mats tend to catch debris and trap moisture under the hair, predisposing the area to skin disease. Bacteria and fungus thrive under mats in warm, moist conditions, causing what are commonly known as "hot spots." Also, be sure to check for mats under the ears. Once mats are formed, the hair must be separated by hand or trimmed off. Cutting out mats can be tricky if the mat is close to the skin and an infection is present under it. These areas are sensitive, often painful, and require careful handling. Some dogs, if severely matted, must be sedated by a veterinarian to remove their mats, because the discomfort is too much for them to bear. If you do try to cut out a difficult mat, go slowly and be sure your scissors are the type described previously with rounded tips. MOST MATS MUST BE CUT OUT WITH A SCISSORS. Sometimes small isolated mats can be carefully brushed out if the dog tolerates it, but stop if it is painful.

Dealing with mats takes time and patience. It's much easier to brush your dog regularly. If your dog is one of those types where all the brushing in the world wouldn't keep the coat straight, regular clips and the use of a coat conditioner will help to keep the hair tangle-free.

Many owners have been led to believe that poodles don't shed their coats, but this is not the case. Actually, the hair is shed, but because of the kink in the hair coat, it remains in the hair. Poodles require frequent grooming to remove this dead hair and prevent mats.

STEP 5: Brushing

Set up your brushing on a regular schedule, according to the needs of your dog's coat. Brushing out the coat completely will prevent mats as well as giving you the opportunity to thoroughly check the dog's skin for any problems. This is a special time that you spend with your dog. If you begrudge the time the grooming takes, the dog may sense your feelings and become difficult to handle.

Approaching the brushing with a positive outlook and as an opportunity to spend quality time with your dog will make grooming a pleasurable experience and one that your dog will enjoy in the future. I talk to my dogs while I'm brushing them, constantly reminding them how beautiful they will look when I'm finished. I also try to begin with the area where they most like being brushed and do this area again at the very end. This helps to reinforce the enjoyable impression of the grooming process.

My toy poodle, Lily, loves to be brushed. But what she really loves most is getting her nails polished. When the groomer first polished her nails I protested, not really liking the painted poodle look.

But Lily overruled me; she made it perfectly clear that she liked the polished nails by running around and showing them off to everyone she came into contact with.

STEP 6: Clipping

If your dog requires clipping, you will need a great deal more patience if you plan to do it yourself. To tolerate clipping, dogs must be trained. Of course, it's best if they get used to being clipped from the time they are puppies. Some dogs need less clipping than others, but standing on a table for any length of time can be extremely boring for your dog. It's best to make your dog feel very secure by introducing the process slowly.

Be sure the grooming surface is nonslip, or use a vinyl tablecloth on top of your table. Let your dog see and smell the clippers both off and while they are running to reassure her that the noise and vibration will not hurt. If she displays a great deal of fear and becomes unmanageable, don't proceed beyond this step. Wait until the next day and repeat the introduction of the clippers. If necessary, continue this step for several days, until she is calm in the presence of the clippers. Then you will be able to proceed with the clipping with fewer problems. Allowing for this period of adjustment will pay off in the long run. Forcing a dog to submit to clipping when she is frightened can cause worse problems the next time you try to clip her. Dogs remember bad experiences and may demonstrate even more unruly behavior the next time. Don't give up when dealing with a frightened dog. Eventually almost all dogs will adjust to being clipped.

It's important to look at the situation from the dog's point of view. When a dog is frightened and you try to force it to be clipped by excessive restraint, a fight usually results. Then the dog has accomplished what it set out to achieve—avoiding the clipping—and has also created a strong negative feeling for herself and for you. Neither of you will look forward to the next clipping session, at which time your negative feelings of dread and animosity may communicate to your dog, making the situation even more difficult.

Once in a while you will have to use some force to restrain a dog, but avoid it if at all possible. Many horses I have owned required training to accept being clipped. If you think a dog is difficult to restrain, imagine a 1,000-pound horse! The same technique is effective for horses, resulting in a horse that is easy and safe to clip.

Don't think that after one session your dog will thereafter behave when being clipped. It can take up to six initial clipping sessions to work through your dog's difficult behavior and establish positive association with the grooming procedure. Allow for idiosyncracies in your dog and try to work around them. Remember that he's a unique individual too. One of my poodles was ticklish over the end of his nose. When I used the clippers on his nose and around his whiskers it drove him crazy. When I tried using scissors to trim this area, no further disobedience occurred. Another one of my dogs is very ticklish on her back feet near her pads. If I clip very quickly she tolerates it, but slow clipping will cause her to jerk her foot and no amount of discipline will make her stop.

Check your clippers frequently to be sure they are not overheating and causing discomfort to your dog. Clipping too close can cause clipper burn, resulting in a scraped-looking area. This usually happens on the face, but it can occur anywhere on the body. Clipper burn also relates to the angle of the clippers to the skin when clipping; try to maintain a 45-degree angle.

The frequency of clipping depends on your dog and how fast her hair grows. Most poodles require reclipping every six to eight weeks. Other breeds, such as chows or Saint Bernards, may only need a seasonal clipping in the late spring or summer. If you're not sure about your dog, ask a groomer's advice.

Do not think that clipping is distressing to a dog. Most dogs feel good after they've been clipped, and some even show off their new haircuts by strutting about. A few dogs are wallflowers after they've been clipped, but even they seem to feel better.

Once the clipping is finished, it's time to give your dog a bath. Some people like to "rough-in" by doing the close clipping and form the haircut, then bathe the dog, and, at the end, finish clipping the coat after it's been dried and brushed out. Bathing before clipping seems to make the skin more sensitive and prone to clipper burn.

STEP 7: The Bath

Each dog has different requirements for bathing according to his health and environment. Mother Nature didn't design dogs for bathing, so it's best to keep baths to a minimum. If your dog lives indoors most of the time and carries an odor, he may require more frequent baths. In no event should a dog be bathed more than once a week at the absolute maximum. Brushing the dog on a regular schedule will also reduce the need for bathing by helping to clean the coat, distributing the body oil through the hair, and removing dead hair.

If you have a problem with fleas (which I'll discuss shortly) and your dog is getting frequent flea dips, always bathe your dog before dipping. This helps the dip stay on the hair because there are fewer oils to prevent the dip from coating the hair. Also, dogs should always be bathed when they are getting clipped. This is a good bathing schedule, provided your dog doesn't get dirty in between clips.

Puppies can be a real challenge. Resist the urge to give them daily baths, no matter how messy they get. Every time you get a puppy wet there is a small risk of illness. So I recommend as few full baths as possible with spot cleaning as needed. Don't bathe more often than once a week—this will protect the coat and decrease the stress level.

Bathing Products

There are an abundance of bathing products on the market, and making a choice can be very confusing. Should you use a flea shampoo, a medicated shampoo, or a conditioning shampoo? Should you use a conditioner after shampooing? What about hot-oil treatments? There are almost as many choices for dogs as there are for people. Again, your dog's needs will help you determine what to buy.

Always check the label of any shampoo or conditioner that you are considering. Avoid using products with harsh detergents and alcohol, because they can be very drying to the skin. If frequent bathing is required, try to use as mild a shampoo as possible. Remember, Mother Nature didn't design dogs to be bathed and the oils in the coat are diminished when a dog is bathed. So pay special attention to the products you use and be sure to brush your dog after the bath to stimulate circulation to the skin and restore natural oils to the coat. If your dog is going to the groomers, check the products being used. My own poodles once experienced problems with a particular shampoo used by a groomer. This shampoo resulted in a nice fluffy coat but after about a week the hair was so stripped of oil that it tangled and matted very easily.

Let's look at the various products on the market:

Shampoo

Regular Shampoo—Choose a natural shampoo for dogs or for people. (Some of the companies listed under "Product Suppliers" in the Appendix make good pet shampoos.) If using human shampoo, DO NOT USE IT FULL STRENGTH. Dilute it half and half with water. One of my favorites is Dr. Bronner's Oil Base Soap in almond. It's a liquid that cleans but does not dry out the coat.

Medicated Shampoo—If your dog has skin problems, a medicated shampoo may be helpful. Medicated shampoos are sold in a variety of types with sulfur, betadyne, coal tar, and such an added aid in controlling some skin problems. Generally sulfur and betadyne shampoos are used to combat excessive bacteria growth on the skin. Coal tar is used as a conditioner and is often recommended when dry skin accompanies a skin disease. I don't recommend antidandruff shampoos intended for humans, because they are very strong. Medicated shampoos can be used in conjunction with conditioners, but always check the label to make sure no problems will result. Ask your holistic veterinarian or groomer for a shampoo recommendation according to your dog's skin condition.

Flea Shampoo—Commercial flea shampoos contain insecticides to kill the fleas. Puppies under 16 weeks of age may become ill from these insecticides, which are toxic. Herbal flea products have become very popular, but even these natural products can have drawbacks. Like their toxic chemical counterparts, some natural products can also cause skin reactions such as itching and redness. Although herbal flea shampoos can be safely used on most dogs, I have seen dogs have allergic reactions to citronella, pennyroyal, and eucalyptus. Always test a small area of skin before saturating the entire dog with a new shampoo. If you are used to the flea-control or killing abilities of chemical flea dips, you should be aware that natural products are safer but the results are more variable and sometimes less impressive in terms of actual flea control. However, this is a small price to pay for having less toxic poisons on your dog's body.

Another option to flea shampoos made with toxic insecticides is to use a detergent-based shampoo, work up a good lather, and leave it on for 10 minutes. This usually kills most fleas. And yet another alternative to flea shampoos is adding Avon's Skin-So-Soft to the rinse. Do not use it full strength but dilute it half and half with water and pour over the dog as a final rinse. It can be left on to dry and act as a flea repellent. When using flea shampoos, remember that the shampoo does not have a residual effect. You are only killing the fleas on the dog, not preventing fleas from jumping on. (Also see "Fleas" on page 260 for further information.)

Conditioning Shampoo—These shampoos usually have an oil base that coats the skin and hair. Some can be very soothing to irritated skin and others help keep the hair untangled. Read the label carefully to make sure it's the correct shampoo for your dog.

Conditioners

Creme Rinse—This is the most common type of rinse available. It works to detangle the hair and may even help to keep the hair tangle-free for a short while. It can be rinsed off or left on to dry. If using a product made for humans, always dilute it half and half with water. Oatmeal conditioners are popular today, because they soothe the skin and decrease irritation.

Moisturizing Rinse—Used to hold moisture in the skin, this type of rinse may leave an oily coating on the hair.

Hot-Oil Treatment—A hot-oil treatment can be very effective to soothe dry, irritated skin and condition the hair. This treatment can be applied once every two weeks if necessary. Hot-oil treatments for animals are available from most veterinarians and in many pet stores. Some kits also include compatible shampoo and other skin care products.

Where to Give a Bath

So you've got the shampoo and you're ready to get that dog soaped up, but where is the best place to do it? There are several things to consider—safety, comfort, and convenience. Of course, one major factor is the size of your dog. Choose a location where you can control your dog, preventing her from jumping out. The main locations to choose from are: bathtub, sink, shower, and yard.

Bathtubs are probably the most frequently used dog bathing venues and may be the easiest. Bathtubs with sliding shower doors are my favorite because the dog cannot easily escape while being bathed. But the problem with bathtubs is that they can be hard on your back. If you have back problems, I'd suggest another choice. Many people take their dogs in the shower with them, which can work well and make the job a bit easier, especially with large dogs. Sinks often work best for small dogs. Yard bathing works well for large dogs—if things get messy there's no cleanup necessary. Of course, when you bathe in the yard you are dependent on an outside water faucet, with only cold water. In extremely hot weather, this might work but it is a problem in cold weather or when you're dealing with a young, sick, or sensitive dog. It may be possible to run a hose to an inside water faucet, allowing you to adjust water temperatures. Wherever you bathe your dog, use a spray nozzle to control the water flow.

Bathing Procedure

If you take the following steps, bath giving will be a bit easier on everyone's nerves:

1. Gather everything you'll need:

- several thick towels
- shampoo, conditioner, and/or dip
- spray nozzle and hose attached to faucet
- hand-held hair dryer

2. Adjust the water temperature to lukewarm. Always test the water before putting your dog in it to avoid excessive temperatures that might harm him.

3. Wet the dog's entire coat, including the face.

4. Apply the shampoo and work in over the entire body. DO NOT GET SHAMPOO IN EYES, NOSE, OR EARS. Some dogs manage to get shampoo in their eyes no matter what precautions you take. If your dog is one of them, apply an ointment of liquid tears (available in the contact-lens section of your drugstore) to protect the eyes during the bath. If water gets in the ears, inflammation or infection could result. Put cotton balls in the ears if this is a problem with your dog.

5. Rinse the coat thoroughly. Be sure no soap is left on the skin—it could cause irritation.

6. Make sure the coat is clean. One shampooing should be enough, but if the coat still seems oily or dirty, repeat the shampooing.

7. If you are using conditioner, apply according to label directions. Let it set a few minutes so maximum benefit can be derived.

8. Rinse conditioner off thoroughly.

9. Towel-dry.

10. Blow-dry completely. Blowing your dog dry will help to cut down on the stress experienced by the body when it's completely wet. In nature when a dog gets wet, the coat sheds off a lot of the moisture due to the oil in the coat; therefore the dog is not really as wet and takes only a short time to dry. But because domesticated dogs usually don't have enough oil in their coats, drying takes longer. Many dogs get cold and are stressed. This is especially true for puppies, which should always be thoroughly dried after a bath. When drying a puppy with a hand-held blow dryer, start on the lowest setting until the puppy gets used to it and then work your way up to a higher setting. If you constantly run your hand through the coat as it's drying, you will be able to assure that the setting is not too high for the dog's comfort level. Dry the chest first, then the ears, followed by the rest of the body.

Dealing with Fleas

When bathing a dog who is covered with fleas, I always try to kill the fleas before doing the bath. If you just start bathing the dog, the fleas tend to scatter and jump off. I don't like them jumping on me and infesting the area where I am bathing the dog. Spray with a quick-kill product that has a pyrethrin base and immediately wash it off in the bath. (Also see the section on "Flea Shampoos," p. 72.)

Dealing with Skin Infections and Injuries

Shampoos can cause irritation if the skin is infected, making matters worse. Consult your holistic veterinarian to recommend a shampoo. Medicated shampoos containing chlorhexidine, sulfur, or betadyne are most commonly used for dogs with skin infections.

If your dog has been injured and has an open lesion, it is important not to get shampoo in it; shampoo can be very destructive to cells and will prolong the healing process.

6

A Healthy Diet

Prescription for Health: A High-Quality Diet

If this is the only chapter you read in this book, I will be content; a high-quality diet is the most crucial ingredient to your dog's health. A commitment to optimum health and longevity for your dog *must* include a high-quality diet. And that does not necessarily mean going out and finding the most expensive food available, though better foods generally do cost a bit more.

A healthy diet for your dog does not have to break the bank. But a commitment to diet—as natural and high quality as possible—will be well worth your efforts and any additional cost. As a veterinarian, I can tell you that the dog's diet has a direct correlation to health and longevity. Remember the old adage: An ounce of prevention is worth a pound of cure. The price tag for quality food fed now will reap years of love, friendship, and loyalty.

I am a holistic veterinarian; therefore, I have a vast array of both traditional and holistic options from which to choose in treating a dog. Sometimes my sole prescription is a change to a high-quality diet that frequently solves the health problem, eliminating the need for any other kind of veterinary treatments.

When Luke, a 95-pound chocolate Labrador retriever, first came to see me he was like so many dogs I see every day: he had a sparse, dry, flaky, dull, and coarse coat; his frequent scratching indicated uncomfortable, itchy skin; his lethargy indicated a lack of energy; and he suffered from frequent attacks of gas. Because Luke's owners had come to accept these symptoms as normal for him, they considered him to be a healthy dog.

When I first met Luke his diet consisted of a discount store generic brand of kibble that contained a high percentage of soy protein. I put him on a lamb- and rice-based food and then, a few weeks later, switched to a high-quality chicken- and corn-based food, which was more readily available in the area where Luke and his family live. A few times a week his owners added natural culture yogurt and acidophilus powder to his diet to help eliminate the problems with gas.

Within six weeks Luke was a vibrantly healthy dog: his coat was shiny, thick, and smooth; his skin was clean and his incessant scratching had stopped; his increased energy was apparent to all; and his bouts of gas all but disappeared.

The truth is that your dog's health is a reflection of his diet, and the overall quality of that diet determines what resources are available to his body to fight disease. The only exception to this statement would be hereditary ailments and, even then, some of these ailments can be less severe with a high-quality diet. Therefore, the ingredients in the dog food have significant importance.

When you switch to a high-quality diet, ongoing health problems may disappear within days or weeks. But even dogs who appear healthy will gain an elevated vitality; this new energy and the signs of improved health may be imperceptible to all but the most astute and aware owners. When you become sensitive to the little signs that your dog is feeling younger and more vital, you will value the difference a natural high-quality diet can make. Some of the signs that I may see immediately are a shinier coat, less "dog odor," fewer bowel movements, and fewer digestive problems (gas). But the greater value comes from the long-term benefits of internal cleansing and supplying the correct nutritional building blocks to the body to maintain optimum health.

It is regrettable that Madison Avenue has led people to believe that government standards for pet foods will lead to optimum health. When confronted with the huge variety of dry kibble, canned foods, semimoist foods, and treats to select from, the public has been told that they are all scientifically formulated and are good and safe for our dogs. But the fact is the experts who put together the government standards for pet foods have far lower standards than I believe are necessary for optimum health.

In a recent article in a professional journal, Dr. R. L. Wysong argues that pet food companies should not be allowed to label their foods 100 percent complete, because the study of nutrition is ongoing and new discoveries make old absolutes untrue. He says,

> The best way to see the reasonableness of removal of the "100% complete" claim is with an analogy, a human parallel. How many parents would take the advice of a pediatrician who placed a packaged food product on the exam table and told the parent that this is the only product they should feed the child day-in, day-out, for the child's lifetime, and further that they should be sure to not feed any other foods because that might unbalance the product? Even if the pediatrician gave assurances of nutrient analyses that exceeded required minimum levels, feeding trials, and even if the label guaranteed "100% complete and balanced," how many parents would accept such counsel?[1]

The pet food industry and federal regulatory agencies have led us to believe that these cans and bags of food are all that our dogs will ever need. But, as Dr. Wysong points out in his article, to claim that any food is "100% complete" would indicate that pet food manufacturers know everything there is to know about animal nutrition. The fact is that less is known about animal nutrition than human nutrition—and certainly no one in the scientific community is given credit for knowing with 100-percent certainty a human's nutritional needs. It's clear that the opposite is true. From time to time medical researchers identify nutrients that are required by the body that were unknown previously. This is one of the reasons I feel a top-quality food that exceeds government nutritional standards is needed to assure vibrant health.

Many veterinarians don't even ask what you are feeding when you bring your dog in for a yearly checkup or for a visit due to an illness. Like your own medical doctor, many veterinarians have lim-

1. R. L. Wysong, D.V.M., "The Myth of the 100% Complete Manufactured Diet," *Journal of the American Holistic Veterinary Medical Association*, February–April, 1992, vol. 11, no. 1, p. 17.

ited training in nutrition, so many of them do not focus on the link between health and diet. Fortunately, this is changing as scientific findings continue to prove conclusively that vital link. More and more medical doctors and veterinarians are becoming aware that we are what we eat. This old axiom is as true when it comes to your dog's health as it is for your own. As more and more owners understand this obvious connection between diet and health, they are moving toward natural diets for their dogs.

In my clinic, questions concerning diet are a routine—and important—part of any exam, and the owner's responses are always recorded on the patient's chart. Sometimes, as with Luke, a change in diet can be the sole prescription I make to clear up a health problem. When the dog has been fed a low-quality diet for a long period of time, however, it can be difficult to correlate an illness to any one cause. When a change in diet leads to an improvement in the condition, I know that I have identified the primary source of the problem. In any event, an upgraded diet is an important step in the treatment of even the most advanced health problem.

I have seen truly dramatic examples of almost immediate results from a switch to a high-quality diet. For instance, the owner of a breeding kennel was concerned about a very low conception rate. She bred Yorkshire terriers and Lhasa apsos. When I suggested the switch to a high-quality food she was concerned about the extra cost but agreed to try it to see if it would make a difference. In the very next heat cycle the conception rate improved by 75 percent, proving that the high-quality food was indeed cost-effective. And the owner realized too that this improved breeding rate was an indicator of increased overall health among her dogs, potentially cutting down on future veterinary bills.

It is often the small, sensitive dogs who are the most susceptible to poor-quality diets. I have found Yorkshire terriers to rank the highest in this category. Not only is their breeding ability often affected, but their coat condition and thickness of the hair are excellent barometers of their overall health. Some Yorkshires can be so sensitive to certain foods that when these foods are eaten, they go into seizures resembling epilepsy. This is an extreme example of how diet affects the body.

What's Wrong with Most Dog Foods Today?

It's not surprising that most people are overwhelmed with the choices of dog foods available today. After all, they each claim to be nutritionally complete. Most owners don't distinguish between dry kibble, semimoist food, and canned food—aren't they all nutritious and safe foods?

Whether the foods are dry or canned, they are marketed to entice owners through appealing shapes and sizes, fancy packaging, and clever advertising. Because people have so little basis for deciding what food to feed their dog, they often decide to buy a food solely because it is formulated for their dog's age group. Or owners can be persuaded to buy a particular food because it is less expensive or, conversely, because it is touted as a "premium" brand and it costs more than other foods. Often people make their selection because TV commercials swayed them; they have no real way of knowing whether this is really the best food for their dog.

For many owners, price is a major consideration. When I ask people what they are feeding, most (especially the owners of large dogs) answer with one of the commercial brands of dry kibble, which appears to be the most cost-effective food available. Some people just buy huge bags of whatever brand is on sale. Admittedly, we cannot all spend as much as we would like purchasing dog food. But in this chapter I hope to convince you that the better foods end up being more cost-effective in the long run. After all, if you are feeding a food that the dog's body cannot fully utilize, he will be unable to break down the nutrients and readily absorb them.

Often these supermarket dog foods have been devised to remind us of "people foods" such as hamburger or cheese. We are being led to the erroneous conclusion that our dog will like it better if it looks like our own foods. Your dog does not care about the color, size, or shape of his food. He *does* care about the smell, taste, texture, and flavor.

Unfortunately, many of these foods are manufactured and fed at the expense of our dogs' health. The semimoist foods are the worst; I consider them to be the "junk foods" of the pet food industry. Most semimoist foods are made to resemble hamburger, chunks of meat, or cheese. They contain a high percentage of artificial flavorings, preservatives, and sugars, which keep the food in that ever-moist state. The protein is of low quality and is difficult to digest. When owners tell me they are feeding semimoist foods, I ask them to take a look at the colorful hamburger-like stools that are produced when semimoist foods are part of the diet. That is usually enough to convince them that this food is being poorly utilized by their dog's body.

Although semimoist foods top the list of foods to avoid, other types of commercial dog food are also culprits in causing dietary problems. Many dog food manufacturers substitute ingredients when availability is a problem. They word their ingredient lists on the packaging to give them leeway, allowing for these substitutions.

Because I ask about the dog's diet as a part of every exam, I have on occasion been able to link illnesses to specific brands of foods. During times when my clinic was overrun with gastrointestinal upsets (i.e., upset stomachs) I was able to link each dog to a recently purchased bag or can of the same brand of food. The symptoms can vary and include vomiting, diarrhea, lack of appetite, eating grass, and drooling. Often the owners had been feeding the same major brand of food for a long period of time with no problems, when suddenly a particular batch of the food caused problems. This could be because the company substituted one ingredient, used a lower-quality ingredient, or stored the food improperly, creating rancidity. Once the dog was taken off the food, the symptoms disappeared.

For single-dog homes, this is an unfortunate but easily resolved problem once the culprit has been identified. However, I have dealt with entire kennels of up to 250 dogs that all had severe diarrhea due to a problem with a specific brand of food. (Imagine dealing with that mess?) In one case, the problem was traced to a local mill that produced the dry food. The manufacturer had been unable to obtain the ingredient that they usually used for a particular mineral and substituted another ingredient that contained that same mineral. Unless a pet food manufacturer is committed to the highest-quality ingredients, they will make these substitutions as the need arises, often because one ingredient is unavailable or because another ingredient will cost less.

To sum up what's wrong with dog foods today is to look at the whole picture. The majority of foods are produced to appeal to the public for sales purposes and not for our dog's optimum health. Quality control of ingredients is not always maintained, and added nutrients are not always digestible by the dog. Generally, the higher quality the ingredients, the more usable they are by the dog's body, requiring less food and producing fewer stools.

What's in Most Dog Foods?

The ingredient list on a bag or can of dog food will usually include terms such as *meat meal, meat by-products, poultry by-products, soybean meal, bonemeal,* and so on. Most use a combination of these ingredients, and they are listed according to the percentage of ingredient.

Do not assume that more "meat" ingredients make the food a higher-quality protein. Some sources of meat protein are lower quality than others. And some vegetable sources, such as soy protein, may or may not be high-quality protein, depending on the quality and processing of the actual ingredient used. Also, because dogs were not designed to digest soy protein, much of it is not utilized as protein by the body. Some dog foods promote the fact that they contain a high percentage of protein. However, a high-protein diet is too much protein for most dogs to metabolize and thus it is unnecessary.

In his book *Pet Allergies,* Dr. Alfred Plechner says this about many common foods:

> . . . poor-quality excess protein over the long-run is a prescription for kidney disease. The kidneys have to process and excrete the toxins and nitrogenous waste products from protein breakdown. But nature never designed canine or feline kidneys to handle the volume of impurities that comes their way. The result is fatigued, irritated, damaged and deteriorated kidneys after several years of life. Scar tissue replaces healthy tissue and cannot perform the normal task of filtration. Waste products are retained in the body instead of being excreted. These poisons often collect in skin tissue and cause shabby coats and itchy, dry or scaly skin, a situation that mimics an allergic dermatitis. Left untreated, the toxic buildup leads to vomiting, loss of appetite, uremic poisoning and death.[2]

2. Alfred J. Plechner, D.V.M., and Martin Zucker, *Pet Allergies: Remedies for an Epidemic,* 1986, J.P. Enterprises, p. 14.

Most people assume that the percentage of protein on the label indicates exactly how much protein their dog will be getting from this food. But the analysis does *not* tell you the quality of the protein or how much protein your dog will be able to digest from that food. The digestibility of the protein to the dog's body depends on the type of protein it is and the processing it underwent. So the question really is: To what extent can the dog's body break down these ingredients and extract protein from them? If the protein source cannot be properly digested, a protein deficiency might occur, even though you think you are feeding a food with an adequate amount of protein.

To help you understand this point, think about a rawhide chew toy. In a chemical analysis rawhide has a very high percentage of protein. But I'm sure common sense would tell you that the protein in rawhide is not a highly digestible substance and therefore is relatively unavailable to the body for absorption. Unfortunately, many of the protein sources used in dog food are also low-quality.

What is true of protein is also true of other components of food. For instance, fats in the food are a necessary nutritional component. But all fats are not the same; all carbohydrates are not the same; all vitamin and mineral supplements are not the same. The quality of all of the base products used to formulate the dog food determines the overall quality of the food and its ultimate effect on the dog's health.

Another vital consideration is the processing of the ingredients. Often the meat or soy has been so overprocessed that its protein content is not easily assimilated by the body. This is especially true of dry and semimoist foods.

Some breeds are more sensitive than others to specific ingredients. Labrador retrievers and Doberman pinschers are often sensitive to soy protein. A large number of these breeds have skin problems, many of which disappear when placed on a soy-free diet. Akitas and German shepherds are often sensitive to both soy protein and wheat cereal products and often do well when placed on a rice cereal base food.

Yet another consideration is the category of pet food ingredients called "by-products," which often include diseased and decayed meats and meat considered nonedible for humans; the term *by-products* is used in conjunction with meat, poultry, beef, and such. The government standards actually allow by-products to include diseased chicken, beef, or pork; tankage from cooked or condemned carcasses; undigestible parts of carcasses such as ligaments, tendons, and cartilage; and parts of the animal you probably wouldn't consider as food at all, such as feathers, beaks, and hooves. Most commercial pet food companies simply list a general term such as *meat or poultry by-products* on their labels and do not define the exact contents, even though they are often made of so-called 4-D animals—dead, dying, diseased, and disabled. I'm not exaggerating—*4-D* is an actual term used in the meat industry to define categories of meat. Most pet foods are not inspected by the United States Department of Agriculture (USDA).

These by-products are considered acceptable for commercial pet foods because they have been processed at such high temperatures that they are considered sterile. Of course, processing at these temperatures also destroys many nutrients. (The pet food industry tries to compensate for this by adding isolated vitamins, minerals, and amino acids to make up for what was cooked away or missing in the first place due to low-quality ingredients.) In any event, I certainly wouldn't want to eat a cancerous tumor that the government calls "safe" because it has been sterilized. Nor do I think pet foods that contain these ingredients are nutritious for our beloved companion animals.

But not all by-products are the same. A number of natural pet food companies are now manufacturing superior pet food made with quality ingredients. The ones I approve of use human-quality meats or categories of meat that fall into the "by-products" definition which I consider acceptable sources of safe protein, including human-quality whole chicken carcasses and top-quality beef and lamb carcasses. However, just because a company calls itself "natural" does not mean they pass the test. You have to check them out. Read labels and brochures and, if necessary, call the company to ask about the ingredients they use.

Recently the Association of American Feed Control Officials (AAFCO), the regulating agency of the pet food industry, changed the labeling rules, making it more difficult to distinguish by-products that are acceptable (according to my standards) from by-products I consider unacceptable. Prior to this new ruling an acceptable by-product ingredient such as lungs was listed as such. Now the lungs must be listed as a by-product. In this case AAFCO has ruled that the consumer should be told less about an ingredient rather than more.

Following this logic, all by-products are equal—which is simply not true. This makes it difficult for the average person to know whether the by-products in a particular food are safe. Fortunately a manufacturer has the recourse of listing the types of by-products in parentheses, giving you information necessary to determine if the specific by-product ingredients are acceptable. Some natural pet food companies use only USDA inspected meats, allowing nothing in their food that falls into the category of by-products. Clearly this is an even better solution to the question and will provide a higher-quality diet.

On the labels of most commercial foods you'll also see the word *meal*. Some examples include meat meal, poultry by-product meal, bonemeal, and other variations. This is another term that encompasses a great deal of slaughterhouse refuse that has been ground up into a "meal." In addition to the inclusion of diseased parts, some bonemeal has been found to contain unacceptable levels of mercury and lead.

Other ingredients used in most commercial pet foods often include rancid or moldy grains, rancid oils, and other refuse from food processing plants that are not considered fit for human consumption. One leading "veterinary" brand of pet foods includes peanut hulls, listed as a source of fiber. I don't know about you, but I don't consider ground-up peanut hulls a "food" I want my dog to eat. Corn husks join the peanut hulls in the catchall phrase "vegetable fiber"; hydrolyzed chicken feathers become "poultry protein products"; and ground bones can legally be listed as "processed animal protein."[3]

Unfortunately, harmful chemical preservatives and other artificial additives are the norm in most pet foods. Unless you are a chemist or an unusually well-educated consumer, it is difficult to read a label and distinguish between the multisyllabic words of many ingredients to know which ones are harmful. For instance, it may list methionine, which is an amino acid (the components of protein); cobalamin, which is vitamin B_{12}; or sodium selenite, which is a mineral. All of these are beneficial ingredients.

Chemical preservatives, on the other hand, are highly suspect. Many of the preservatives commonly used in pet food have been linked to serious health problems, including liver damage, increased cholesterol, brain damage, weakness, loss of consciousness, and a

3. Ibid.

host of other problems. Some of these preservatives have been linked to cancer and even as a cause of death. They include sodium nitrite, sodium nitrate, butylated hydroxyanisole (BHA), butylated hydroxytoluene (BHT), monosodium glutamate (MSG), sodium metabisulfite, and ethoxyquin.

I've listed only a few of the host of chemical preservatives commonly used. As an example of the specific problems linked to one type, ethoxyquin, studies have indicated that it blocks the uptake and utilization of the mineral selenium. Selenium deficiencies have been linked to cancer and heart disease. Ethoxyquin has also been found to inhibit the uptake of glucose, resulting in a problem with carbohydrate metabolism in the body. Studies show that a wide range of bodily functions and other health problems are linked to ethoxyquin, including increased caries, cataracts, decreased fertility, sterility, hair loss, skin problems, cardiomyopath, and kidney and liver cancer.

Natural pet food manufacturers use natural preservatives such as vitamins C (sometimes listed as ascorbic acid) and E (sometimes listed as tocopherol), which is another reason they often cost a bit more.

Other additives used in most commercial foods include dyes, flavor enhancers, stabilizers, and thickeners, many of which are also suspected of causing health problems. Additionally, various forms of sugar (including corn syrup) and excessive salt are used to entice a dog to a particular food.

I can't say enough about the importance of a manufacturer using good quality ingredients. And that brings me to another point. Unless a meat has been organically grown, it may contain residues of pesticides and antibiotics that are passed along in the food chain. Residues of these toxins lodge in the fat of the body and are passed along to humans and pets when the animals are used as a food source.

In her book *Nontoxic, Natural and Earthwise,* environmental researcher Debra Lynn Dadd gives the following statistics:

> In the United States, almost 2 billion pounds of pesticides are applied to our land every year, including food crops. In 1987, an EPA [Environmental Protection Agency] report ranked pesticides in food as one of the nation's most serious health and environmental problems. Pesticides are among the most deadly of chemicals: ac-

> cording to a report from the National Academy of Sciences, 30 percent of commercially used insecticides, 50 percent of herbicides, and 90 percent of fungicides are known to cause cancer in animal studies. Ironically, pesticides aren't even doing their job. Since they were first developed after World War II, pesticide use has increased ten times; during that same period, crop losses due to insects has doubled. Often less than .1 percent of the chemicals applied to crops actually reach target pests. Pesticides used in agriculture have contaminated nearly all the air, water, soil, and living beings of the entire planet.[4]

A recent newspaper article on this subject adds the following information:

> Insect resistance to pesticides is also increasing. Currently, 600 of the most significant pests, including insects, weeds and plant diseases, are resistant to one or more classes of chemicals that had been developed to control them. . . . Excessive use of toxic chemicals has also produced the unwanted result of creating pests out of species that had not previously caused any noticeable harm. "Spider mites are now a problem worldwide as a direct result of the use of DDT, which killed their natural enemy," [Sheila] Daar added.[5]

There is hope for us still. Organic farmers use techniques such as crop rotation, disease-resistant crops, nontoxic products, and beneficial insects such as ladybugs, spiders, lacewings, and parasitic wasps that feed on the problem insects. Hopefully, governments around the world will wise up and realize that our earth is a precious resource that we must respect. (See the Appendix for books and organizations that offer more information on these issues.)

It would be very expensive to feed a household of large dogs a homemade diet of all-organic or home-grown food. So, until we stop the agricultural practices that are creating this situation, most of us have no choice but to feed these commercially raised meats. That's just one more reason to uplift the quality of the diet as much as pos-

4. Debra Lynn Dadd, *Nontoxic, Natural and Earthwise,* 1990, Jeremy P. Tarcher, p. 77.
5. Karen Dardick, "No Pests, No Poisons," *Los Angeles Times,* June 14, 1992, p. K11.

sible through the other suggestions in this chapter, giving the body nutrients, enzymes, and antioxidants to promote health.

Buster, a miniature schnauzer, is an example of a dog who responded poorly to the typical dog food on the market. He suffered from a sensitive stomach; vomiting was a normal part of his life. He had a dull coat and erratic behavior. On my recommendation, Buster was switched to a natural diet—in his case a chicken- and rice-based food containing no preservatives or artificial colors or flavors. Because of his sensitivities he was put on distilled water, since it contains no minerals; a vitamin and mineral supplement was mixed in his food.

Buster's vomiting diminished during the first week on the new regimen and gradually stopped within four weeks. His coat became shiny and healthy and his behavior that of a model dog. He continues to do well but had relapses of vomiting and poor behavior when he was given table scraps that contained artificial ingredients.

A High-Quality Natural Diet

I hope you are now convinced that a high-quality diet is crucial for your canine friend. She deserves it, and it need not cost a great deal more than you are currently paying. Homemade food is certainly the best choice, and I'll tell you how to make it. But if you're like me, finding time to prepare homemade food is difficult. So if that task is beyond you, don't despair; there are high-quality commercially available pet foods, which I'll discuss later in this chapter.

Whether you make your own homemade food or simply add fresh ingredients to a commercial food, it is important that your dog's diet include raw ingredients that provide the energy inherent only in fresh foods. This energy is destroyed with cooking. It is essential that our food contain some of this life energy for a proper balance of health to be maintained. Just imagine if your diet consisted primarily of canned or dried food. The processing necessary for either canning or drying removes the life force; it's all dead, cooked, and processed. You would feel the difference in your body if you never had fresh, raw vegetables or fruits. Raw meat also contains this inherent energy, but processing it as dog food removes the life energy.

Enzymes, the protein molecules that break down and digest our food, are another important component of a high-quality diet. Without the proper enzymes, the food we eat does not get properly digested and therefore nutrients are not absorbed by the body. New research is proving that enzymes have a far greater role in nutrition than previously understood. In addition to the role enzymes play in digesting food, they are involved in every metabolic process—including the functions of the immune system, the bloodstream, and the organs. A leading researcher in enzyme nutrition, Humbart Santillo, goes even further in describing the role of enzymes by stating that all cellular activity is initiated by enzymes.

Enzymes are found in raw food, but most are destroyed when food is cooked. The body also has its own supply of enzymes that it calls upon to digest any enzyme-deficient foods we (or our dogs) eat. If you eat a diet of only cooked foods, you are requiring your body to produce most of the enzymes to digest that food, because the majority of enzymes in the food have been destroyed in the cooking process. Since most dogs get almost no raw food, their bodies must draw on enzyme reserves from organs and tissues, which may cause a metabolic deficiency.

Many research studies support a strong correlation between enzyme deficiency and diseases, both acute and chronic. There are two ways to combat enzyme deficiency—feed more raw foods and add an enzyme supplement to your dog's diet. Several veterinary enzyme supplements are now on the market. Because specific types of enzymes are needed to digest proteins, fats, starches, and cellulose, a good enzyme supplement must have a correct balance of enzymes to be effective. Some are better than others, so check the Appendix for product suppliers of top-quality enzymes.

Raw foods that can be fed to your dog include carrots, alfalfa sprouts, lettuce, broccoli, zucchini, raw meat, and uncooked meat bones. Many dogs also like fresh fruits—I find apples and peaches to be favorites. (See the chart entitled "Raw Foods to Add to the Diet," on page 92.) Be careful not to overfeed raw foods when you first add them to the diet. Your dog's body will have to shift gears to digest raw food; excessive amounts eaten at one time could cause diarrhea. It is best to start slowly and gradually increase the amount of raw foods you are feeding.

Many dogs enjoy raw meats. In the wild, raw meat was the

standard fare for canines before we domesticated them, so it is closest to their natural diet provided by Mother Nature. However, the dog ate the whole carcass of his prey, including bones, intestines, and the contents of the digestive tract. If you have not fed your dog raw meat before, start very slowly with small amounts, because digestive upsets could result. It is best to feed organic meat if at all possible. Buy the meat from a store with a big turnover so it is more likely to be fresh. To avoid feeding meat that is too old, check dates carefully and keep raw meat refrigerated for no more than two days before feeding.

Meats that are commonly fed raw are beef, lamb, chicken, and turkey. Because it is difficult to ensure that poultry is free of bacterial contamination such as salmonella, I prefer feeding it cooked. If you do choose to feed raw poultry, find a clean source. There has been increasing concern over the possibility of parasites in raw beef and lamb—another reason it is important to shop at a reputable meat store. I do not recommend either raw pork or fish due to the possibility of parasites in the raw product. Organ meats such as liver, heart, and kidney can be used, but do not feed any one exclusively. (While liver is an excellent source of nutrients, its role as the body's filter system means it may also contain a number of toxins.) Alternating muscle and organ meats is best; do not feed the same source of raw meat all the time.

Feeding raw meat two or three times a week can be beneficial to your dog's health, providing an alternative source of nutrients. Wash all raw meat thoroughly before mixing it into your dog's food. Be especially careful to wash chicken and turkey, which can be exposed to salmonella bacteria during processing.

Raw meat bones should be large round knuckle bones, so dogs cannot swallow them. Raw vertebrae bones from beef, lamb, or chicken are okay for chewing, providing that your dog does not attempt to swallow the vertebrae whole. It is *cooked* chicken bones, beefsteak bones, and pork- or lamb-chop bones that you must *not* feed because they can splinter while the dog is chewing them and cause tears or blockage in the throat or intestines. Find a meat shop—preferably one in a natural foods store—that you know to be clean, and always wash the bones thoroughly before feeding.

It is okay to feed raw eggs to your dog, but feed only the yolk on a daily basis. The egg white, when fed raw daily, blocks the production of a certain protein, resulting in a dietary deficiency. (This is not a problem with cooked eggs. Both the yolk and white of cooked eggs can be fed daily.) It is okay to feed a whole raw egg once a week, but be sure that the egg has a clean shell and is fresh. Organic eggs are best because antibiotics are not used in their production.

Raw Foods to Add to the Diet

Here are raw, natural items you can add to any food to upgrade its nutritional content and add life energy to the diet:

Raw meat:	Raw beef or lamb, or organ meats such as liver, heart, or kidney; or, as a treat food, raw bones (give large round knuckle bones or raw vertebrae bones from beef or lamb). Add ⅛ to ¼ cup of raw meat for each 10 pounds of your dog's weight to any commercial or homemade food. Organ meats should be fed in small amounts and no more than three times a week.
Raw vegetables:	Experiment to find the raw vegetables your dog likes best. Try grated carrot, zucchini, chopped lettuce, green beans, or broccoli. (Avoid raw potatoes; they often cause digestive upsets.) Add ⅛ to ¼ cup for each 10 pounds of your dog's weight to any diet.
Raw egg:	Feed only the yolk on a daily basis if desired; the white can be included once a week. Get fresh organic eggs from range-fed chickens if possible. Can be added to either homemade or commercial food daily if desired.

Garlic:	Add ½ clove of minced fresh garlic to the food for each 10 pounds of your dog's weight, or give a capsule of Kyolic or other high-potency garlic (see "Giving Tablets and Capsules," page 197).
Acidophilus:	Choose an acidophilus product in capsules, powder, or liquid form from the refrigerator section of a natural foods store. Give ¼ to ½ teaspoon (or one capsule) once a week.
Yogurt:	Mix in the food a plain, natural culture yogurt. Feed several times a day mixed in a food or as a treat if your dog is suffering from digestive upsets or is on antibiotics; otherwise, add to the food occasionally, up to several times a week. Give ⅛ to ¼ cup for small dogs or ½ to ¾ cup for large dogs.

Vitamin and Mineral Supplements

Because you want to be sure your dog is getting all of the nutrients needed for optimum health, I recommend adding to any diet a vitamin and mineral supplement formulated for dogs from one of the natural pet products companies. These products come in a powder which can be mixed in the food or as wafer-sized pills. I don't recommend giving a vitamin and mineral supplement that contains *medicinal* herbs (such as rue, nettle, goldenseal, or ginseng) since these herbs should not be given on an ongoing basis. *Food* herbs such as garlic and parsley can be given daily. Whether your dog's food is homemade or canned, it is difficult to predict the quality of the ingredients used. And, even if you buy the freshest organic foods available, because of the depletion of nutrients from the soil for the last few decades, you can't be sure that they contain all the vitamins and minerals your dog needs. It can take many years of organic farming to once again give the soil the mineral balance intended by Mother Nature.

Commercial dog foods contain added vitamins and minerals to replace the nutrients that were destroyed in the cooking and processing of the food, and to ensure that they meet the nutritional standards on the label. But, once again, you have no way of knowing the quality of these vitamins and minerals. Many health experts feel that supplements made of isolated vitamins and minerals are not assimilated and absorbed as well as those made of whole foods. Therefore, I suggest adding a natural whole-food vitamin and mineral supplement such as Anitra's Vita-Mineral Mix or Pro-Tec's Body Guard on a regular basis to assure that there are no deficiencies in the diet. Make sure the brand you select contains no chemical preservatives and no artificial colors or flavors.

One common ingredient found in many natural pet foods, supplements, and vitamins is yeast, which is extremely high in the B-complex vitamins. However, there is a controversy about feeding yeast because some animals have a sensitivity to it. Yeast can be a source of excessive gas and cause abdominal problems. Many people believe it helps to repel fleas, but studies are indicating it has no effect. It is possible that the quality of the yeast is a factor because not all companies use high-quality brewer's or torula yeast in their products. Additionally, it is possible that problems develop when an owner feeds too much yeast. The small amount present in some natural foods and supplements may provide an acceptable source of B-complex vitamins without creating any problems. If you are feeding any food or other product containing yeast and your dog develops a skin irritation, stop feeding it to see if the problem abates. If so, your dog may have a yeast allergy and yeast should be eliminated from the diet thereafter.

I do not recommend giving isolated vitamins or minerals, except for specific health problems. One exception is the recommendation to add extra vitamin C to the diet for puppies of large and giant breeds, which I'll discuss later in this chapter in the "Feeding Puppies," section.

I am often asked about the need for extra calcium for expectant mothers, nursing mothers, and puppies. (I'll discuss the calcium needs of puppies later.) Pregnant and nursing dogs should *not* be given extra calcium supplements, because it causes a substantial diminishment of the dog's own ability to produce calcium in the body. For a pregnant dog, this can be disastrous at whelping time when high amounts of calcium are suddenly required by the body for milk production. The body that is accustomed to getting a large amount of calcium through dietary supplements will be unable to produce enough calcium to meet this demand. The result can be a condition known as eclampsia, which usually develops one to three weeks after whelping.

Because the body has used all its available calcium and is unable to respond to further demands, a resulting hypocalcium (low calcium in the body) causes symptoms such as disorientation, trembling, stiff muscles, and eventually convulsive seizures. High temperatures (up to 107°F) can also accompany this life-threatening syndrome. It is most common in small breeds such as Chihuahuas, toy poodles, and terriers. In my own practice I have seen it most frequently in miniature dachshunds. To prevent eclampsia, the diet should include a normal calcium/phosophorus ratio of two to one. You probably don't have to be concerned about the calcium content of the diet; as long as you are following the recommendations for a high-quality diet the proper amount of calcium will be present.

Antioxidant Supplements

If we could have the advantage of looking into the future, it is entirely possible that the discovery of *free radicals* will be considered one of the most important breakthroughs in understanding the immune system and its ability to combat disease and degenerating conditions, including aging. Free radicals are highly volatile atoms that have at least one unpaired electron. This free electron causes a chemical reaction and leads to cellular damage when it becomes attached to another element. Free radicals can be extremely toxic. More than 30 years of research have proven that these overreactive molecules cause cellular damage. The cell damage from large numbers of free radicals has been linked to many degenerative diseases responsible for aging.

High concentrations of free radicals result from stresses on the body that weaken the immune system. These stresses include chemicals in the food chain, polluted air and water, heavy metals such as mercury and lead, and exposure to radiation. Free-radical activity in the body is also increased by a high amount of fat in the diet, especially rancid and heated oils. But free radicals are not all bad—the body actually requires minute amounts of them to remove a virus or bacteria from the body. It is high concentrations of free radicals that represent the challenge to your dog's health.

When the body is confronted with an overabundance of free radicals, it springs into action with its own free-radical defense system composed of an array of body-produced enzymes called *antioxidants,* which are sometimes referred to as free-radical scavengers. (Earlier in this chapter I discussed the important role of digestive enzymes. All enzymes have similar roles as catalysts that stimulate certain chemical reactions in the body, but antioxidant enzymes differ in function from digestive enzymes.)

Free radicals become a problem when the body is unable to produce enough antioxidant enzymes on its own to combat high concentrations of these toxic invaders. While you can positively impact on your dog's ability to deal with free radicals by selecting a high-quality natural diet, you cannot totally avoid harmful amounts of free radicals from other sources such as pesticide residues on food and in water, air pollution, and heavy-metal contaminants. Among their many other functions beta-carotene and vitamins C and E are antioxidant nutrients because they play a supportive role in combatting excess free radicals. Also helpful are specific antioxidant supplements made from whole food sources such as sprouted wheat that promote the antioxidant enzyme supply of the body such as Bioguard and Vitality from Biogenetics. (A dog that has a food sensitivity to wheat is generally able to take these supplements with no problem. This is because the protein gluten is found in significant amounts in a grain of wheat but not in wheat sprouts.)

Dr. Peter R. Rothschild, and Zane Baranowski, C.N., explain the results of using antioxidant supplements:

> Physicians and veterinarians utilizing whole food supersprout concentrates to improve the nutritional status of their patients report a long list of positive benefits that can only be related to an improved nutritional standard. These benefits include diminished joint pains and inflammation, more energy, better circulation, and, most importantly, significantly reduced recovery time after sur-

gery or other types of convalescence after severe stress conditions such as physical trauma. Clearly, the degree to which a patient is well nourished does affect their ability to cope with stress. Apparently, whole food sprout concentrates supply the right nutrition for these circumstances. Due to the growing understanding of antioxidant enzymes, pharmaceutical companies are also pursuing the development of new compounds including [the antioxidant] SOD. These products, unlike whole food, contain isolated enzymes and could potentially create imbalances. Such new products will, of course, be regulated as drugs and require prescriptions. Fortunately, we have whole food "supersprout" concentrates at our disposal to naturally assist our body's maintenance of adequate antioxidant enzymes.[6]

Garlic, Acidophilus, and Yogurt

Other foods that can promote your dog's health include garlic, acidophilus, and yogurt. It has long been held that garlic has many claims to health improvements. In dogs it has also been helpful in repelling fleas. But it is also effective in supporting the immune system and treating digestive-tract problems. Many dogs just plain like the taste of garlic. But to be effective, it is important to use at least one-half of a clove of raw minced garlic mixed in the food for every 10 pounds of body weight (one-eighth to one-quarter clove for tiny dogs) or a capsule- or liquid-form high-potency garlic such as Kyolic. You can give the capsules as you would any pill (see p. 197) or open it and mix the powder into the food. Give one capsule or ½ teaspoon for each 20 pounds of body weight.

Both acidophilus and yogurt can be very beneficial to dogs suffering from gastrointestinal upsets such as diarrhea, vomiting, or excessive gas because they replenish the natural "friendly" bacteria in the system. It is especially important to give either acidophilus or yogurt to your dog if an antibiotic has been prescribed, because antibiotics interfere with the balance of bacteria in the body.

Acidophilus is available in capsules, powder, or liquid form in the refrigerator section of any natural foods store. If the dog is taking

6. Peter R. Rothschild, M.D., Ph.D., and Zane Baranowski, C.N., *Free Radicals, Stress and Antioxidant Enzymes—A Guide to Cellular Health,* University Labs Press, 1990, p. 4.

antibiotics, give one-fourth to one-half teaspoon of acidophilus (or one capsule) daily while the antibiotics are being given and for three days afterward. For general health maintenance, this same dosage is suggested once a week.

In addition to aiding the system with natural bacteria, yogurt provides a soothing coating to the digestive tract. Often dogs with excessive gas can be fed yogurt to help relieve this problem. For a healthy dog, adding yogurt to the food several times a week provides a different source of protein and a continual source of digestive bacteria to the gastrointestinal system. Buy plain yogurt made from a natural culture.

What About Feeding Dairy Products?

Cow's milk, cream, and half-and-half should not be fed to your dog; they often cause diarrhea since dogs don't have the proper enzymes to digest these products. Cottage cheese can be fed and is an excellent source of protein that is easy to digest. You can feed cottage cheese up to three times a week. If your dog is ill, cottage cheese can be fed daily. Goat's milk is okay because it is naturally homogenized and easy to digest. Goat's milk also has a more complete nutrient balance than cow's milk. Natural cultured yogurt is also a good addition to the diet as discussed above.

Homemade Food

There's only one way to be absolutely sure that your dog is getting the best: Make it yourself. Many of my clients have perfected the homemade diet and have it down to a science. One owner even came up with the consummate recipe and submitted it to a dog food company.

Here are some cautions about implementing the recipes given below for homemade dog food:

1. Although brown rice is recommended, some dogs' digestive tracts are unable to handle the bulk and react with digestive upsets. This is particularly true with less active dogs who have slower diges-

tion. If this happens, soak the brown rice overnight, add a half cup more water, and cook longer. If you use oatmeal as the grain, you may have the same problem, particularly when there are too many husks in it. Again, soaking the grain overnight, adding more water, and cooking longer will usually circumvent these problems.

2. Prepare small quantities of the food so you don't have to store it more than three days in the refrigerator. Or, if you want to make large quantities, keep only three days' worth of food in the refrigerator and freeze the rest in small containers. It should be fresh when served; frozen is next best. Make sure it is at room temperature before feeding.

3. Use top-quality ingredients; organic meats, grains, and vegetables are always the best. Use fresh ingredients when possible and avoid frozen or canned sources. This allows the homemade diet to contain as much natural energy and nutrition as possible. It's easy and inexpensive to grow your own sprouts; they are a source of superfresh nutrients. Most health food stores sell special sprouting jars. You might also want to grow some wheat grass in a pot on the windowsill by planting wheat berries. When the grass is a few inches tall, you can make this pesticide-free "lawn" available to your dog. Or, cut the wheat grass into small pieces and mix into your dog's food.

4. Switch to the new diet gradually, allowing your dog's digestive tract time to adjust. At first you can mix one part of the new food with three parts of the old food (a 25/75 percent ratio); then, in a few days or a week, feed half new food mixed with half old food. In another few days or a week, mix three parts of the new food with one part of the old food. Finally, in another few days or a week, feed only the new food.

5. Be careful about leftovers; you don't want to feed spoiled food.

Fix-It-Yourself Basic Diet

This is a good basic diet for adult dogs. See special recipes later in this chapter for Hypoallergenic Diet, Reducing Diet, Restricted Protein Diet, and Homemade Puppy Food.

Grain	Use cooked brown rice, oats (usually in the form of oatmeal), corn, wheat berries, wheat bulgur, barley, rye, or millet. If you use oatmeal or corn, increase the amount to one-half more. Use rye as an alternative occasionally in either a cooked whole grain form or try crumbled rye crackers (buy the no-salt variety). (*Note:* Although brown rice is preferable to white rice, some dogs may suffer from digestive problems and do better on a mixture of half brown rice and half white rice until their systems get used to the extra bulk.)
Protein	Use raw,* boiled, or broiled lean hamburger, chicken, turkey, or lamb. Choose lean meat with a little fat. Up to three times a week you can substitute one-half of the meat portion with cooked beans, lentils, or tofu, if desired.
Vegetable	Experiment to find the vegetables your dog likes best. Try grated raw zucchini, yellow squash, or carrots; chopped alfalfa sprouts; lightly steamed broccoli, asparagus (most dogs love it), corn, green beans, turnips, parsnips, or peas. Try other vegetables to see how your dog responds, but avoid onions and cabbage because they can cause digestive upsets. If your dog doesn't like the vegetables at first, try chopping them finely and mixing well into the food.

*If using raw meat, review pp. 91–92 for precautions to assure freshness and avoid harmful bacteria such as salmonella.

Oil	Choose any high-quality vegetable oil: safflower, corn, sesame, wheat germ, sunflower, flaxseed, or extra virgin olive oil. Or buy an oil supplement for pets from a natural pet food company. During the winter months give extra virgin olive oil or cod-liver oil a few times a week. *Note:* High-quality oils are cold pressed and should be refrigerated after opening. Wheat germ and flax-seed oil are extremely high in nutrients but turn rancid easily. These oils should be refrigerated as soon as you get them home—even before opening. Omega Nutrition manufactures a high-quality flaxseed oil that's an excellent source of the Omega 3 fatty acids.
Vitamin and Mineral Supplements	Choose a vitamin and mineral supplement formulated for dogs from a natural pet food company. Be sure it is made of natural whole food ingredients and contains no preservatives or artificial ingredients. Use according to directions on label. (See Appendix for product suppliers.)
Enzyme Supplement for Dogs	Use according to directions on label.
Antioxidant Supplement for Dogs	Use according to directions on label.

Fix-It-Yourself Basic Diet—Quantities

Use the following chart to determine how much food to make per day. Multiply these quantities to make food for more than one dog or to make more than one day's supply. Remember that each dog's metabolism differs and these are only approximate amounts.

DOG'S WEIGHT IN POUNDS	5	10	25	40	60	80
Grain	½ c.	1 c.	2 c.	2½ c.	4 c.	5 c.
Protein	2½ T.	⅓ c.	⅔ c.	1⅛ c.	1⅓ c.	1¾ c.
Vegetables	1 T.	⅛ c.	¼ c.	⅓ c.	½ c.	⅔ c.
Oil	¼ tsp.	½ tsp.	1 tsp.	1½ tsp.	2 tsp.	2½ tsp.
Vitamin & Mineral Supplement	Use according to directions on label.					
Enzyme Supplement	Use according to directions on label.					

Choosing a Commercially Made Natural Dog Food

Superior-quality pet foods survive in the marketplace even though they usually cost more, because of the results that owners see in their dogs—clear indications that the higher-quality food is having a positive impact on their dog's health and vitality. These high-quality pet food companies know that people will continue to pay a bit more because of this noticeable difference. Their main criterion of doing business is based on this edge they have on the more commercial competitors. The standards of production and balance of ingredients are of the highest importance to companies whose products are truly high quality, supporting the old adage, you get what you pay for. The major food manufacturers are beginning to realize that they must produce high-quality foods in order to compete with natural pet food companies, some of which have been around for years.

This does not mean that I endorse all foods that are labeled "natural," "premium," or "veterinary prescription." Some of them are good, while other brands contain the same questionable ingredients as their more commercial competitors: artificial flavorings and colors; chemical preservatives; by-products that include low-quality meats; overprocessed protein; and so-called vegetable fiber such as peanut hulls. For some the word *natural* is a marketing gimmick rather than a commitment to quality.

Remember that companies are required to list the ingredients according to the amount of each contained in the food. The first ingredient listed is the largest quantity, and so on down to the smallest percentage represented by the final ingredient in the list. You will note that water is usually one of the top ingredients. One natural brand of canned food I have used seems fairly dry, so I mix water with it before serving. With this food I know I'm getting more for my money because I'm not paying for them to water it down to the normal texture of canned dog food.

Other ingredients in a high-quality food will be natural sources of vitamins, minerals, and other supplements. Natural preservatives such as vitamins C and E are used in these foods instead of the potentially harmful chemical preservatives, including BHA, BHT, sodium nitrite, sodium nitrate, MSG, ethoxyquin, and so on. Other potentially harmful additives such as color and flavor enhancers are eliminated.

In addition to better quality meats, some of these companies even use pesticide-free grains in their foods. A few natural pet food companies offer lamb and rice diets for dogs who are allergic to the more common meats such as beef and chicken. Another company currently offers a variety of gamelike meats, which some dogs find more palatable, and that do not contribute to irritation of the skin. Several natural dog food companies also manufacture vegetarian foods.

Most of the commercial pet food companies use artificial colors and low-quality ingredients as fillers and binders to assure the same color and consistency from batch to batch. The top natural pet food companies don't use fillers and binders—so a slight color and consistency variation can result from time to time.

Remember, even if you feed a commercial brand of food, you can make it better. It is easy to supplement it by adding fresh ingredients such as raw meats, vegetables, eggs, yogurt, and garlic as listed earlier in this chapter. Mixing these foods into the natural pet food you buy will add the beneficial vitamins, minerals, and enzymes contained only in fresh, raw foods. I suggest adding them on a daily basis or, at the very least, several times a week.

Also, don't be afraid to occasionally add leftover "people" food to your dog's meal. Many dogs enjoy it when salads, vegetables, and meat scraps are added. Adding these leftovers from time to time will not appreciably affect the dog's nutritional balance as long as you do it in moderation. But remember to avoid foods that are overprocessed and full of preservatives such as white bread and baked goods. Also, don't feed sugary or salty foods.

When you switch to a new food, your dog may reject it because she is accustomed to the artificial flavor enhancers, sugars, and excessive salt in the old food. If this is the case, just take it slowly. Mix one part of the new food with three parts of the old food. Then, in a few days or a week, change the ratio to 50–50. In another few days adjust the ratio so the diet consists of three parts of the new food to one part of the old food. After another few days feed only the new food.

Most dogs are able to accept the new food when it is gradually introduced in this way. In some cases a dog goes through a detoxification process when the artificial preservatives are removed from the diet. If this happens, the herb milk thistle can be given (dosage depends on the brand of milk thistle and its potency; check with a holistic vet for the proper dosage), or the homeopathic remedy nux vomica can be given three times a day at a potency of 6C. (See "Herbs," p. 163, and "Homeopathy," p. 165, for more information.)

What About a Vegetarian Diet?

While dogs can be quite healthy on a vegetarian diet (unlike cats who require meat), I don't recommend it for most dogs. Mother Nature designed the canine digestive system to break down and utilize meat proteins most efficiently. The cereal proteins in vegetarian foods often lack the full range of amino acids (the components of protein) required by the dog's body, sometimes resulting in protein deficiency problems. These problems can show up in a variety of ways, depending upon which amino acid is missing or insufficient. A more serious possible long-range consequence of this type of amino acid deficiency is the development of early arthritis. This effect has been documented by researchers performing clinical food trials over many years' time and is an unfortunate, painful, and sometimes permanent result of vegetarian diets fed to dogs. I have treated several dogs with early generalized arthritis that were fed exclusively vegetarian diets for many years; most of these vegetarian diets were homemade. The natural foods companies that are now making vegetarian foods have balanced these amino acids, and therefore they are much safer than a homemade vegetarian diet.

I *do recommend* vegetarian diets in dogs who are protein sensitive and tolerate cereal-source proteins better than animal-source proteins. In any event, a vegetarian diet should not be fed to puppies or other dogs whose protein needs are high. Unless there is a specific medical reason, I do not recommend an all-vegetarian diet.

Choosing Between Canned and Dry Food

Because most owners are accustomed to feeding dry food, I am frequently asked if it is acceptable. Some natural pet food companies are now producing higher-quality dry foods—foods that are made of better grade ingredients and that do not contain the vast array of artificial ingredients and preservatives that are found in most dry foods.

There is no question: canned food is preferable to dry food. Though the canning process destroys nutrients, it is not as harmful as the processing of dry foods. There is less alteration of the chemistry in the canned alternative, and canned food is generally higher in fat, supplying more calories per pound than dry food. Pound for pound, it can be cost-effective to switch to canned food. Because dry food contains less fat, it may not have enough calories for very active dogs or nursing mothers.

If cost is a major concern for you, how about a compromise? Try feeding half canned and half dry foods. But get them from a company that uses high-quality ingredients and omits the artificial chemicals and preservatives.

Choosing a Brand of Natural Dog Food

For your convenience, the companies I currently find acceptable are listed in the Appendix. Be aware, however, the companies sometimes change management and/or the ingredients in their foods. Just because I have listed a company, do not assume that they will always maintain high standards. Keep ever vigilant; monitor your dog's coat and skin as an indicator that the food remains high quality. You must make it your business to check the ingredient list on the label. Perhaps you'll want to call (most have toll-free numbers) or write to the companies and ask for information on their standards and sources of ingredients. Remember, both the specific types of ingredients and the quality are important to the final product.

Here are some questions to consider when looking for a high-quality food: Does the company use meats, vegetables, grains, and other ingredients that are fit for human consumption (such as USDA meats) instead of "pet consumption" ingredients? Do they use natural ingredients instead of chemicals to preserve the food? Do they exclude artificial fillers, binders, coloring agents, and flavor enhancers from the food?

Choosing a Formula That's Right for Your Dog

Canned and dry foods are available in various formulas, depending on a dog's specific needs. These formulas differ in a number of ways, including the ratio of proteins, grains, and vegetables; the types of meat and vegetable proteins; and the amount of sodium. Most natural pet food manufacturers use similar categories:

Maintenance Formula: for adult dogs

Growth or Puppy Formula: for puppies and pregnant and lactating bitches

Senior or Weight-Loss Formula: lower calorie and sodium levels for the slower metabolism of older dogs and dogs who need to lose weight

Endurance or Active-Dog Formula: for extremely active dogs or working dogs

Allergy Formula: formulas that exclude common foods which some dogs are allergic to, such as wheat, corn, soy, dairy, chicken, and beef

Vegetarian Formula: for dogs with meat-sensitive allergies

Note: If your dog is pregnant or lactating, check the labels to see which formula the manufacturer recommends.

How Much to Feed?

When your dog is switched to a higher-quality diet, she will probably eat less. That is because all of the nutrients are being offered in a highly digestible form; her body no longer needs as much in order to get everything it requires to operate efficiently. Also, the dry foods available from some natural pet food companies are made with a process that retains more nutrients. The pelleting or soft-cooked methods of processing produce foods that are more compact, so your dog will not require as much food cup for cup as she does with other commercial brands that have been made by the more common extrusion process.

To determine the correct amount to feed your dog, I have included a chart that will give you an idea of the amount needed for your dog's weight per day. However, it is important to remember that each dog is unique and has its own metabolic rate. Some breeds, such as terriers and shelties, are naturally more active and often have a higher rate of metabolism than other dogs their same sizes. So this chart should be used only for general guidelines and adjustments made for your own dog's unique requirements.

General Guidelines on How Much to Feed

DOG'S WEIGHT	CUPS OF FOOD PER MEAL
10 lbs. or less	½ cup or less
10 to 25 lbs.	½ to 1 cup
25 to 35 lbs.	1 to 1½ cups
35 to 50 lbs.	1½ to 2 cups
50 to 75 lbs.	2 to 3 cups
75 to 100 lbs.	3 to 4 cups

Note: Foods vary considerably in density; a cup of one food may equal a cup and a half of another brand. Also remember to add the supplements to each meal according to the chart in the "Fix-It-Yourself Basic Diet": vitamin and mineral supplement, oil, enzyme supplement, and, if you choose, an antioxidant supplement.

Another way to determine how much to feed is to ask your veterinarian if your dog's current weight is appropriate. Or weigh your dog and record it. Then, as you adjust the quantity of food to determine the correct amount, weigh your dog each week. If you are feeding a commercial food, check the label for suggested amounts. To determine the amount of a new food for a dog who is at the correct weight, lower the amount of food being fed by one-fourth. Then reweigh the dog in a week and make sure she is maintaining her weight. If so, you have hit upon the correct amount of food for your dog.

If the dog is underweight, add one-fourth more food to the diet and reweigh in a week's time to make sure she is gaining. For overweight dogs, do not make drastic changes in the amount of food. Decrease the quantity by one-fourth for one week and by one-third for a second week. Then reweigh the dog and adjust so the weight loss is gradual. For most overweight dogs, a loss of a half pound a week is ideal.

For elderly dogs increase meals to three times daily. Decrease the amount fed in each meal, so you are feeding the same amount of food daily.

Need for Fresh Water

Dogs require a source of fresh water at all times. If water is not available, dehydration can occur faster than most people realize, particularly in hot weather. Water is not only a vital source of fluids but also contains essential minerals needed by the body.

When I stress the importance of pure drinking water, owners often question me—after all, they often see Scottie out in the yard drinking from a mud puddle and he doesn't seem to get sick. I point out that dogs who regularly drink from unpure sources of water such as ponds often build up a tolerance to most of the common bacteria found in the water. However, if a serious disease-producing bacteria has formed in the water source, even these dogs can become ill.

I have noticed that mud puddles and algae green ponds seem to attract dogs to drink. I'm not sure why dogs like that terrible-looking water. Perhaps there is an appealing taste to it—or maybe it's the panicky reactions of owners that lead them to drink it. While they often get away with it with no ill effects, I have treated many cases of gastrointestinal upset associated with contaminated water sources.

More and more, people are questioning the safety of their water supply. Even though municipal water authorities continually guarantee the safety of the water they provide, there is no question that public confidence in water safety has eroded. People concerned about the purity of their drinking water are choosing in ever greater numbers to install water filters on their home faucets or buy bottled water. If you buy bottled water, be aware that many sources of much of so-called spring water are questionable. It is a sad but true fact that much of our groundwater throughout the country has been affected by numerous contaminants, including pesticides, insecticides, heavy metals such as lead and mercury, and other industrial wastes. Also, bottled water that is labeled "drinking" water is sometimes no better than your own tap water. Because laws governing the sale of bottled water vary from locality to locality and are often vague, look into your state and local government regulations.

I don't recommend giving your dog distilled water, because the distilling process eliminates essential minerals. However, I have occasionally had patients who had problems with bottled water that was enriched with minerals; the added minerals produced vomiting and diarrhea. For these sensitive dogs, distilled water has been used, together with a natural mineral supplement added to the food to compensate for the minerals missing from the water.

An in-home water purification system is another good option. Several different types are available. Before you invest in one of these systems, I suggest doing some further research. An excellent assessment of these devices is in the "Water" chapter of *Nontoxic, Natural and Earthwise* by Debra Lynn Dadd.

If you believe the tap water in your home is unsafe for you to drink, then don't give it to your dog. Your dog is just as susceptible to potential illness or toxicity as you are. Choose wisely for your own drinking water and then give that same water to your dog.

Whatever your choice of pure water, it should be kept fresh in your dog's water bowl and available at all times. The container should be washed daily. Choose a water bowl that has smooth surfaces so bacteria and mineral deposits don't build up.

If your dog is an outside dog, check water supplies frequently. In the summer keep the water free from algae and bacteria buildup by cleaning the bowl and changing the water daily. Winter water supplies must be kept ice-free. Water-heating devices are available for use in cold climates to prevent water from freezing. Remember, your dog can dehydrate in cold weather also, so always be sure his water supply is fresh and plentiful.

Serving Your Dog's Meals and Storing Leftovers

I suggest feeding twice a day approximately 12 hours apart. When you do feed, leave the food available no more than 20 to 30 minutes. If there is any food left after that time period, discard it or refrigerate it until the next feeding. Making food available only twice a day will aid the digestive process. Dogs who have food available all day long and munch on it from time to time are constantly having to go through the process of digesting food, which means the blood supply is focused on digestion rather than on other bodily functions.

It's best to serve your dog's food at either lukewarm or room temperature. If yours is an indoor dog, serve the food in an out-of-the-way corner of the room where he can eat without distractions.

The use of plastic food bowls has been implicated as a health concern, because the plastic may leach into the food. All plastics release some undetectable fumes, especially when heated. This "outgassing" means the fumes can pass into the foods that are served or stored in the bowl or container. While this may seem to be a minor issue to you, it's just as easy to use stainless steel, glass, or ceramic bowls for food and water. You may also want to store any refrigerated leftover food in a glass container for the same reason. I don't recommend storing canned food in the can. Most cans are made of aluminum and sealed with lead. After the can has been opened and oxygen gets into the can, the lead and aluminum can affect the food. It may be minimal, but over time the effects can build up in the body. We just don't need any extra stresses on the body.

After you've added raw food to the meal, don't heat the food at all. Even putting the food in a microwave for a few seconds to warm it destroys some of the beneficial enzymes. Instead, a container of food that has been stored in the refrigerator can be placed in a pan of hot water for 5 or 10 minutes until it is room temperature or lukewarm.

Treat Foods

My own dogs seem to live for their treat foods, and they truly enjoy having a variety to choose from. They run the gamut from store-bought treats to "people foods" they love. Treat foods should be just that—a special treat fed only once or twice a day. Treat foods are not nutritionally balanced; they should be given in small amounts so they don't interfere with or take the place of a balanced meal.

Commercially available treats include those that are made to resemble round bones or sausages and hard biscuit treats shaped like bones, little squares, or cookies. Most of them contain artificial flavoring, coloring, and preservatives. Again, you must read labels carefully to avoid harmful ingredients. In addition to the harmful additives, these products should be avoided because they contain high percentages of sugar and complex carbohydrates which encourages the buildup of tartar (dental plaque) on the teeth.

Some natural pet food companies make acceptable dog biscuits and other treats without those harmful additives. One company makes a lamb-based biscuit for dogs with sensitive skin and food allergies. Or, you can make your own biscuits with the recipes that follow. You can even buy bone-shaped cookie cutters.

In my household it is quite challenging to find treats that work for both dogs due to the age differences in Kelly, my 17-year-old miniature poodle and Lily, her young companion, a 5-year-old toy poodle. Because each dog has her own particular favorite taste and some can be very finicky, you will need to experiment with different flavors to discover the treats your dog prefers. Do not limit your testing to meats and biscuits—many dogs enjoy vegetables and fruits. Try both raw and lightly steamed vegetables. I have known several dogs who love asparagus, turning down bits of steak for a spear!

Feed only a small piece at a time when trying vegetables and fruits; the dog may like the taste, but a digestive upset such as diarrhea or excessive gas may result.

Cooking methods also make a taste difference for some dogs. Kelly and Lily, like me, definitely prefer oven-baked meats to boiled meats. I have noticed what tastes better to you will often be more appealing to your dog as well.

The size of the treat must be considered. A toy poodle cannot be expected to enjoy German shepherd–sized bones. This is an extreme example, but I'm constantly surprised when I see treats wasted and discarded simply because they are too large for the dog to eat.

The geriatric dog will sometimes have few teeth to chew with, so consider this when selecting treats. Kelly decided a few years back that she would retire from eating the hard biscuit-type bone treats, preferring pieces of meat or cheese that she can chew without difficulty.

Beef jerky is also an excellent treat for the older dog, but remember to avoid commercially made products that are full of chemical preservatives. Also, because it is rich, high in protein, and high in sodium, do not give it more than once a day. Here's a recipe for homemade jerky sure to win your dog's "Treat of the Month" award:

HOMEMADE BEEF JERKY

1 lb. sliced flank steak or brisket (slices should be ¼ inch or less thick)
½ cup soy or tamari sauce
¼ teaspoon garlic powder
¼ teaspoon black pepper

Combine soy or tamari sauce, garlic powder and pepper. Dip the slices of beef into the sauce. Arrange slices on a rack which is placed over a shallow pan. Do not overlap pieces. Bake 10 to 12 hours at 150 degrees.

Rawhide chew-toys can be a great treat, but most are processed with arsenic, bleach, lye, and/or chemical preservatives. There is no labeling required to tell you how the rawhide was processed, so be wary. Some natural types of bones are now available from natural pet products manufacturers.

Chocolate is toxic to dogs, particularly dogs who are unaccustomed to "junk food" in their diets. Signs of chocolate toxicity vary according to how long before the chocolate was consumed. Salted nuts and chips can contain enough salt to cause death in a small dog unused to large quantities of salt all at once. Recently I treated a miniature poodle for acute chocolate and salt toxicity. While her owners were out, Missy got hungry and raided the cupboards of a large bag of chocolate-covered peanuts and a bag of chocolate-covered raisins. Intensive emergency care saved her life, but a week later she returned to the clinic with severe liver failure as a complication of the ordeal. Unfortunately she died three days later.

ACCEPTABLE TREAT FOODS

- Meat pieces—lean
- Raw meat bones (large round knuckle bones or raw vertebrae bones from beef, lamb, or chicken)
- Vegetables
- Fruits
- Cheese
- Popcorn—plain or air popped (Do not feed excessive amounts)
- Cottage cheese
- Yogurt
- Tofu
- Dried fruits (Be sure they do not contain sulfur or other preservatives)

FOODS TO AVOID

- Fatty meat pieces
- Processed meats such as bologna, hot dogs, etc.
- Salted nuts and chips
- Candy
- Chocolate

Among the gourmet canine delights in her book, *The No Barking at the Table Cookbook*, Wendy Boyd-Smith includes lots of healthy recipes which her dogs, Webster and Max, have given the seal of approval. My Kelly and Lily have tried a couple of the biscuit recipes and could not agree more.* Here they are:

*Both of these recipes are from *The No Barking at the Table Cookbook* by Wendy Boyd-Smith, published by Lip Smackers, Inc., P.O. Box 5385, Culver City, CA 90231-5385; phone: 310-641-0578.

COOKIES WITH CHICKEN BROTH

Max's Midnight Snack

(48–60 cookies)

2 cups whole wheat flour
⅔ cup yellow cornmeal
½ cup shelled sunflower seeds
2 eggs mixed with ¼ cup low-fat milk
2 tablespoons corn oil
½ cup chicken broth

Glaze: Beat 1 egg; lightly brush on cookies before baking. Preheat oven to 350 degrees. In a large bowl, mix dry ingredients and seeds together. Add oil, broth and egg mixture. Your dough should be firm. Let sit 15–20 minutes. On a lightly floured surface, roll out dough ¼ inch thick. Cut into shapes and brush with glaze. Bake for 25–35 minutes until golden brown. Take out and cool. Store cookies in an airtight container.

GARLIC SNAPS

(6–8 dozen)

1½ cups wheat germ
1 pound cooked boneless chicken, white and dark
1 cup low salt chicken broth
2 cups whole wheat flour (more may be needed)
2 cloves fresh peeled garlic
1 cup yellow cornmeal
2 tablespoons brewer's yeast (optional)
Garlic powder

Glaze: Beat 1 egg; lightly brush on cookies before baking. Preheat oven to 350 degrees. In a large blender or food processor, gradually puree chicken and garlic, slowly adding chicken broth. Transfer the chicken puree into a large bowl. Mix in wheat germ and brewer's yeast. Slowly add flour and cornmeal until the dough becomes stiff. Knead the dough for 3–5 minutes. Let it rest for 5–10 minutes. On a lightly floured surface, roll the dough into a ball.

Boyd-Smith adds: "As Webster and Max like their crackers thin, I have found that the best way to do this is to split the ball into four sections and roll each section into a hotdog shape. Wrap these in plastic wrap and chill for 30 minutes. Slice into very thin chips. Place the chips on a lightly greased cookie sheet (I always use Pam Spray when lightly greasing my cookie sheets), and brush with glaze. Lightly sprinkle with garlic powder and bake for 25–40 minutes. Halfway through, turn. As the crackers cool, they will become hard. Leftover dough can be frozen for up to 3 months."

Food Allergies

There has been a lot of recent publicity about food allergies in dogs. I am grateful that this problem is finally being recognized and addressed by a broad spectrum of the veterinary community. I have found food allergies to be the cause of some of the most puzzling dermatitis cases I have seen.

The most common manifestation of food allergies is via skin problems. If your dog's coat is dry, dull, and flaky, and the dog is being fed a good diet, then food allergies must be considered. In most cases, treating the dog for food allergies should be tried before allopathic medical treatments such as prescription drugs are given. All drugs used for skin problems have side effects that can be debilitating. And there is growing evidence that these drugs can have long-term effects on the immune system as well.

If food allergies are the cause of the skin problem, it is because the dog is allergic to a particular item (or items) contained in his food—the difficult part is identifying that item so it can be eliminated from the diet.

Some breeds have particular problems with food allergies or sensitivities. Labradors and Dobermans are often intolerant of soy products; some lines of Akitas and German shepherds are sensitive to both wheat and soy in their food. If you have one of these breeds, and symptoms of food allergies are present, simply eliminating foods with these ingredients may eliminate the problems.

If your dog is not one of these breeds, however, then a more diagnostic approach to determining food allergies is required. I have found dogs allergic to all facets of the food groups, including animal protein. I usually start by removing all of the most common problem foods from the diet—beef, soy, wheat, corn, and preservatives. The easiest way to eliminate these ingredients is to feed the homemade Hypoallergenic Diet or one of the special allergy formulas from a natural pet products company.

HYPOALLERGENIC DIET

¼ lb. diced lamb or chicken, boiled or broiled (venison or rabbit may be substituted)
3 tablespoons vegetables (choose from list given in the Basic Diet on page 100)
1 cup brown rice
1 teaspoon oil (choose from oils listed in the Basic Diet on page 101)
Vitamin and mineral supplement (see guidelines on page 93). Add according to label directions.
Add 3 times a week: **½ cup plain unflavored yogurt**

Increase recipe as necessary for quantity needed. Be sure to refrigerate or freeze unused portions. See "How Much to Feed?" page 107, for guidelines.

Gradually introduce the new diet to your dog. For the first three to five days, replace one-fourth of the old diet with the new food by mixing the two together. Then, for three days, mix the new and old diets half and half. Then, for another three days, mix three-fourths of the new diet with the old food. Finally, you will feed only the new food. This method of slowly introducing the new food allows the digestive bacteria in your dog's system a chance to gradually change with the new diet and usually avoids sudden onsets of diarrhea or gas, which develop when a new food is introduced too quickly into the diet.

Only in extremely severe cases of skin problems do I alter this gradual modification of the diet. In these severe cases I feed only rice for three to seven days, which helps cleanse the system. Then I add chicken or lamb to the rice for another three to seven days, finally adding the vegetables and the rest of the ingredients in the Hypoallergenic Diet. Add vitamin and mineral supplements back into the diet last.

During this time it is important to closely monitor the dog's skin and behavioral responses to the diet. If food allergies are the culprit in causing the skin problems, sometimes I see a dramatic lessening of the symptoms almost immediately. Do not expect overnight changes in your dog's skin. It frequently takes about four to six weeks for maximum changes to occur in the skin and coat, so be sure to allow enough time on the new food for results to be seen.

If food allergies are the cause of the skin problems and this new homemade diet eradicates them, you can stick with the new diet indefinitely. If you want to switch back to commercial foods, however, you must do so gradually, again proportionately mixing the two foods together as described earlier.

When switching to a commercial food or adding ingredients back into the diet one at a time, watch for sudden changes in the skin such as itching, redness, or hives, indicating a sensitivity to that particular food or ingredient. Behavior changes such as restlessness or irritability should also be noted as indicators of a problem food or ingredient.

When diet changes are made, care must be taken to make sure the new diet meets all the dog's nutritional needs. The simplified diet I described earlier—feeding only rice and then, after three to seven days, adding chicken or lamb—must be followed for only the short time indicated to prevent nutritional deficiencies. It is vital that you add vegetables to the recipe to provide the necessary vitamins and minerals for a balanced diet. Whenever you are altering your dog's diet, it is best to consult with a veterinarian regarding the changes you're considering.

When you begin making changes in the dog's diet, keep a written record of the dietary changes you are planning. Then keep track on a daily basis, noting the date and the foods you fed, as well as the symptoms and any changes you note. I also recommend taking a picture of the dog so later comparisons can be made.

Other Special Diets

Check with your veterinarian before using a special diet. If excessive weight loss or weight gain occurs, ask your veterinarian to help you adjust food levels for your dog's specific needs.

REDUCING DIET

¼ lb. chicken (no skin), boiled or broiled
½ cup cottage cheese or natural cultured yogurt
4 cups vegetables (choose from those listed in the Basic Diet on page 100)
Vitamin and mineral supplement (see guidelines on page 93). Add according to label directions.
1 tablespoon oil (see guidelines on page 101).
Enzyme supplement (see guidelines on page 90). Add according to label directions.
Add 3 times a week: **½ cup plain yogurt.**

Multiply recipe as necessary for quantity needed. Make sure to refrigerate or freeze unused portions. See "How Much to Feed" for guidelines on amount to feed.

RESTRICTED PROTEIN DIET

¼ lb. ground beef, chicken, or lamb, boiled or broiled
⅛ cup vegetables (choose from those listed in Basic Diet on page 100)
2 cups brown rice
1 egg (soft boiled)
½ cup boiled sliced potato or wheat bread crumbs
Vitamin and mineral supplement (see guidelines on page 93). Add according to label directions
1 tablespoon oil (add oil only if meat used is chicken or lamb); choose from the oils listed in the Basic Diet on page 101)
Enzyme supplement (see guidelines on page 90). Add according to directions on label.

Increase recipe as necessary for quantity needed. Make sure to refrigerate or freeze unused portions. See "How Much to Feed?" for guidelines on amount to feed.

Feeding Puppies

Because puppies vary in their developmental processes, they should be judged individually for the proper time to supplement the mother's milk with puppy food, beginning the weaning process. While the mother (referred to in canine circles as the bitch) is nursing her puppies it is important to watch her closely. If she begins to lose weight even though she is eating as much food as possible, she may not be able to provide her puppies with enough nutrients. At this point it is critical both for the mother's and puppies' health to begin supplementing her milk with special puppy food.

The puppies' health is a reflection of the quality of their mother's milk. If the bitch is on a high-quality diet, you can be sure that the correct nutrients are available for the milk she is producing. While she is feeding her puppies she will eat more food in order to produce an adequate milk supply.

Just as with an adult dog's diet, a homemade diet is best for your puppies. If you are unable to make homemade food, however, follow the same guidelines as detailed in the adult dog food section to select a high-quality commercial food formulated specifically for puppies.

Here is a good basic puppy food which will supply all the puppies' nutritional needs:

HOMEMADE PUPPY FOOD

***1 cup regular hamburger (not lean) or chicken with fat left on**

1 cup grain (see grains listed in Basic Diet on page 100)

**Note:* Eggs can be substituted for half of the meat two or three times a week. When substituting eggs, add 1 teaspoon of oil. Choose from oils listed in the Basic Diet on page 101.

¼ cup vegetables, minced (see vegetables listed in the Basic Diet on page 100)
¼ cup goat milk, cottage cheese, or natural cultured yogurt
Vitamin and mineral supplement from the health food store. Add *only after weaning* and according to label directions.

While I normally don't recommend giving isolated vitamins or minerals unless there is a specific health problem, research indicates that puppies of large and giant breeds can benefit from extra vitamin C to promote cartilage formation. Many breeders of dogs prone to hip dysplasia have incorporated vitamin C into their feeding program to help prevent the problem from developing. The initial vitamin C dosage should be low, usually about 100 mg, and gradually increased. A general guideline would be about 500 mg daily for 25-pound puppies and up to 1,000 mg daily for puppies over 25 pounds. The dosage will vary with the size of the puppy and the puppy's tolerance level. If too much vitamin C is given, diarrhea or loose stool will result. This can be easily remedied by reducing the amount of vitamin C until the stool is firm.

People often ask about giving extra calcium to puppies. This is a controversial subject. I have seen calcium supplementation given most often to large breeds. Unfortunately, giving excessive amounts of calcium supplements (which often contain vitamin D as well) can result in metabolic imbalances and sometimes lead to severe clinical illness. I have seen problems arise when extra calcium was given in an effort to make puppies grow faster. A particularly distressing experience involved a lovely eight-month-old Great Dane puppy. The puppy was experiencing digestive upsets of undetermined origin. She was not "ill," but vomiting and diarrhea had been occurring with increasing frequency and the owner noticed decreased urination. The puppy was on a puppy food diet with the additions of high levels of calcium, phosphorus, and vitamin D, as well as milk and cottage cheese. X rays revealed mineralization of the stomach, kidney, and other soft tissue areas. This puppy was getting so many minerals in her diet that her body began storing them in hardened bonelike form in these organs and soft tissue, which was a life-threatening problem. Unfortunately, her condition was advanced and irreversible by the time she came to me as a patient. She died about a year later.

Although this was an extreme case, I keep the X rays available to demonstrate to clients why excessive supplementation is not advisable. It is best to use a well-balanced puppy food and let the dog grow at Mother Nature's own pace.

Normally puppies begin the weaning process sometime between the age of three to five weeks. Watch the mother; she may decide the weaning time herself and begin to feed the puppies less and for shorter periods of time. If you are using a homemade puppy food, it should be mushy; if you are feeding a dry food, soak it in warm water until it is mushy.

Put the mushy food in a flat pan. To introduce the food, start with one puppy and put a tiny amount of the food on your fingertip. Then let the puppy lick your finger or gently put your finger in the puppy's mouth. Keep repeating the process with little bits of the food as long as the puppy cooperates. Then go on to the next puppy.

FIGURE 5

It may take a few sessions until the puppies get the idea that this mushy stuff will nicely complement their mother's milk and can indeed be considered a food alternative. The first few sessions will require individual puppy cleanup afterward. Offer this mushy food twice a day at first. Then, as the mother decreases her nursing, increase the puppy food feedings to three to four times a day. Let the puppies eat as much as they want in each session. In the fifth to sixth week a small amount of hard puppy food can also be introduced at each meal. Most puppies enjoy chewing on it. By the sixth week, the puppies should be able to eat dry food.

Once the puppies are fully weaned and eating only puppy food, feed them approximately every four hours with a total of four feedings during the day until they are about four months old, then decrease to two meals a day. Some toy breeds may require more frequent feedings. Also, for toy-breed puppies, I suggest keeping honey water available at all times. Put one teaspoon of honey into each cup of water in the bowl.

Giant breeds such as Great Danes, Saint Bernards, or Newfoundlands mature slowly and may require puppy food, which has a higher percentage of protein, up until the age of one and a half or two years.

Tips on Weaning Puppies

1. Do not overfeed puppies. Puppies who grow too fast or become overweight can be prone to metabolic bone disease.
2. Do not leave the mother in the same room with the puppies at feeding time. She may eat all of the puppies' food.
3. Do not use cow's milk to soak puppy food or supplement the diet; it usually causes diarrhea. Do not use puppy food that comes coated with powdered milk; it often causes digestive upsets.
4. Do not leave large, full water bowls with the puppies. They may fall in and not be able to get out and thus drown. Make water available to the puppies in a shallow bowl at the point in the weaning process when the mother is no longer nursing very often.
5. Be sure to clean the puppies after each feeding; moist puppy food left on paws and other areas can create an environment for skin infections.
6. Because parasites such as roundworm can be passed from

the mother to her puppies before they are born, worm puppies at two to three weeks of age and repeat again in another two weeks. Ask your veterinarian to recommend a *mild* wormer. I prefer Strongid, which is also sold under the name Nemix.

7

Breeding, Neutering, and Spaying

Animal shelters take in millions of stray or unwanted dogs each year. The conditions at most shelters are crowded, smelly, and stress-filled. If you don't believe that overpopulation of dogs is a problem, spend the day at a large city shelter. The number of dogs euthanized (put to sleep) on a daily basis is enormous. But, in a way, these shelter dogs are the lucky ones. At least they don't have to suffer anymore. Many areas don't have adequate control or are overcrowded, resulting in a surplus of homeless dogs.

The sight of a thin, starving dog, loaded with parasites and often diseased, is heartbreaking. Even more tragic is when owners drive unwanted dogs to the country and drop them off. Many people do this because they believe the dog will be able to survive in the country. Unfortunately this is usually not the case. Our domesticated dogs have lost most of the instinct that would enable them to catch wild animals as a food source. Very few can survive in the wild. Most of the time they starve to death or are killed for attacking pets—who are fairly easy prey—in their attempt to catch food.

Recently an unwanted dog was dropped off in my neighborhood. I live in the country, with woods and a stream nearby. It probably seemed an ideal area to someone abandoning a dog in the country. This dog got into people's trash, stole pet food that was left outside, and became a killer of cats and small dogs. A retriever type of dog, he was swift and silent, closing in on unsuspecting little animals and breaking their necks in one practiced shake of the head.

I became aware of the dog when he tried to grab my toy poodle one night while we were out walking. It was a close race, but I got to Lily first and had to aggressively chase the retriever away. Two days later he tried to get Kelly, my 17-year-old poodle, and again I chased him off into the woods. Fifteen minutes later, after rifle shots rang out from my neighbor's house, the retriever's reign of terror had ended. In this case the dog suffered, the neighborhood animals suffered, and the people suffered. Some of my neighbors lost their pets, and for several weeks we all had to resign ourselves to the somber knowledge that the only possible outcome of this siege would be the eventual death of the retriever. Whoever got the chance would have to kill him because he had become too vicious to catch. Because one person was irresponsible in the handling of an unwanted dog, that dog and an entire community suffered.

The Facts About Neutering and Spaying

Spaying of female dogs requires major abdominal surgery and, in most clinics, an overnight stay. This surgery is actually called an ovariohysterectomy—both the ovaries and uterus are removed. Most dogs tolerate the surgery very well. Because veterinarians perform it so frequently, most are proficient at it, completing the operation in a relatively short time and thereby reducing the stress on the dog.

Recovery from spaying varies with the individual dog, because each dog tolerates and interprets pain differently. Some dogs just slow down, resting for a few days, then gradually return to their same old selves. Small dogs often exhibit the most pain, requiring a longer recovery period and a little more tender loving care. Do not push your dog while she is convalescing. Restrict activity for at least a week, then watch her carefully for another week. It's amazing to me how quickly most dogs recover from this or any other major surgery compared to the recovery time needed by people.

If your dog isn't eating at least a little food by the second day after surgery, call the veterinarian. Very sensitive dogs may be helped by mild pain relief such as homeopathic arnica or buffered aspirin. But be sure to check with your veterinarian before administering any medications to your dog, even aspirin; it can cause blood-clotting problems or mask important symptoms and therefore should be prescribed by your veterinarian.

When males are neutered, the testicles are removed through a small incision. Because some owners do not feel comfortable with the cosmetic effect of neutering, a vasectomy is an option to neutering. Males are usually kept just one night. They generally need less recuperative time since their surgery does not require opening the abdomen. Some swelling may occur, along with accompanying discomfort. If too much discomfort occurs, an ice pack wrapped in a towel can be periodically applied for 5 to 10 minutes. Homeopathic arnica and Bach Flower Rescue Remedy can also be helpful.

Some males have a congenital abnormality called cryptorchidism, which occurs when one of the testicles has not descended into the scrotal pouch. This testicle can be in the abdomen or in the inguinal canal above the scrotum. To remove this undescended testicle, more complex surgery is required. This problem seems to be more common in recent years, particularly due to the increase of inbreeding. It is important that dogs with this condition be neutered because otherwise the undescended testicle often creates problems.

Keep both male and female dogs quiet and away from other pets and young children when first returning from the hospital and for several days afterward. Be sure your dog starts eating a little by the second day home. It is normal for your dog to lick the incision area, but check it frequently to be sure your dog is not over-licking or trying to pull out the sutures placed in the incision. Excessive licking of the suture area can result in an infection of the incision site. Return for suture removal when specified by your veterinarian, usually 7 to 10 days following surgery. Make sure your dog is having bowel movements within two or three days following surgery.

If the cost of neutering or spaying is preventing an owner from pursuing it, there may be an alternative to a private veterinarian. Most communities have a neuter and spay clinic, and some humane societies offer discounts so neutering and spaying can be affordable.

It's best to spay or neuter your dog at about eight months of age. Females should be spayed before their first heat because this helps decrease the chance of mammary (breast) cancer. Many veterinarians won't spay dogs in heat, and there is a good reason for this. Some dogs in heat tend to bleed more and their tissues are more delicate during this period. These problems require more time, precautions, and considerably more effort on the veterinarian's part. So consider carefully before requesting that your dog be spayed while in heat, though sometimes it is unavoidable. Spaying a dog who is in heat will not stop the male dogs from trying to breed the female. It takes a week or two before the attraction is gone.

Neutering your male dog will help prevent testicular cancer, prostate problems, and the tendency to roam. From middle age on, males are susceptible to testicular cancer, benign tumors (which often cause problems), and prostate enlargement and infection. Neutering helps prevent many problems before they can manifest.

Breeding Your Dog

Even in purebreds, breeding must be carefully considered. Because of indiscriminate breeding, many genetic defects are passed on to future generations. Your dog should be checked carefully to be sure he or she is a good candidate for breeding before starting a breeding program.

Sadly, many people are uninformed about genetic problems that can occur with inbreeding. Inbreeding is the breeding of close relatives, including father/daughter, mother/son, or, worst of all, brother/sister. When these breedings take place, genetic problems are magnified. The resulting abnormalities are usually not readily apparent. Most often the result is internal abnormalities, which become time bombs that owners are unaware of until the dog develops problems. Sometimes they do not show up until well into adulthood.

One litter of rottweiler puppies I treated was a mother/son cross. Of the five puppies, two died after eight weeks of unknown causes, one died at five months of liver failure, one died at seven months of kidney failure, and one had malformed joints in its back legs. That was a very dramatic example of why inbreeding is not recommended.

In another case a Pomeranian was brought in for a cesarean section delivery. Because of improper breeding practices, she suffered from a malformed eye, throat, and internal organs. I pleaded with the owner to allow me to spay the dog after the cesarean section so these genetic problems would not be passed on beyond the current litter.

But she informed me that this was an expensive dog with rare bloodlines and therefore no spay was to be done. This attitude is not uncommon, and unfortunately it's the dogs who suffer and the owners who profit.

Usually it's the dog and an unsuspecting owner who suffer the consequences of inbreeding. To avoid problems, check bloodlines carefully before purchasing a dog. A friend who owned a red Doberman discovered that her dog was a brother/sister cross after he almost bled to death from a small cut. The dog was a hemophiliac, a genetic disorder sometimes found in the Doberman breed. A two-year-old pit bull I examined recently was in heart failure and severely anemic. The dog had Rocky Mountain spotted fever and a congenital heart defect. Apparently the illness had been severe enough to strain the heart past its capacity. Upon questioning the owner I learned that the dog was a mother/son cross, which explained the medical problems. Educating the public about neutering, spaying, and responsible breeding is one of the challenges that face veterinarians and all those associated with the pet industry.

"But I don't want my dog to get fat and lazy" is the most common reason I hear for refusing neutering or spaying. Although many people believe weight gain and lethargy are inevitable after these procedures, this scenario is not necessary. It is true that a sudden change in hormonal balance is sometimes a shock to the body, putting too large a burden on the remaining hormone-producing glands, and the metabolism slows down as a result. Ideally the adrenal gland should take over to fill some of this hormonal deficiency, but sometimes the change is so abrupt that this doesn't happen. Traditionally there was nothing that could be done except to put the dog on a diet and give it vitamins. Now, with acupuncture and homeopathy, the entire problem can be avoided. Many holistic veterinarians automatically include acupuncture and homeopathy treatments with the surgery. However, if your dog has this problem, even if it's long-standing, acupuncture and homeopathy can make a difference.

The homeopathics will be prescribed according to your dog's symptoms, so before you consult with the veterinarian, keep a careful record of behavior and eating habits and anything that seems unusual to you. Although I have had good results using homeopathics alone, the response is quicker and often more effective if acupuncture is used in conjunction with homeopathics.

8

Holistic Veterinary Care

Holistic Versus Allopathic Veterinary Medicine

Dog owners seek out a holistic veterinarian for many reasons. But the overwhelming factor is that the alternative—allopathic medicine—has not maintained their companion animals in the desired state of health. The advantage of holistic veterinarians is that they combine the knowledge and skills of "regular" allopathic medicine with the holistic approach, thereby offering the animal a broader range of healing possibilities. In the next chapter I will give an overview of major holistic modalities used in veterinary medicine today: homeopathy, acupuncture, herbs, chiropractic, Bach flower remedies, magnetic therapy, oxygen therapy, and aromatherapy.

My objective in practice has always been to get the dog well using the *safest*, most *effective* method possible. Please note that the word *quickest* is not a part of my objective. Although holistic treatment can sometimes bring fast results, it is often more gradual. Faster is not always better. A holistic veterinarian is thorough, leaving no step out of the diagnostic process. I am a firm believer in knowing what you're treating whenever possible.

Recently a golden retriever named Rusty was under my care because she was suffering from pain. Chiropractic adjustments would relieve the pain and symptoms would disappear after each treatment.

Each time, however, there would be a gradual return of pain over the next few days. After repeating the adjustments on several visits, I felt an X ray was in order. The X ray indicated a bullet lodged in the muscle tissue near the area that was requiring adjustment.

Although there was no way to know how long the bullet had been there, as a hunting dog, Rusty could have suffered this undetected wound years earlier. Now it was obviously causing problems with fibrous adhesions and a decrease in the energy available to that area. After removal of the bullet and a few additional chiropractic adjustments combined with acupuncture, all symptoms disappeared.

Sometimes it is not that easy, and even sophisticated technology and laboratory tests do not yield a definitive diagnosis. A Chinese pug named Chang was recently brought to me with severe upper respiratory symptoms resembling a cold, including sniffles and sneezing. He was depressed and not eating. I couldn't pinpoint a diagnosis. Chang had already been to an allopathic veterinarian and had been taking a wide array of antibiotics, with no response. I suspected a virus and treated the dog using holistic methods—acupuncture, homeopathics, and herbs. In this case the results were swift and dramatic—by the next day Chang's fever was down, he was eating, and his energy had improved. Complete recovery followed in four days.

This case demonstrates another advantage of holistic medicine, because we can use guiding symptoms to establish treatment when regular diagnostic methods don't provide enough answers. Most holistic methods of treatment were established before laboratory testing was available and therefore had to rely on different methods for diagnosis and treatment.

For instance, when using acupuncture, a holistic veterinarian can use pulse diagnosis to check energy meridians for deficiencies as well as checking for sensitive acupuncture points. (See more on pulse diagnosis on page 195.) In homeopathy the important or guiding symptoms for each remedy can be found in volumes of *Materia Medica*. And chiropractic has shown that certain physical problems are associated with the areas of the spine that require adjustment.

It is this broader range of available diagnosis and treatment that first interested me in holistic medicine. Using allopathy I found that many medical problems were either not treatable or required drug therapy that was potentially harmful to the dog. My own miniature poodle, Coco, had a chronic neck problem that frustrated me for years. Coco loved to play and sometimes was overly enthusiastic, thinking he could run, jump, and turn around all at once at full speed. His neck would go out of alignment and he would be in agony for several weeks. The only treatments allopathic medicine had available for him were pharmaceuticals: steroids, painkillers, and muscle relaxants. After several weeks on these drugs Coco's symptoms would disappear and he would return to play.

I had not been practicing holistic medicine long when Coco injured his neck again. This time I treated him with a chiropractic adjustment and acupuncture and, to my surprise, he was symptom free in two hours. These holistic treatments did not have the negative side effects of the drugs. In addition, they had a wonderfully positive side effect: with the proper realignment of the neck and reestablishment of energy, Coco's symptoms did not recur with the frequency previously seen.

I'm the type who likes to see results before judging the effectiveness of different forms of treatment. Coco's rapid recovery with holistic methods compared to many weeks with allopathic medicine confirmed to me the effectiveness of holistic medicine.

While I have seen dramatic physical changes with holistic medicine, the positive results go even further. Most holistic modalities also address the mental well-being of a dog. This is another aspect of holistic medicine that is a tremendous advantage when treating an animal. Dogs are capable of a full range of emotional disturbances, many of which are tied in to their owner's emotional well-being. An increasing number of companion dogs seem to be affected by this bond, particularly those who are confined to apartments. The dog often becomes so close to its owner that an owner's emotional upset can so affect the dog's own emotions that he becomes physically ill.

Little Peaches, a cream colored Peke-a-Poo, arrived in my clinic vomiting, depressed, and suffering from diarrhea. After doing an extensive exam, I was unable to pinpoint any specific medical problems. But I did note that Peaches was sensitive to her owner's every move and change in voice. When I inquired about possible emotional influences in her home, the owner admitted there was a lot of turmoil in the home due to the serious illness of one family member and the owner's own high level of stress.

I put Peaches on a diet that was more digestible with fewer fats. I also prescribed digestive enzymes and, most important, a Bach flower remedy for her emotional upset. The Bach flowers were effective and Peaches returned to normal by the next day. In addition, I gave the owner instructions on how to avoid future problems by using the Bach Flower Rescue Remedy at highly stressful times.

Trauma can also produce emotional and behavioral changes that are difficult to diagnose and are not easy to correct. Bach flower and homeopathic remedies are often effective in dealing with these problems, though they are usually more gradual and don't work as fast as the methods I used on Peaches.

Most holistic veterinarians combine all the resources, technology, and treatments of allopathic medicine with a wide range of more natural, holistic modalities. This gives us a wider variety of treatment possibilities and often a safer and healthier method of treatment.

Finding a Holistic Veterinarian

It's important to find a holistic veterinarian that both you and your dog like. Just because a veterinary clinic advertises that they are "holistic" does not mean the veterinarians at the clinic are well versed on a range of holistic modalities. Ask about affiliations with professional associations, years of experience, and the specific holistic modalities the clinic specializes in. Several sources of holistic veterinarians are listed in the Appendix: the American Holistic Veterinary Medical Association, the International Veterinary Acupuncture Society, and the National Center for Homeopathy.

If you are unable to find a holistic veterinarian in your area, it is possible to work long distance with a veterinarian as long as you have a consulting veterinarian locally to do examinations and any necessary tests. The long-distance veterinarian will require information obtained by the "hands-on" veterinarian. If you pursue this type of arrangement, be sure that your local veterinarian is agreeable to working in this manner.

Once you have narrowed the field and found more than one holistic clinic that would work for you, here are some additional factors to consider and ask about over the phone:

- Is your facility an outpatient clinic or a full-care hospital?
- Do you board dogs?
- Do you have separate rooms for hospitalized dogs and cats?
- What if my dog requires special treatment? Does this clinic provide 24-hour care? Do the veterinarians perform complex surgeries and provide special anesthesia?
- How many veterinarians are on staff and what are their qualifications? Are they male or female? (You may be more comfortable with one sex or the other.)
- How does the veterinarian feel about owners getting a second opinion from another clinic in case of a major health problem?

Once you have gone through the basic checklist, it's time to get down to the finer details. At this point you will need to visit the clinic and meet the veterinarian. After that initial introduction, you will have a new list of things to consider:

- Is the outside clean and well kept?
- Is your first overall impression favorable?
- Are you comfortable in the waiting room?
- Is the receptionist friendly and helpful?
- Is the clinic clean and the color scheme appealing?
- Are the employees wearing uniforms that are neat and reasonably clean?
- Do you like the way the staff handles your dog?
- Read any posted signs to be sure the clinic policies match your own needs.
- Ask about hours, emergency services, etc.

Let's look at some of these points in greater detail. The waiting room is an area where you and your dog will spend time, so it's important to feel very comfortable there. The waiting room can also be a reflection of the veterinary practice itself. If the color scheme is appealing, and the furniture designed for your comfort as well as your pet's comfort, you will probably find that the staff will follow suit, with caring, thoughtful personnel and progressive medicine. This is simply a rule of thumb and by no means is it always true, but it is one indicator to look for.

If you are uncomfortable in the waiting room it can be due to a variety of reasons and is not always because of a lack of something. This was evidenced by a clinic I visited several years ago. The floor in the waiting room was carpeted, which caused a great deal of emotional upset to owners whose dogs urinated on it—a common occurrence in veterinary clinics.

How the staff reacts to problems such as accidental urination is one indication of how they will handle your dog. In most clinics this type of accident is so common that the problem is dealt with quickly with a "no muss, no fuss" attitude. However, I have been in clinics where owners were scolded and dogs disciplined. The scent of previous accidents is very obvious to a dog's keen sense of smell. When that smell is combined with the excitement of a car ride and the exposure to other animals in the waiting room, the probability of accidental urination is high. So most veterinary offices don't get upset about these incidents.

Once you've observed the general attitude of the staff, then watch the way your dog is held during the examination. Of course, if your dog is excited or resists the exam, then more restraint may be required. However, a good veterinarian will have methods to hold and restrain your dog that will not cause harm. I keep a selection of soft nylon muzzles on hand for the more nervous or aggressive dogs. The new style of muzzles slips on easily and does not cause the dogs any discomfort. Often when we use them on a known biter right away, there is much less fuss on the dog's part as he learns that he must behave when the muzzle is in place.

I am always adamant that the owner accompany the dog into the examination room. If you're not comfortable doing this and your veterinarian does not insist on it, do it at least once to see how your dog is handled.

I recently had a nasty experience with a Pekingese because the owner had never accompanied Willie into the exam room, where he had obviously had some rough treatment. It happened one day while I was visiting Willie's owner, a new acquaintance. Willie had not finished his breakfast that morning, which worried his owner, so I volunteered to do a brief exam. She was a quiet and gentle lady and Willie seemed much the same. While he laid on my lap I started to gently palpate Willie's stomach region, checking for discomfort. However, before the exam had barely begun Willie leaped up and began to viciously attack me. As I stood up he bit at my legs and leaped and snapped at my hands.

When we eventually quieted him down I discussed the radical change in Willie's behavior with his upset owner. She admitted that she never accompanied Willie into the exam room when they visited the vet and that he always seemed upset when he came out. Since she had never witnessed what occurred behind the closed door, she would just allow him to calm down and hope that he would forget the upsetting experience.

I explained to her that something was very wrong for Willie to react in that way. Willie's association with a veterinary exam was obviously a negative and stressful one, indicating that he had been mishandled. A good veterinarian can examine a dog in a gentle manner. Unfortunately, Willie's experience had created a potentially dangerous behavior pattern that might lead to biting a small child one day in the future.

It is important to know all the behavioral patterns your dog can exhibit. When being examined in the veterinarian's office many dogs become nervous and show aggressive behavior like Willie's. Often the owner's presence helps to reassure and calm the dog as well as making the owner aware that the dog can behave in an unruly manner. In case the owner ever has to administer first aid at home, this knowledge will forewarn him or her to take precautions if aggressive behavior is anticipated. Fortunately, after years of practice, my reflexes are quick and I was unharmed by Willie's unexpected frightened response, even though it was too close for comfort.

Once you have evaluated how the veterinarian and staff handle your dog, you want to check on the policies of the clinic to make sure they fit your needs. Check the hours and ask about emergency arrangements. Some animal hospitals handle their own emergencies, and some areas have centralized emergency hospitals. Also ask about payment policies. Very few clinics offer credit; however, many take credit cards and checks, with some also honoring pet insurance programs.

If your dog has special needs, check to be sure that all procedures that your dog may need now or in the future are provided for. Not all clinics have a full range of highly technical medical machines, but most have X-ray capability along with other basic equipment. The more complex and expensive items such as the ECG (electrocardiograph) machine, ultrasound, or fiberoptic devices are not available in every clinic. If your dog requires a special type of diagnostic equipment which an otherwise desirable clinic doesn't have, the clinic may be able to arrange a referral just for that particular test. Referrals are common in veterinary practice just as in human medicine, and most veterinarians will not hesitate to refer to a colleague who specializes in a particular field.

The practice of getting a second opinion from a veterinarian at another animal hospital has become more common in recent years. Each veterinarian views this in a different light, which is why it's advisable to ask the veterinarian's views on this topic in your first meeting. A doctor who is secure and open-minded will encourage an owner to seek further advice from other sources if he or she wishes when the case at hand is a difficult one. If you plan to get a second opinion, let your veterinarian know of your decision early on, because it may save you from repeat lab work or diagnostic expenses.

Finding Other Health Care Professionals

It's amazing how many animal specialists there are today. For many years groomers and obedience trainers were the only animal care professionals available other than the veterinarian. With a growing concern to meet the needs of our animal companions, the field of professionals now available includes nutritionists, herbalists, animal massage therapists, psychiatrists, and animal communicators and behaviorists.

When selecting any of these professionals, I'd advise a procedure similar to that outlined previously for choosing a veterinarian. Don't be shy about checking out any health care professional you consider taking your dog to. This way you will avoid unpleasant surprises. At the very least you can learn about the reputation of the person you are considering by asking around. A good source of information is your veterinarian. Fellow pet owners, pet stores, and health food stores may also be able to give you leads on a good holistic professional. Advertisements in the Yellow Pages will also give you a good lead. Additionally, you may be able to reach a regional veterinary medical association that can answer your questions. Some states have specific laws concerning what pet health professionals can do legally and what they cannot do.

It may not be so easy to find professionals in the more esoteric areas, such as those who communicate with animals and animal massage therapists. Your own skill at interviewing prospective professionals will be important in determining if you feel the person is someone you want to trust. (See more on "Animal Communicators" on page 27.)

The Checkup

The annual checkup is often the only time I see many of my patients, so I always give a thorough physical exam. This is completed prior to any regularly scheduled treatment, including vaccinations. It is particularly important to do a careful exam on those dogs approaching old age, to try to catch developing health problems. Occasionally with an older dog I suggest laboratory blood work so a baseline of that dog's normal values can be on record in case any problems should arise in the future. This is particularly important with dogs whose owners travel frequently or are unable to monitor the dog themselves. Then, if the dog has health problems in the owner's absence, medical attention can be more prompt.

Each veterinarian conducts an exam differently. If a dog is nervous, I begin by giving him Rescue Remedy (see "Bach Flower Remedies," p. 160). To begin the exam I like to palpate or feel the entire dog, starting at the tip of the nose and working my way back to the tail. Special attention is given to the teeth, checking for tartar buildup, broken teeth, and infected gums. Dogs require teeth cleaning just like people. Any problem with the teeth and gums can be a source of infection affecting your dog's overall health and must not be taken lightly.

Several years ago a dog was brought to me with an incredible list of complex health problems. Sasha had undergone a major diagnostic workup, extensive surgery, and was taking a lot of medication for a gastrointestinal problem. Although the problem was stable, he refused to eat. The owner had been to several different veterinary clinics with no success. Finally, as a last-ditch effort, she decided to try a holistic approach and came to me.

The complexity of Sasha's problems was mind-boggling. The owner had brought along records from previous veterinarians. Having copies of medical records is always important when you get a second opinion or leave a clinic because you decide to try a different veterinarian. You are entitled to copies of your dog's medical records and X rays. They will be very helpful in guiding the new or consulting veterinarian, because they give details about tests and treatments that have been followed.

After reviewing the dog's medical history I set about doing the exam. I was shocked to find that because there was so much dental tartar on the dog's teeth, the inside of the mouth was cut and bleeding. No wonder she wasn't eating; it was obviously very painful to her. The owner had been told by the other veterinarians not to worry about this, because the dog's condition prevented the anesthesia that would be needed to do a thorough teeth cleaning.

My technician and I were able to accomplish the job with a little patience and no anesthesia. Some dogs must be anesthetized for teeth cleaning, but luckily Sasha was very cooperative. She returned home and the owner called to say she had started eating again immediately.

The same attention should be given to the ears, checking the outside as well as inside. Here in the South where parasites are prevalent, the outside of the ear and tips are checked for evidence of scratching or fly bites, and the insides for signs of ear mites. Because a moist, humid climate increases the incidence of ear infections, these problems often show up in the summer. Early detection helps prevent damage to the ear as well as avoiding a deep-seated infection.

The rest of the body is examined in a similar fashion, checking the skin, the hair coat quality, and the anal glands, which are located on either side of the anal opening and often become impacted. Then I run my hands down the legs and look at paws and nails, making sure there are no ingrown nails. Ingrown nails can be very painful and often go undetected by owners. The dewclaw, the high first claw on the inside of the leg, often becomes ingrown. The longest ingrown nails I have cut out extended almost 2 inches into the dog's leg. Imagine how painful that must have been.

Checking for external as well as internal parasites is always part of the yearly exam. If evidence of flea or mite (commonly called mange) infestation is found, I discuss various solutions and control measures. We check for internal parasites through a fecal sample, which is either brought in by the owner or obtained from the dog during the exam. It is checked for eggs of internal parasites such as roundworms, hookworms, and whipworms. If internal parasites are found, a wormer is prescribed. Internal parasites are less common than they used to be because many heartworm medications contain compounds that kill these parasites.

Heartworms are checked for, even if the dog has been on a preventive. Heartworms are long spaghettilike worms that inhabit the heart. They eventually cause shortness of breath, coughing, and lead to death within a few years. Heartworms are well established throughout the United States, and I have found infestations even in dogs on preventives. Because heartworms are carried by mosquitoes, be sure to check with your veterinarian about which months of the year to have your dog on this medication in your area. In some colder climates heartworm preventive can be discontinued during some winter months. In the South, however, there is no break in the mosquito season, and dogs should remain on the treatment year-round.

Some of the most tragic cases of heartworm-positive dogs have come from the misconception of being able to discontinue treatment in the winter, or the belief that a house dog is not exposed to mosquitoes. Unfortunately I have seen many cases of dogs in both of those categories infested with heartworms. Although heartworms are treatable, it is a treatment regimen I prefer to avoid if possible. Many times the heart has already been damaged by the time heartworms have been diagnosed. I recommend a heartworm check every year, even for dogs on heartworm preventive. (See the discussion of these topics in the "Health Problems" section at the end of the book for detailed information.)

During the exam I always discuss the diet and note it on the chart. If a change is necessary, I discuss the options with the owner, from making homemade food to commercially available natural brands. Some of my clients live in remote areas that only have supermarket pet foods available. In such cases I help them find a food containing no preservatives and no soy products. Others are willing to buy natural pet foods by mail order from a distributor or manufacturer. (See addresses in the Appendix.) We also discuss the raw foods and other supplements that should be added to upgrade the quality of the food. (See chapter 6.)

Continuing with the exam, I evaluate the overall appearance of the dog. I like a bright, energetic look with a healthy coat and correct weight for the dog's body. Hair color is also noted. Is it the same color it used to be, or has a black dog turned brown? This type of change can be a warning sign of physiological problems. Is the dog walking with her normal gait or is she moving with a sideways motion? Is his overall attitude depressed or defensive? If the weight is excessive, diet alternatives are discussed and possible contributing medical problems are evaluated. Many cases of glandular disorders such as hypothyroidism are first evidenced when the dog's coat becomes dull and sometimes changes color.

Any potential problem is addressed in the yearly exam, treating it the same as a human's annual physical exam. The objective is to keep your dog's health at optimum performance.

Symptoms of Illness

If your dog starts to exhibit any health problems or major behavioral changes, you should call the veterinarian to report them. Some symptoms, like vomiting, are clear warning signs of trouble. Others are more subtle. Here are some indicators that should be checked out with the veterinarian—at least with a phone call:

- Vomiting or diarrhea, especially if continual. Prolonged vomiting or diarrhea could lead to dehydration.
- Not eating, or diminished appetite.
- Radical change in behavior—such as sudden aggressive tendencies.
- Excessive sleeping (change from normal).
- Lethargy; dog shows lack of energy.
- Limping or change in movement.
- Constipation.
- Breathing problems.
- Urinating or defecating in the house.

An owner knows his or her dog better than anyone else. Be alert to any indications that your dog is not up to par and report them to your veterinarian immediately. You could be detecting a health problem early on, leading to a big difference in the severity of the prognosis. If you go away and have someone else take care of your dog, be sure they are alert to any symptoms of illness.

Hospitalization

If your dog needs 24-hour care, make sure the veterinarian you choose offers it. Visit often to check on your dog's condition, lend encouragement, and cheer her on to recovery. Unless the diet must be changed due to medical problems, bring your dog's own food so she will have the reassurance of eating food she is used to. Some dogs only eat for their owners, so alert the staff that you will come for feedings if necessary. Bring a blanket or towel and special toys from home to give your dog reassurance and the comforting smell of home. Advise the veterinarian of your dog's habits and normal feeding schedule.

Ask the veterinarian if dogs who are hospitalized in the clinic get walking exercise. Here in the more relaxed atmosphere of the South many clinics walk dogs outside, whereas this is rarely offered in the city. If there is no medical reason your dog can't exercise, arrange to take her on walks yourself if necessary.

9

A New Standard for Your Dog's Health

Owners are with their dogs all the time; often they just don't see the gradual decline in health, which is, unfortunately, commonplace. Even in young dogs problems such as greasy skin, lack of energy, or unpleasant odor are all too frequent. Owners have no barometer against which to measure the small, often imperceptible decline in health, so they often don't realize that their dog is not in top form.

The minor health problems that often go unnoticed in dogs are not even considered as "health problems" by most people. But astute veterinarians and owners know that even minor problems are often symptoms of a bigger problem brewing.

In Chapter 8 we covered the noticeable signs of a health problem, such as repeated vomiting or diarrhea. But what are the small changes that signal a decline in health? Let's look at some criteria:

SIGNS OF HEALTH	SYMPTOMS OF ILLNESS
Good energy, even in an old dog	Lethargy
Healthy skin and coat (for some breeds, shiny coat)	Dry and scaly skin, greasy skin, or bald patches

SIGNS OF HEALTH	SYMPTOMS OF ILLNESS
Bright and clear eyes	Dull, cloudy, or reddened eyes
Correct weight	Overweight or underweight
Pleasant smell	Foul odor
No digestive problems	Gas

The "symptoms" of illness listed here are signs that the body is not properly digesting and assimilating nutrients, eliminating toxins and other wastes, or dealing with the stresses imposed on it. When your dog's body is overwhelmed by too many of these factors, it becomes sluggish; it's unable to operate efficiently. All of these symptoms can be precursors to the possibility of a major health problem down the road. All too often I see dogs with arthritis, cancer, diabetes, and other life-threatening diseases, which don't develop overnight. A natural diet and holistic treatment are the best ways to maintain health and correct these conditions before they take hold.

The body does its best to detoxify through normal channels—the liver, spleen, and kidneys. If these organs are overloaded or in a weakened state, other organs, including the skin, will begin to show toxic changes. All of the symptoms of illness listed previously indicate that the body is fighting to detoxify itself. The immune system is often affected by the excessive toxicity. Chronic or long-term detoxification will deplete the immune system, which is the body's defensive shield against illness.

A strong immune system wards off invading bacteria, viruses, allergens, and carcinogens. But it can be weakened or compromised by a buildup of toxins in the body due to the side effects of medications and vaccinations; preservatives and additives in food; chemicals and pollution in the air, water, and soil; psychological stresses; or lack of circulation (due to lack of exercise). Then, when the dog's body is attacked by any of these factors, the overburdened immune system is unable to defend the body and illness results.

Let's look at some of these stresses in greater detail.

Stresses from Antibiotics, Steroids, and Other Medications and Medical Procedures

Overuse of medications is commonplace in today's world—for both people and pets. In fact, there is now a term for the health risks associated with the overuse of medications. *Iatrogenic* disease means "physician induced" illness, usually as a result of the long-term negative side effects of pharmaceuticals. The drugs used in allopathic medicine often interfere with the body's natural defenses. Many are designed specifically for the purpose of suppressing the body's own responses. Repeated use of these pharmaceuticals often leaves the immune system in a weakened and ineffective state, unable to cope with further stresses and therefore open to new diseases or infections.

In the next chapter I'll explain the differences between a holistic veterinarian, like myself, and those who practice allopathic veterinary medicine. For now, suffice it to say that a holistic veterinarian does not rush to prescribe pharmaceutical medications, due to their negative side effects, drawing instead on a host of natural remedies whenever possible.

Some owners misuse drugs by keeping leftover medications that were prescribed in the past. If you have leftover medication, do not give it again unless specifically directed to do so by your veterinarian. Prescription medications are given for specific problems, and in specific potencies and dosages. Also, many medications are given in a course, meaning that they must be given for a certain period of time in the prescribed dosage to be effective.

Any medication alters the body's natural balance (though natural remedies such as homeopathics do not alter this balance as much as allopathic medicines). For example, a dog's ear canal has a natural balance of bacteria and yeast. If this balance is altered through the use of drugs such as antibiotics, either the bacteria or yeast may reproduce in larger numbers and affect the balance, resulting in an ear infection. Here in the South this delicate balance in the ear canal is frequently upset by excess moisture because of the humid climate. Yeast, thriving on the moisture, quickly takes over the ear canal. A medication is prescribed to control the yeast and bacteria, allowing their natural balance to be restored.

Many times I have treated dogs with a history of yeast infection in the ear. Owners frequently treat a recurring infection with medications they have on hand, usually an antibiotic. Often the infection becomes markedly worse after treatment because the antibiotic kills off the very bacteria needed to maintain a balance with the yeast, allowing the yeast to grow unchecked. Additionally, antibiotics overtax the liver and the kidneys because these organs must break down both the antibiotic itself and other toxins in the system.

In fact, antibiotics are commonly prescribed for many health problems when the body would be better off dealing with the infection without them. In his book, *Natural Health, Natural Medicine,* Andrew Weil, M.D., says:

> Antibiotics are powerful medicine that should be reserved for situations that demand them, for instance, when the immune system cannot contain a bacterial infection or when a bacterial infection establishes itself in a vital organ like the heart, lungs, or brain. Another strong reason to be cautious about overuse of antibiotics is the possibility of selectively breeding new strains of antibiotic-resistant, more virulent bacteria. Even people who are aware of that danger seldom realize that frequent use of antibiotics can lead in the long run to weakened immunity.[1]

Another common type of medication, the family of drugs known as corticosteroids, have earned a bad reputation in the holistic medical community due to their many negative side effects. Corticosteroids have come to the public's attention recently as immune suppressants used for transplant patients. They are also widely used for treatment of allergies, inflammatory conditions, and autoimmune diseases, and are available in pills, injections, and topical creams.

Dr. Weil also warns us about these pharmaceuticals:

> Steroids cause allergies and inflammation to disappear as if by magic. In fact, the magic is nothing other than direct suppression of immune function. I have no objection to giving these strong drugs for very severe or life-threatening problems, but even then I think they should be limited to short-term use: no more than two

1. Andrew Weil, M.D., *Natural Health, Natural Medicine,* Houghton Mifflin, 1990, p. 192.

> or three weeks. I deplore prescription of steroids for illnesses of mild or moderate severity or for months and years at a time.[2]

The side effects of corticosteroids are the same for dogs as for people: weight gain, increased appetite, increased urination, Addison's disease, and Cushing's syndrome, among others. Unfortunately the use of these drugs has been more widespread during recent years due to the increase in allergy problems and the relatively few methods of treating some of these problems. I realize that there are some severe cases where corticosteroids must be utilized (such as acute shock); in most cases, however, I prefer to thoroughly investigate the problem first by looking at the cause of the symptoms. If the problem is an allergy, then I seek the underlying cause that has weakened the immune system to allow it to react in this manner. Certain breeds have genetic deficiencies that are associated with the immune system. Some of these immune problems are just deficiencies, whereas others are actual autoimmune syndrome or self-destroying syndrome. Breeds that are known for this kind of immune system deficiency are Akitas, Lhasa apsos, and Shih Tzus.

The holistic veterinarian also uses X rays, tranquilizers, and anesthetics sparingly, because these procedures can be stressful for the body to detoxify. Excessive stress should be avoided when possible to keep the immune system healthy. When it is necessary to take an X ray or use a sedative, a holistic veterinarian can assist the dog with the detoxification process by giving a homeopathic remedy.

Vaccinations affect the immune system by stimulating a particular part of it, so an antigen is formed for each of the diseases for which your dog is vaccinated. The antigen acts as a memory for the body and allows a very fast response to protect the body when that particular disease attacks it. When vaccines are used, the protection process can take up to two weeks to be fully active. If many vaccines are used at once, the immune system can be tied up and not function efficiently. In addition, other areas of the body react to the vaccines, resulting in side effects. Some of these side effects are noted immediately, whereas others can take years to manifest, causing problems. In some areas of the country vaccines must be used because they are currently the only effective protection against certain diseases. How-

2. Ibid., p. 193.

ever, vaccinations should be given sparingly to avoid overburdening the immune system and diminish side effects.

(Also see chapter 10 for more on each category of prescription drugs.)

Stresses from Chemicals in the Food Chain

The immune system is constantly being bombarded with challenges from outside the body as well. In the last few decades there has been increased awareness of the toxins in our environment, which are adversely affecting our sources of food and water. Today most soil used for growing crops is treated with chemical fertilizers that break down into various chemical elements and are selectively absorbed by plants. Occasionally this selective absorption results in a concentration of a chemical that reaches toxic levels. The toxicity of crops from fertilizers is variable depending on the weather conditions during the growing season.

Another problem with crops is the use of pesticides. Residue from these chemicals also remains on the crops when harvesting occurs. And, of course, the fertilizers and pesticides eventually affect our groundwater supplies. Even minute amounts of these chemicals can build up over time with deleterious results.

Once the crops are harvested, they become a part of our food chain in two ways: some become the grains that feed us and our companion animals, and other crops are fed to the livestock that are later slaughtered as people and animal food. It is through this latter category that the chemical imbalances in the plants can be passed along and incorporated into the meat we feed our companion animals. Because of the unique digestive systems of cattle and sheep, the pass-along of toxins and chemical imbalances is an even greater problem when these meats are fed.

Yet another problem with the meat we feed our companion animals is the use of hormones and antibiotics given livestock, which build up in the muscles and organs of the animals. The residue from these hormones and antibiotics is then passed along when the meat becomes a part of the food chain.

Of course, we can't monitor the condition of the crops or the meat that is used in our dog's food, so we have to rely on the pet food manufacturer to do this for us. Even if you feed only homemade food, you can go no further than the butcher's assurances that the meat is top quality.

As I discussed in chapter 6, you also want to avoid any foods with harmful by-products, preservatives, and low-quality protein. Additionally, some dogs are allergic to specific ingredients such as soy or wheat. We must try to decrease the stresses on the immune system as much as possible. Even if your dog is fed a totally pure diet, the immune system is constantly being challenged by numerous other stresses in the daily environment. So a diet free of excessive chemicals is just one more way to practice preventive medicine.

Some pet food manufacturers have stricter quality control standards than others, monitoring and testing the meats and grains they use. But, unfortunately, most dog foods contain chemical imbalances and impurities that are a constant stress on the detoxification system, which eventually affect the immune system. That's another reason why I suggest buying food from a reliable natural pet food manufacturer, or making your own when possible.

Stresses from Chemical Hazards in Our Yards and Cupboards

We are also paying a price for our gardening practices. As the world becomes more environmentally conscious, there is increased public awareness of the hazardous chemicals that are used on our yards and gardens. Some people go so far as to warn you with a sign like the one I saw in a front yard: "Warning: Chemical yard treatment may be poisonous to pets and feet." I guess they're just covering their liability. But it's clear that the chemical industry knows how hazardous the pesticides are. Imagine, people spray their yards, gardens, and trees with these products and then actually allow children and pets to play in that yard.

Companion animals may ingest or inhale these chemicals, causing just one more stress on the detoxification system and the immune system. Usually it's the long-term effect of these pesticides that I'm concerned about, but every now and then a patient comes in with serious symptoms relating to this type of chemical poisoning.

One morning a pug named Mitzy was brought in by her owner with complaints of uncoordinated movements and vomiting. She had been experiencing this reaction off and on for a couple of days. After in-depth questioning, we narrowed down the times of each episode to right after the walk outside. The owner then remembered that her neighbor had recently sprayed his entire yard, treating grass, bushes, and trees. Fortunately, after a few days of hospitalization, Mitzy was well enough to go home. Not all dogs that suffer this kind of poisoning are so lucky.

There are now safe insecticides that use pyrethrin, a natural product obtained from flowers, as the active ingredient, though even pyrethrin can be toxic if your dog is overexposed to it. A number of books are now available on natural gardening and yard care, giving environmentally safe methods and products as alternatives to the chemicals that can be poisonous. Remember, though, that even products with natural ingredients such as pennyroyal and eucalyptus must be used with caution because some dogs have allergic reactions to them.

Carcinogenic and other toxic chemicals are found in household cleaning products as well as paints and solvents. Use natural products whenever possible. When you clean your floor, a residue of the cleanser remains on it. Any chemicals in that cleanser can be absorbed by your dog's skin or ingested when he licks his paws.

Stresses from Smog, Lead, and Other Environmental Contaminants

Sometimes it's hard to diagnose a problem that is stressing the immune system. This is the situation I encounter when working on an allergy case that is unresponsive or only partially responsive to therapy. All too often I find that the problem is environmental pollution, such as smog. Allergy responses to environmental pollution are more common than we realize and often go unrecognized. One way I am able to determine this is through detailed questioning of the owners. As I question them, they come to realize that the dog is fine when traveling outside the city, but the allergic reactions reoccur within 24 hours of returning home. (Of course, this is true only when they travel to an area free of smog.)

Another hazard that is being studied is the long-term effects of lead poisoning on both people and animals. One study concluded that lead contamination in our soil is the cause of many health problems. The amount of lead is high primarily in neighborhoods near freeways. This lead contamination is a frightening remnant from the days when "leaded" gasoline was standard, proving that unsafe industrial and manufacturing practices can haunt us for years to come.

One of my own dogs had a severe allergy problem due to environmental pollution, so I understand the frustration experienced by my clients. Some animals are less able to handle this kind of toxic burden on the system, probably due to genetics. I've had good results in treating these animals with a combination of homeopathy and acupuncture. Of course, the best solution is the drastic one of moving to a smog-free environment. That's the one I opted for when I moved away from Los Angeles.

Stresses from Emotional Issues

The growing link between emotions and health for people has become an accepted part of medicine. A new field of medicine, called *psychoneuroimmunology,* studies the interconnections between the mind (psycho), the nervous system (neuro), and the immune system (immunology). All of us who love companion animals know that, just like people, they respond to changes in their environment, illness or death of a loved one, and the emotional well-being of the owner.

If these emotional issues can result in suppressed immune response for a person, there is no reason to believe the same is not true for our pets. It is just one more factor affecting health and well-being. Bach flower remedies (see page 160) and aromatherapy (see page 158) have proved effective in treating emotional issues.

Identifying Stresses on the Immune System

There are many theories concerning the increase in immune deficiencies in recent years, and there may not be just one answer. With each dog it could be variable, a combination, or just a single agent that affects the system. After taking a thorough history, I try to pinpoint the underlying cause and eliminate it if possible.

In addition, I review other factors in the dog's food and environment that might be a source of toxins or allergies and set about eliminating them. I put the dog on a diet free of preservatives, soy proteins, and wheat. Next a vaccination history is looked at and, if necessary, a nosode is used to negate side effects from previous vaccinations. (See "Vaccinations and Nosodes," p. 183.) Any products used on the dog are recorded, from shampoo to flea products, nail polish, and such.

Then the home environment is investigated, including the type of bed the dog sleeps in, the plants in the home and yard, and the type of carpet in the home.

I ask the owner about other possible influences, such as emotional upsets in the home. I know my dogs are extremely sensitive to my moods, and their behavior changes when I become upset. In particular, my toy poodle, Lily, will often have digestive problems and a poor appetite if I'm upset.

This detailed approach to diagnosing is characteristic of holistic medicine, emphasizing study of the whole dog, including her environment, diet, and even her mental well-being. The results are often worth the extra time spent with this type of in-depth examination. All phases of the dog's life are considered to have a bearing on her health and are integrated into the final diagnosis. This is not to say that the original complaint is not strongly considered; however, as in the case of treatment of allergies, the root cause must be found and dealt with to prevent a recurrence.

In one allergy case I was presented with, Rory, an adult Chihuahua who was nearly hairless, constantly chewed on his skin. After a thorough investigation, we found the dog was allergic to the Scotchgard on a newly installed carpet.

In another case, Casey, an aged West Highland terrier, was itching and losing hair with no apparent changes in the home environment. This breed has very sensitive skin and a delicate immune system. A series of events sparked the problem here: first a rabies vaccination had been administered (one month earlier), then relatives with children visited (this dog was unaccustomed to children), and finally, because no yard work had been done that spring, crabgrass had grown up in the yard.

Casey was already somewhat sensitive to crabgrass, and the added emotional strain of children in the house, together with the immune system stress of the rabies vaccine, were enough to cause a full-scale allergic reaction to the crabgrass. He was treated with a homeopathic nosode for the rabies vaccine, a homeopathic nosode for the crabgrass, and a Bach flower remedy for the emotional upset. A month later his hair was almost grown back and no further problems were experienced.

The consideration of the entire dog is important to understanding the symptoms. In many instances if these dogs were taken to a regular allopathic veterinarian there would have been very little investigation into the root cause. Instead a drug would be prescribed to stop the itching and hair loss—probably a steroid. With the irritant still present (the carpet in the case of Rory and the crabgrass in the case of Casey), the signs would have returned once the steroids wore off. At this point more steroids might be prescribed or further diagnostics, such as skin testing, would be done.

Unfortunately, with the passage of time, getting an exact diagnosis might be more difficult because the owner may not remember all of the details from the onset of the problem. The already sensitized immune system may be overreacting to several things by that time, thus making sorting out a clear history and initial cause that much more challenging. So, although the holistic approach may be more time-consuming initially, the results can be rewarding and well worth the extra effort.

10

A Guide to Allopathic and Holistic Veterinary Treatments

Many of the holistic modalities used for humans have been adapted for veterinary medicine as well. The most common holistic methods in use today are the ones discussed in this chapter: acupuncture, aromatherapy, Bach flower remedies, chiropractic, herbs, homeopathy, lasers, magnetic therapy, and oxygen therapies. Nosodes, a homeopathic medicine used to counteract a specific bacteria or virus, are discussed later in this chapter in the section entitled "Vaccinations and Nosodes." As always, a high-quality diet gives an important boost to the immune system. Obviously this is even more critical at a time of illness. Since nutrition is covered in depth in chapter 6, we will forgo further discussion on diet issues here.

The holistic veterinarian has all of these methods to choose from and the standard allopathic treatments as well. I have grouped the major allopathic choices together later in this chapter. They are antibiotics, anesthetics and tranquilizers, cortisone and other steroids, diuretics, mineral oil, surgery, vaccinations, and X rays. One type of pharmaceutical drug—that used in prevention and treatment of heartworms—is discussed in Part II, page 273, under "Heartworms."

In many cases, the combination of several holistic treatments is advised. For instance, herbal remedies, acupuncture, and homeopathy can all be utilized simultaneously. If a serious condition warrants a pharmaceutical drug or an invasive medical procedure, the addition of complementary holistic remedies can make the difference that leads to successful treatment and rapid recovery.

Acupuncture

Interest in the ancient healing art of acupuncture has increased over the last 30 years. The dramatic health benefits that can be derived from acupuncture are becoming widely known and veterinarians have taken notice. A course offered by the International Veterinary Acupuncture Society (IVAS) teaches veterinarians the basics of acupuncture. This organization also certifies veterinarians in the field of acupuncture. Each year the attendance in this course has steadily increased. If you want to find a qualified veterinary acupuncturist, ask if he or she has trained with the IVAS or been certified by them.

The general public has been exposed to veterinary acupuncture in magazine articles and on TV talk shows, leading to growing acceptance of this form of treatment. I am still surprised, however, when a client who has never shown interest in holistic medicine asks about acupuncture as an optional treatment for their pet. Most of the time this is prompted by an acquaintance who had successful treatment with acupuncture. Many of my clients whose dogs receive acupuncture eventually seek acupuncture for themselves when they observe the improvement in the dog's condition.

Misconceptions and fears about acupuncture have made some people wary about considering it as a treatment for their dog. Among the questions I'm most frequently asked are: "Doesn't it hurt?" "Are the needles safe?" "Is it expensive?" "Does it take a long time?" "How can that little needle stuck in my dog fix anything?" These questions are not unreasonable and should be answered so an owner feels confident about the treatment. There is very little discomfort experienced by the dog when the needles are placed in the acupuncture points. The points are specific places along lines or meridians of energy that correspond with specific functions of the body. If there is a problem with an area of the body, the acupuncture point corresponding with that area is treated.

Most treatments take from 5 to 20 minutes once the needles are in place. During the treatment, endorphins, a natural pain-regulating product of the brain, are released. Occasionally this leads to sleepiness. Many animals learn that this sensation is very pleasant and they are enthusiastic when returning for treatments. It's one of the few times in practice I've had dogs run in and jump on the table, eager for treatment to begin.

In addition to inserting needles, some conditions require different types of stimulation to further enhance the treatment. Minute electrical impulses can be incorporated in the treatment by attaching clips to the needles. These impulses are very small and often are not even noticed.

Another variation of acupuncture is called moxibustion. In moxibustion an herb, mugwort, is burned and used to heat the needles or held near the acupuncture point to stimulate it. Although moxibustion is applied to many conditions, this is a particular favorite of many arthritic dogs because it simultaneously applies heat over painful areas and stimulates the acupuncture point.

Sometimes for minor recurring problems I teach the owner to use acupressure, also known as Shiatsu. Acupressure is similar to acupuncture but instead of using a needle to stimulate the specific points, a hard firm pressure is applied with the fingers. If you don't hit the precise acupuncture point you can't do any harm, so acupressure is a safe method for owners to use.

I have used acupuncture successfully in treating many diverse medical problems. In describing it, I realize it sounds deceivingly simplistic considering the phenomenal healing I have witnessed. Acupuncture is best known for the treatment of spinal disorders, particularly disc problems. However, many other skeletal problems as well as physiological conditions respond to this treatment. Skeletal conditions such as arthritis, hip dysplasia, and joint inflammation can be greatly improved following treatment.

Of the many dramatic results I've seen, one of the first cases in which I used acupuncture stands out. Perhaps it was because I was still a little skeptical, but the striking results in this case left no doubts in my mind concerning the role of acupuncture in a holistic practice.

The dog was a huge German shepherd mix weighing in at around 90 pounds. Sheba was 13 years old, a fairly advanced age for a large dog. The owner had brought X rays of both front feet, which showed severe advanced arthritis involving all the toes and extending up to her front knees. Sheba walked slowly and with great care; she was obviously in great pain. After reviewing the X rays and examining her, I gave her hopeful owner a poor prognosis due to the extent of the arthritis, but agreed to try acupuncture treatment to see if some relief was possible.

I didn't hear back from the owner, so I called a week later to see what the response had been. She reported that the day after the treatment Sheba got up, behaving in a normal manner, running and jumping with no sign of pain. There had been no return of symptoms during the week and the owner was delighted. Sheba received two additional acupuncture treatments. After that she only came back for additional treatments whenever stiffness recurred, usually after the monthly hiking trip.

Many physiological disorders, such as kidney problems, elevated liver enzymes, viruses, glandular imbalances, and allergies, can also respond to acupuncture. Just recently I was presented with a 12-year-old Dalmatian with elevated kidney enzymes, indicating that about 75 percent of her kidney function was gone. This can be the beginning of kidney failure; it was potentially life-threatening. It is difficult to treat and improve a condition like this using traditional methods.

I recommended acupuncture combined with homeopathy, and went on to perform the treatment. This patient had come through a referring veterinarian who called me two weeks later, wanting to know what I had done to that dog. I explained the acupuncture and homeopathic treatment hesitantly, because I am used to the negative reactions of allopathic veterinarians. To my surprise, what I had initially interpreted as hostility was actually great excitement. He explained that the dog's follow-up lab work showed greatly reduced kidney enzymes. Then he asked me for a detailed account of the treatment and wanted to know how he could learn to do it!

Acupuncture is one of the most fascinating modalities within Oriental medicine. It is a constant source of discovery and learning for me, since I have repeatedly seen how a simple insertion of a needle can influence the entire physiology of the body. An acupuncturist's goal is not only to correct a patient's symptoms, but to balance the energy system of the entire body so the problem will not recur. This rebalancing is often noticed by owners because they see that not only has the original problem disappeared, but the dog seems more energetic and happy.

Practitioners of acupuncture are pushing this form of treatment to new horizons. Dr. Are Thorsen, a veterinarian and acupuncturist in Norway, recently presented a way to treat cancer utilizing acupuncture and homeopathy, which he has developed over many years. The treatment is amazingly simple, using only two acupuncture needles most of the time. When I've used this cancer treatment the owners are always skeptical at first, but they become believers when the tumors gradually disappear. The basis of the treatment is to rebalance the body's energy where it is deficient, not to treat the cancer as an entity itself. This method is not effective 100 percent of the time, but many complex forms of cancer have responded to treatment and I have found it very valuable.

Since acupuncture has been around for thousands of years, why wasn't this cancer treatment available sooner? Sometimes it takes the right person with the right motivation. Dr. Thorsen is also an acupuncturist for humans. His motivation was the "hopeless" cases of cancer in children, who were referred to him after all other treatments failed. As a father himself, he wanted to help these children. I was touched when Dr. Thorsen related the stories of terminally ill children being carried into his clinic. His decision to try his unorthodox acupuncture treatment as a last resort gave me insight into the courage and motivation that this pioneering healer possesses. The treatment was then adapted to animals and many veterinary acupuncturists throughout the world now use it.

Even when no symptoms of illness are present, I often check the dog's acupuncture points just to make sure none of them are deficient, especially in older dogs. If an acupuncture point is deficient, I recommend acupuncture treatment to avoid the development of actual symptoms due to this decrease in energy. Although the old premise "If it's not broken, don't fix it" has merit, sometimes things are in the process of breaking, and we can prevent a full-scale breakdown with some regular maintenance.

Also see the section on lasers on page 169 for additional methods of healing aligned to acupuncture.

Aromatherapy

The use of scents in our culture has been confined mostly to perfumes and bath oils. Today, however, there is a growing awareness of aromatherapy, the use of essential oils in healing. Aromatherapy is one of the oldest forms of healing and preventive treatment, dating back to ancient Egypt. Much was forgotten and lost through the centuries, but aromatherapy gained popularity once again in the 1920s, developing a following in Europe. Herbalists and other natural healers kept alive the art of treating with essential oils derived from plants, and today the popularity of aromatherapy is expanding. The essential oils used in aromatherapy are complex parts of the plant, found in concentrated form and very volatile.

In his best-selling book, *Perfect Health*, Dr. Deepak Chopra explains why aromatherapy works:

> The language of taste is limited to sweet, sour, salty, bitter, astringent, and pungent. The nose, on the other hand, understands a vast vocabulary of smells, amounting to about ten thousand different odors if you have a well-trained beak. The odors that can be detected by the nose must first dissolve in the moisture of the nasal tissue and are then passed on by specialized olfactory cells straight to the hypothalamus in the brain. . . .
>
> The fact that smells go straight to the hypothalamus is very significant, for this tiny organ is responsible for regulating dozens of bodily functions, including temperature, thirst, hunger, blood sugar levels, growth, sleeping, waking, sexual arousal, and emotions such as anger and happiness. To smell anything is to send an immediate message to "the brain's brain," and from it to the whole body. At the same time, the message of an odor goes to the brain's limbic system, which processes emotions, and to an area called the hippocampus, the part of the brain responsible for memory, which is why smells bring back past memories so vividly.[1]

The essential oils used in aromatherapy are harmless to tissue; however, they have many properties. Some are antiseptic or bactericidal, and others act like antibiotics and antivirals. These oils work

1. Deepak Chopra, M.D., *Perfect Health: The Complete Mind/Body Guide*, 1991, Harmony Books, p. 152.

with the body to promote healing by stimulating and supporting the body's own healing abilities. Essential oils are often used in conjunction with other forms of natural healing such as herbs and homeopathics.

If you are in doubt about the effectiveness of essential oils, try a bath with a particular essential oil and notice how you feel afterward. Recently a friend was visiting and complained that she had not been sleeping well because of so much stress. After a long, tiring day she was still unable to sleep, so I made her a warm bath with the essential oil hops, an excellent relaxer, before bed. Because she stayed in the tub for such a long time, I became concerned and knocked on the door to check on her. She said the bath was so relaxing she wanted to stay and savor the relief. She slept soundly that night and has used aromatherapy ever since to combat the stress in her life.

In the "Health Problems" section at the end of the book I have included aromatherapy where appropriate in the actual treatment of problems. The essential oils recommended will be inhaled through the lungs where the fumes then cross over into the bloodstream and are carried throughout the body. If you are skeptical that the smell of a particular essential oil can cause a physical reaction, remember that smelling salts and ammonia have been widely used to revive people who have fainted or are about to faint. Then there is the less pleasant but very graphic example that glue sniffers have provided, proving that a fume or gas can have a strong effect on the physical well-being of the body.

Essential oils can also be absorbed through the skin. Since it is difficult to predict the health and condition of the skin, however, the inhaling method is preferred unless a lung problem is present.

Dr. Chopra has found aromatherapy to be a helpful adjunct to natural treatment in both placating a symptom and relieving stress. However, he also notes that patients who did not respond to other treatments for conditions such as migraine headache, back pain, skin rash, and insomnia were helped by aromatherapy.[2]

Just as a certain perfume may appeal to you more than another or may change to a different odor on your skin, the essential oils interact with each dog's body chemistry differently. The dog's diet is the main factor that influences this reaction.

2. Ibid., p. 154.

How to Use Essential Oils

Once you have decided on the specific essential oil you want to use, there are several ways to use it. While your dog is resting or sleeping, put 10 drops of the oil into a cup of hot water and place it near his head. If you have a way to keep it warm, such as a coffee warmer, do so for about a half hour. Special aroma pots that are warmed by the heat of a candle are available as well.

Bach Flower Remedies

Bach flower remedies are similar to homeopathics (see page 165) because they are prepared in a similar manner. In many ways they are also related to the use of herbs, since they are derived from Nature's pharmacy. However, Bach flowers are prescribed specifically when a dog's mental condition needs altering.

Bach flower remedies were developed by Dr. Edward Bach, a homeopathic physician, early in this century. He discovered that certain plain essences, prepared homeopathically, could effectively treat emotional problems and upsets. Bach flowers can be prescribed by the owner with little problem, because there will be no ill effects if you pick the wrong one. However, if you have selected the proper remedy or combination of remedies, you can often see positive results.

I have used Bach flowers most often when there is high stress in a household and the dog is having physical symptoms as a result. Extreme experiences such as car accidents, trauma such as dogfights, or fires can leave a dog so upset that he will not interact with people. In these instances I use one of the most frequently prescribed Bach flower remedies, which is called Rescue Remedy. It is actually a combination of several of the remedies. Rescue Remedy can calm and return a mental state to normal after an upset. This is one of the most remarkable remedies, because it acts very quickly and the effects are lasting. Rescue Remedy can also be used by the owners when an emotional upset occurs due to the loss of a pet or a distressing medical condition. I have often recommended that owners take it, and found that most people responded well and were better able to handle the traumatic situation.

When a dog is not responding to treatment, I often try Bach flowers to see if the source of the problem is emotional. It is amazing how even one dose will improve the physical condition by first acting on the mental. One of the regular boarders in my clinic, Katy, is 14 years old and has chronic kidney problems. Katy's symptoms worsen with the stress of being away from home. A Bach flower remedy is all it takes to settle her in on the first day, and we are then able to avoid vomiting and diarrhea during her whole stay. Another patient, Andy, gets nervous at dog shows and often develops abdominal pain, diarrhea, and an elevated temperature. A mixture of several Bach flowers has resolved all of these problems, enabling Andy to continue his show career as a real trouper.

There are 38 Bach flower remedies to choose from, each corresponding to specific emotional states. You can combine up to four remedies if more than one remedy seems to be called for.

To Prepare and Use Bach Flower Remedies

- Bach flower remedies come in small "stock" bottles. They last a very long time because you take only two or three drops from the bottle and put them in a 1-ounce dropper bottle. (If you are using more than one remedy, put two to three drops of each remedy in the bottle.) The dropper bottles are dark in color to keep sunlight from the liquid, and they're available in glass or plastic. Buy the glass bottles if you can. Then add a teaspoon of brandy. (The brandy is used only as a preservative and is not absolutely required.) Fill the bottle to the top with distilled or spring water. Next, succuss the bottle vigorously *108 times* by holding it in one hand and lightly hitting it against the palm of your other hand. As you'll learn in the section on homeopathy, succussing the bottle 108 times is a principle of homeopathics.
- Be sure to put a label on the bottle so you'll know the specific Bach flower remedies you've used. Two or three times a day—or more often for acute problems—put a dropperful of the liquid into your dog's water, food, or directly into her mouth. Give that specific remedy until the bottle is used up or the condition has been remedied.

Bach flowers are a very useful adjunct to holistic therapy, opening the door to a whole new form of treatment. They are readily available at many health food stores if you want to investigate Bach flowers on your own. Also, a number of books are available describing their use. You can also order Bach flowers and books on this method through the mail directly from Ellon Bach, the U.S. supplier of Bach flowers or from mail-order catalogs. (See address in Appendix.)

Specific Bach flower remedies to use are given in the "Health Problems" section at the end of the book.

Chiropractic

The structure of the body has an intricate balance, from the most obvious, the bones, to the less obvious, the immune system. When I was first introduced to this concept I was very skeptical. However, after doing chiropractic adjustments on countless animals I have been convinced that more is affected than we realize when the bones are out of alignment. The most striking example of a correlation between the alignment of the bones and the immune system is with viral infections. Viruses are difficult to treat, but I found acupuncture and homeopathy to give the best results. Then, when I began adding chiropractic adjustments to the regimen, I found that the animals responded even more quickly and required less treatment overall.

A slight misalignment can cause many problems. One of the most noticeable is a change of disposition. One day a Chihuahua named Cory was brought to my office, accompanied by her two companion Chihuahuas. The two companions had known medical problems and were scheduled to start holistic treatment. Cory was just along for moral support, because she was the leader of the group. I noticed that Cory walked with her head tilted sideways. Her owner told me that Cory had this problem for several years and had been to several specialists as well as a veterinary school with no conclusive diagnosis being offered.

One of the specialists thought an inner ear infection might be the cause, but no response to the medication was noted. Inner ear infections can be very difficult to treat, and my curiosity got the better of me as I listened to Cory's history. After treating the other two dogs,

I asked if I could examine Cory. Like many Chihuahuas, Cory had a definite attitude and it was obvious she usually got her way. However, after a few minutes of talking we became friends and she allowed an exam. My first step was to check the range of motion of her neck. Ever so gently I turned her head first to the left, and then to the right, the direction of the head tilt. As I did this there was a sudden loud pop that startled me as much as Cory. Not expecting this, I immediately stopped the exam and Cory, much to everyone's surprise, straightened her head for the first time in several years and moved it from side to side. Her neck had been out of alignment, and during the exam I had unknowingly adjusted it back into the correct position. Cory took it all in stride, going on about her business as if she was adjusted every day.

Her neck remained in normal position and her owner later reported a significant improvement in Cory's disposition. Obviously she had been in some discomfort, which was now relieved. In other cases similar to Cory's I have noted a defensive attitude as well. I believe this is because the dog would be unable to protect himself or react quickly in a threatening situation if she was unable to turn her head.

It would be nice if all cases were as simple as Cory's. However, a skeletal alignment check is part of the routine exam in my clinic so any problems can be corrected before they become major. A certification program in veterinary chiropractic is now available, and many holistic veterinarians are adding this modality to their practices.

Herbs

The use of herbs lost popularity with the advent of modern medicine, even though the pharmaceutical industry began through the use of Nature's own vast and bountiful harvest of the plant kingdom. In fact, many of today's drugs are still derived from herbs and others are synthetic versions of herbs. Because herbs are natural products, pharmaceutical companies cannot patent them and make huge profits.

Unfortunately, pharmaceutical drugs are often used at a great expense to patients, both animal and human. Adverse drug reactions are so common that Andrew Weil, M.D., a leading researcher on natural medicine, says that "Adverse drug reactions account for the lion's share of iatrogenic illness—so common that any dedicated patient is sure to experience one sooner or later. They can be as mild as nausea, hives, and drowsiness or as serious as permanent damage to organs and death."[3]

When the active component is extracted out of an herb, it is no longer in the state Nature provided. Dr. Weil explains:

> In their enthusiasm at isolating the active principles of drug plants, researchers of the last century made a serious mistake. They came to believe that all of a plant's desirable properties could be accounted for by a single compound, that it would always be better to conduct research and treat disease with the purified compound than with the whole plant. In this belief, they forgot the plants once they had the active principles out of them, called all the other principles "inactive," and advanced the notion that prescribing refined white powders was more scientific and up to date than using crude green plants. . . . Drug plants are always complex mixtures of chemicals, all of which contribute to the effect of the whole. . . . In general, isolated and refined drugs are much more toxic than their botanical sources. They also tend to produce effects of more rapid onset, greater intensity, and shorter duration.[4]

Dr. Weil continues, "Our problems stem directly from the decision of scientific medicine to value the refined white powder over the green plant."[5] However, Dr. Weil does not totally condemn the use of pharmaceutical drugs. For emergency situations we both agree that the quick action of the isolated compound can be lifesaving. Dr. Weil says he prescribes herbs for most conditions and only resorts to pharmaceutical drugs in about one case in 40.

Herbs are used to treat many health problems faced by dogs. Most commonly, they are a wonderful support for the immune system and a boost to vitality. As with drugs, the use of medicinal herbs must be carefully monitored because each dog responds differently.

Herbs commonly used for treating dogs are yucca, Pau D'Arco,

3. Andrew Weil, M.D., *Health and Healing,* Houghton Mifflin, 1983, 1988, p. 97.
4. Ibid., pp. 98–99.
5. Ibid., p. 101.

garlic, psyllium, bladder wrack, goldenseal, and aloe vera. Because the identification, drying, and preparation of herbs require special knowledge, I recommend purchasing prepared herbs. A number of companies sell high-quality herbs that are organically grown. In addition to herbs that are native to America, there is also an upsurge in the use of Chinese herbs. I have also used Chinese patent medicines, many of which are made of herbs, and find them indispensable for certain problems. If you are interested in herbal medicine and have never been to a Chinese pharmacy, I suggest visiting one in the Chinatown area of a large city. The array of herbs and other items used for healing is fascinating.

Herbs can have an unpleasant and bitter taste that dogs do not like, even when mixed with food. I advise using the herbs in pill or capsule form or getting gelatin capsules and making your own pills. Start with small amounts when adding herbs to a dog's diet, allowing their digestive system to adjust gradually. As you increase the amount of herb, watch for signs of vomiting or diarrhea and consult your veterinarian if these signs appear. If side effects occur, it is best to stop using an herb until it can be determined if the reaction is a result of the herb or some other problem. Avoid giving herbs on an ongoing basis. Even food herbs such as garlic should be discontinued periodically for periods of two to five days.

Specific herbal recommendations, are listed in the "Health Problems" section at the end of the book.

Homeopathy

Homeopathy is a system of medicine developed two centuries ago by Samuel Hahnemann, M.D., based on the principle that "like cures like." A pioneer in medical research, Hahnemann found that a substance that produces a certain set of symptoms in a healthy person can cure a sick person manifesting those same symptoms. This was not a new theory. Many centuries earlier, Hippocrates wrote, "Through the like, disease is produced, and through the application of the like it is cured."

For example, the homeopathic remedy allium cepa is made from red onions, which can make your eyes water when you cut them. If you have a cold and your symptoms include a runny nose, a burning sensation on the top lip, coughing, sneezing, and headache, this is the remedy that would probably be prescribed. A cold with a different set of symptoms would call for a different homeopathic remedy.

The homeopathic medicine itself is a very dilute medication (often in parts per million) that stimulates the body's defense systems, allowing the body to heal itself. Usually the effects are gradual, but dramatic changes sometimes occur.

Homeopathic remedies are diluted many times and "potentized" through a method of vigorous shaking or "succussing" between dilutions. The potencies of homeopathic remedies refer to how many times the medicine has been diluted and succussed. They usually range from the low potencies of 3C, 6X, 6C, 12X, 12C, 15X and 15C to higher potencies, such as 200C. The difference between potencies of "X" (dilutions of 10) and "C" (dilutions of 100) is based on the dilution of the original tincture. For instance, a potency of X means one part of the medicine was mixed with nine parts of a dilutant. The dilutant can be liquid (water or alcohol) or powdered lactose (milk sugar). After the first dilution is made, the mixture is shaken (succussed). Then one part of that mixture is mixed with nine parts of the dilutant and is again succussed. This diluting and succussing (potentization) is done a total of 6 times for a 6X potency. If the potency is 6C, one part of the medicine has been mixed with 99 parts dilutant and succussed a total of 6 times. A fascinating phenomenon of homeopathy is that the more dilute the medicine becomes, the stronger its potency.

Because it is so dilute, there is often no chemical residue of the original substance. Yet the less of the original substance is present, the higher the potency. It is this aspect of homeopathy that makes it so difficult for allopathic medicine to accept. In their book, *Alternatives in Healing,* Simon Mills and Steven J. Finando explain it well:

> After a dilution of 9X, however, molecular chemistry suggests that there is no longer likely to be any significant amount of the original substance left in the medicine, and, not surprisingly, this has caused skepticism about the ways the remedies work. Yet homeopaths have found, from repeated experience, that many of these greater dilutions are in fact even more effective than lower dilutions. . . .
>
> Some scientific study is coming closer to understanding how

> potentization works. It is known that a substance leaves behind "footprints" even after it has been greatly diluted. Paul Callinan, an Australian scientist, experimented by freezing remedy tinctures to –200 degrees C; they crystallized into "snowflake" patterns which were different for each remedy. And the more these tinctures were diluted, the clearer their patterns became. Quantum physics tells us that physical substances leave behind energy fields, and in the end, it may be this that will explain potentization fully.[6]

A history of the specific health problem is of great importance with homeopathics, because prescribing is based on the law of similars. Symptoms considered important to a homeopathic veterinarian go well beyond those an allopathic veterinarian would ever consider in making a diagnosis or in prescribing medications. Therefore a homeopathic veterinarian will ask you to keep detailed records of changes in your dog's behavior, habits, or attitudes.

As a regular prescriber of homeopathy, I have found it a rewarding form of medicine that I have used for all facets of veterinary treatment. Sometimes I am able to integrate homeopathy with other types of treatment. For instance, certain cardiology (heart) cases can be assisted by the use of homeopathics. I have been able to take dogs off the toxic forms of medication and use homeopathics instead. Occasionally I get a case that does not tolerate the regular heart medication digoxin, but really needs the benefits of that medication. Digoxin is derived from a plant named purple foxglove and is already very similar to a homeopathic. In its natural state the herb, purple foxglove, is a deadly toxin; but when it is diluted for medicinal purposes, it is a very effective heart medication, prescribed for people and animals.

When I am presented with a dog who cannot tolerate digoxin, I use the homeopathic form of digoxin, in parts per million. This often produces results similar to full-strength digoxin, and the dog is able to tolerate the medication when it is prepared homeopathically.

There are many varied uses for homeopathics, particularly in emergencies. Dr. Michelle Tilghman, of Stone Mountain, Georgia, has developed an emergency kit of veterinary homeopathics, which in-

6. Simon Mills, M.S., and Steven J. Finando, Ph.D., *Alternatives in Healing,* Plume/NAL, 1988, p. 27.

cludes a booklet of instructions. She also gives seminars concerning their proper use. (See Appendix for further information.) These medications are very sensitive and best results are achieved when the choice of homeopathic remedy is made by a careful selection process.

Some homeopathic remedies are safe to be given by owners in low potencies in the same way that you would self-prescribe an aspirin for your own headache. When giving homeopathic remedies, it can take anywhere from minutes to days to see results, depending on the specific problem. When results are not forthcoming, your veterinarian should be consulted.

When giving homeopathic medications, do not give them at the same time as food. If you must give them close to feeding time, allow at least 15 minutes before or after feeding before giving the homeopathic. A homeopathic substance is so sensitive that we want to make sure the body recognizes it and doesn't just assume that it is part of the food.

Because homeopathic remedies can be easily contaminated, it is important that you don't touch them. When using liquid homeopathics, don't touch the stem of the dropper yourself. When using pills, gently tap them from the bottle into the cap. Don't let the dropper or the cap containing the homeopathic remedy touch the dog's body, mouth, or tongue.

Most homeopathics can be obtained in a liquid form for ease of administering to dogs. Drop one dropperful of the liquid on the dog's tongue or under it and hold his mouth closed. *Do not* encourage the dog to swallow—homeopathics are absorbed very quickly through the mucous membranes in the mouth. If you have pills, put 3 or 4 of them in your dog's mouth and hold it closed while they dissolve.

In between uses of homeopathics, store them carefully. Most homeopathics are sensitive to light and heat. Keep them in a cool, dry place out of direct sunlight. Do not leave them in your car, briefcase, or purse, where temperatures may rise. Keep lids on tightly so moisture will not be absorbed; this could change the potency or strength of the medication. Before using a homeopathic liquid check the bottle to make sure no contamination has occurred. Hold the bottle up to the light and look for floating flakes or debris that indicate that the bottle is no longer usable.

It is more important to give a homeopathic remedy than to give the precise potency I have suggested in various places in this book. However, when self-prescribing, don't use a potency higher than 30C.

Hydrogen Peroxide

The hydrogen peroxide used by holistic veterinarians is 35 percent food-grade hydrogen peroxide. It is not the same as the hydrogen peroxide sold in a drugstore. In veterinary medicine, hydrogen peroxide has been used extensively with farm animals and is just now coming into use for dogs and cats. A wide variety of problems have been treated by giving food-grade hydrogen peroxide internally or intravenously. The results have been inconsistent, although there have been some astounding success stories. I have used it for dogs with parvovirus when the case has been severe and no other treatment was effective. In some of these cases the dogs recovered, whereas in others there was no response.

As more research is done, we will better understand how hydrogen peroxide and other oxygen therapies are best utilized, since they hold promise as yet another treatment modality.

Lasers

While many of the modalities and tools of holistic medicine have been in use for thousands of years, holistic veterinarians incorporate the tools of modern technology as well. One tool that I have found to be indispensable is the laser. Lasers range from a penlight size to large tabletop units. Lasers emit wavelengths of light that are used to treat specific problems.

One of the most common applications is the use of the laser at the acupuncture points. (See "Acupuncture," p. 154.) Instead of using a needle the acupuncturist can use the laser to stimulate the point. It is particularly effective in specific cases such as corneal ulcers, muscle spasms, and as an aid to wound healing.

When I was first exposed to holistic medicine I was skeptical of the effectiveness of lasers. Then, while visiting a holistic veterinarian, I scratched the cornea of my eye. I suffered the resultant pain and sensitivity of a corneal injury. It was a minor abrasion, but it was enough to cause discomfort and it certainly put a damper on my planned activities. I was loaned a penlight laser to treat it and was amazed that within 30 minutes my eye no longer hurt. I followed up with one more treatment later in the day and had no further problems with my eye. I became a believer and have not hesitated to use the laser since.

Occasionally I'll use the laser instead of acupuncture needles when a dog is intolerant of needles or when an owner does not want needles used. If the problem is one that is responsive to laser treatment, this is often a handy alternative. It is also a tool that I can teach an owner to use at home when there is a chronic problem or when travel interferes with regular veterinary visits.

In certain cases the laser has been invaluable. I was presented with a dog with a serious puncture wound and the possibility of infection was of great concern. However, even if I had wanted to use drugs, Toby was allergic to antibiotics and many other medications. I used the laser on the wound throughout the healing process and no infection resulted. I have used the laser in this manner many times to avoid antibiotics and stimulate healing. It is a versatile aid to holistic treatment and, with continued research, we are finding many new uses for the laser in veterinary medicine.

Magnetic Therapy

Magnetic therapy, in which a device is used to generate or influence the magnetic field lines on the body, is a healing modality that has been in use for hundreds of years. Presently there are more than 5,000 different magnetic field therapy devices used worldwide. The device is used to expose a body part to a magnetic field, completely penetrating the magnetic field lines of that part of the body. The effect is to increase oxygen utilization and cell function in that area of the body. It is currently being used for treatment of fractures, wounds, degenerative diseases of the legs, circulatory deficiencies, stretched ligaments, and treatment of joints that are out of place. I use this type of therapy frequently for sprains and strains. It's a good holistic alternative because it is noninvasive and, at the same time, effective.

Prescriptive Drugs

Antibiotics

Antibiotics are one of the most common types of drugs prescribed by veterinarians and, unfortunately, also one of the most abused families of drugs. They are stressful to the dog's body because, in addition to killing bacteria, they cause other reactions as well. First, antibiotics kill many of the "good" bacteria that naturally inhabit the digestive system and aid in digestion. When the normal flora (bacteria) of the digestive system are gone, less desirable bacteria flourish and can cause indigestion, illness, or flatulence (gas). You may have noticed these side effects yourself after taking antibiotics. Antibiotics also kill other friendly bacteria in the dog's body, such as the bacteria on the skin or in the outer areas of the reproductive tract.

Antibiotics also cause stress on the liver and kidneys, and certain types are harder to break down than others. The immune system is forced to work overtime as it defends the body from opportunistic bacteria that might take advantage of the imbalance, because so many friendly bacteria have been killed by the antibiotic. For this reason, new health problems can arise from the use of antibiotics. Some dogs develop a fungal infection on the skin because the antibiotic has killed off all the bacteria (both "good" and "bad") and the natural acid/alkaline balance that held the fungus in check is gone. The bottom line is that antibiotics should be used only when absolutely necessary and not as an easy way out.

I am frequently asked about antibiotics and when they are appropriate. A holistic veterinarian has a number of natural healing modalities to choose from which often eliminate the need for antibiotics. However, there are many specific instances when they are truly necessary and should be prescribed, including major infections such as abscesses, puncture wounds, pneumonia, and major organ infections. Even then, holistic modalities should also be employed together with the antibiotics.

An example of a condition that requires antibiotics is pyometra (an infected uterus). Pyometra can be life-threatening. Usually by the time the dog gets to the veterinarian she is very toxic, requiring immediate surgery and strong antibiotics. These patients always recover faster when homeopathy and herbs are used to help in the detoxification process. In these cases the liver is already overloaded due to the toxins from the infection and the strong antibiotics that were prescribed; thus it is important to also prescribe from the range of nutritional and holistic remedies available in order to help the rest of the body cope with the recovery and continuing detoxification.

I always caution owners not to prescribe antibiotics themselves. Many people have a stockpile of antibiotics in their medicine cabinet, left over from past illnesses. I'm always amazed that some are very willing to give these drugs to their dogs. I often see dogs that have been given several different types of antibiotics and are suffering from worse symptoms than when the disease first began. Antibiotics are available in many different types, and each is specific for killing certain types of bacteria. When a bacterial culture is taken, your veterinarian identifies the bacteria and the type of antibiotic that will kill it. If the wrong antibiotic is used, the disease-causing bacteria will continue to multiply and become more established, stressing the dog's body even more. At this point it may be more difficult for the correct medication to kill the bacteria.

Antibiotics work in several different ways. Some kill bacteria on contact, whereas others inhibit bacterial reproduction. Not all bacteria are affected by all antibiotics; some can be resistant to these effects. So if an antibiotic must be used it's imperative that the correct one be prescribed to kill the bacteria as effectively as possible and put a minimum amount of stress on the body.

Antibiotics can be administered through injections, pills, liquid medications, or in drops. When an antibiotic is prescribed for your dog, it is important that you give the full prescription and not cut it short once you start seeing results. If the antibiotic is not given for the full time your veterinarian has prescribed it, the bacteria may not all be killed and the infection could return.

Remember, antibiotics can be very hard on your dog's system and should only be used when absolutely necessary. If you are unsure of a veterinarian's opinion, do not hesitate to go elsewhere for a second or even a third opinion. If a holistic veterinarian is not available in your area, seek a phone consultation with one. Remember, it's your dog. If you want to get another opinion or consult over the phone, a good veterinarian will not stand in your way. In fact, your veterinarian, if he or she is competent and professional, should welcome the second opinion. You can also check with the holistic veterinary organizations listed in the Appendix for referrals.

If antibiotics are necessary, give the dog additional acidophilus and/or yogurt to replenish the "friendly" bacteria that will be killed by the antibiotic (see page 97).

Anesthetics, Tranquilizers, and Muscle Relaxants

I am grouping anesthetics, tranquilizers, and muscle relaxants together, because they all fit into the larger category of sedatives. Although this section of the book deals mostly with pharmaceutical drugs, there are some natural alternatives that can be used as tranquilizers and muscle relaxants. First we'll look at tranquilizers, since owners encounter the possibility of using them more frequently.

TRANQUILIZERS AND OTHER SEDATIVES

Most owners have wanted to use tranquilizers at some point—whether for their own dog or a neighbor's dog who barked all night outside the window. The most common use of tranquilizers is to calm a nervous dog for traveling in a car or plane, and to prevent the accompanying car sickness. Pharmaceutical tranquilizers are not to be taken lightly and should be used with care—if at all. I will list the natural choices first—with certain precautions, they can be safely administered by the owner. Then I'll discuss the pharmaceutical drugs that are most often prescribed.

Thiamine (Vitamin B_1): Thiamine is often found to have sedating effects, but they are variable depending on the animal's ability to utilize this vitamin from the B-complex family. A calm attitude is usually observed when thiamine is given. While the effect is not predictable, some success has been reported in using thiamine as a sedative. Because thiamine toxicity can occur, it is best to check with your veterinarian for the recommended dosage for your dog.

Valerian: This herb is an effective sedative for most dogs. It is usually sold as valerian root in tablet form. Dosage varies for each dog. In general, give one tablet for each 10 to 20 pounds of your dog's weight.

Magnesia Phosphorica (Tissue Salt #8): This homeopathically prepared remedy is often effective for nervous conditions and works well in combination with other natural sedatives. See the homeopathy section for information on how to administer.

Hops: Hops, an herb best known as an ingredient used in making beer, can be very relaxing when used in tiny amounts. Hops also works well when used as aromatherapy. You can buy hops at an herb store, as an essential oil used in aromatherapy (see pages 158f), or as a bath additive for humans.

Melissa: An essential oil used in aromatherapy (see pages 158f), Melissa works well to soothe dogs in upsetting situations.

Love Your Pet Calmer: Sold commercially by a company called Love Your Pets, this product combines many of the previously mentioned ingredients and is entirely natural. It is very effective for calming nervous dogs for travel and for most stressful conditions. Works well with asthmatics.

Acepromazine: One of the most well-known pharmaceutical tranquilizers, this drug is often used to prevent vomiting during travel. Although relatively safe, it should not be used for dogs who have epilepsy, heart problems, or respiratory difficulties (such as asthma). This tranquilizer is broken down in the liver, so it should not be used for dogs who have a history of liver problems. Its effects last from four to eight hours, but can take up to 48 hours to subside in older dogs. It lowers a dog's inhibitions in addition to its calming effects. If you plan to use this tranquilizer on an aggressive dog, be aware that the dog may have more of a tendency to bite after being given the drug, because he will no longer care about the consequences of his behavior. This tranquilizer blocks the dog's ability to realize that he will be punished if he bites. For this reason, use of acepromazine for aggressive dogs can backfire. As with all drugs, it should be used with caution—if at all. It is available in injection form and several different sizes of tablets.

Diazepam (Valium): A mild sedative, this drug is more widely used for humans. Its relaxant effect is usually observed after it is administered, but it does not have the antivomiting effect that acepromazine has. Diazepam does help to reduce convulsions, but is most effective in the injectable form. Care must be taken when using this drug on dogs with heart and liver problems. It is broken down by the liver and cannot be metabolized by dogs with liver problems. It is available in both injectable and tablet form but is most commonly used in injectable form by veterinarians. Its effects last from one to four hours.

Xylazine Hydrochloride (Rompum): This drug acts as a muscle relaxant and calmer, also providing some analgesia (painkilling effect). It can cause vomiting. This drug is broken down by the kidneys and liver, and should not be used for dogs with heart, liver, or kidney problems. It is also not recommended for dogs who are traveling, because it depresses the swallowing reflex, so the dog may not be able to drink water as needed or relieve pressure on the ears during air flight. The duration of these effects is variable. It should not be used with other tranquilizers. This drug is available in injectable form and is reversible.

Muscle Relaxants

Muscle relaxants are used primarily for dogs who are suffering muscle spasms or whose muscles are exhausted due to overexertion. The natural choices can be administered by the owner, but always exercise caution. If muscle spasms are severe take your dog to the veterinarian. I will discuss both natural and pharmaceutical choices.

Selenium and Vitamin E: These nutrients assist in cases in which a deficiency is present or where muscles have been exhausted from overwork or because they were out of shape. These problems are more common in large animals, particularly horses. While not much research has been done on the use of selenium and vitamin E for dogs, they have proved helpful for these problems. Specific formulations of a combination of selenium and vitamin E are available for dogs. The label will give information on the appropriate dosage for your dog.

Calcium: A calcium supplement specifically formulated for dogs is helpful in cases where the muscle is out of shape or overworked. However, calcium is more effective if used prior to the muscle exertion rather than after the problem exists. Give according to label directions.

Magnesia Phosphorica (Tissue Salt #8): This homeopathically prepared remedy aids in relaxing muscles. Use a potency of 6X or 12X three times a day and administer according to the guidelines on page 168. If no relief is seen after one day's treatment, consider another option.

Arnica Montana: This homeopathic remedy decreases inflammation in and around the muscle. Use a potency of 12X or 30X three times daily and administer according to the guidelines on page 168.

Robaxin: This pharmaceutical drug is available in injectable form only and is most safely administered by a veterinarian.

Anesthetics

Anesthetics are a group of drugs that people generally fear, and to some extent this fear is warranted. There is always a certain risk involved in the use of anesthetics, and this risk must be respected. However, the advancement of pharmaceutical technology has provided us with a large variety of anesthetics that can be used more safely than ever before. If your dog requires anesthesia, it would be wise to acquaint yourself with the different types available so you will feel more comfortable about it.

When faced with a procedure or surgery that is absolutely necessary, there is no alternative except to use the safest anesthesia available. In considering elective procedures or surgeries, I avoid complete surgical plane anesthesia whenever possible. This is not always easy to determine because each dog has a different tolerance level for discomfort; where a mild sedation will work for one dog, another may require complete anesthesia for the same procedure. For example, just recently I had to heavily sedate a German shepherd just to clean his ears. On the other hand, my toy poodle Lily is quite stoic and will sit still through ear cleaning and even pulling hair out of her ears with no sedation at all.

Because it is impossible to tell which dogs will be sensitive or allergic to an anesthetic, great care is used when anesthesia is administered. Anesthesia must be detoxified by the body, which puts additional stress on the organ that is responsible (usually the liver or the kidneys), and the dog must be thoroughly evaluated with a laboratory workup before anesthesia is administered. You can't assume how well your dog will tolerate anesthesia.

The best alternative to anesthesia is getting your dog to accept routine grooming and hygiene care (see chapter 5). Dogs who learn to enjoy these procedures at a young age will be easier for the veterinarian to handle during checkups, teeth cleaning, and other medical procedures, and may not require anesthesia or other sedatives. To avoid or lessen the stress of anesthesia, the veterinarian is sometimes able to use physical restraint (which should only be used when absolutely necessary) or a local anesthesic such as lidocaine (which stings a little when injected).

Avoidance of anesthesia during old age is best. When there is an infected tooth or needed surgery, however, it is often necessary to go ahead with the procedure, using a safely administered anesthetic. In this type of situation the most common choices would be a gas anesthesia, isoflurane, or a reversible injectable anesthesia such as oxymorphone, which can be used to give your dog every possible chance for a safe recovery. When delicate anesthesia must be performed on a very aged dog, I would suggest consulting with a Board Certified Veterinary Surgeon.

To be sure you have done as much as possible to ensure your dog's safety during anesthesia, follow your veterinarian's instructions carefully. It is necessary to withhold food and water prior to surgery. This is for the dog's safety—to protect against vomiting during the anesthesia process. If you have ever undergone anesthesia yourself, you are familiar with the nausea experienced during the induction and recovery. Don't be afraid to ask questions of your veterinarian to make you as comfortable as possible with the anesthesia procedure. Your peace of mind will be transferred to your dog, lessening her anxiety as well.

I will give you some general information about the most common anesthesias used by veterinarians today. Research is rapidly advancing, so I expect even safer anesthesias to be available in the near future. There are two types of anesthesia—injectable and inhalant.

INJECTABLE ANESTHESIA

Barbiturates: The most common types of barbiturates are thiamylal sodium (Surital Sodium or Biotal) and thiopental sodium (Pentothal sodium). Both are classified as ultrashort anesthetics. Barbiturates are major respiratory depressants and therefore must be used with great caution. They are eliminated from the body by the liver and kidneys and may cause further injury to the liver if damage is already present. When barbiturates are used recovery from anesthesia is slow and sometimes violent. There is no reversal agent.

Oxymorphone: This type of anesthesia is a morphine derivative. It works well for short procedures and is reversible. Oxymorphone is often used with older animals for minor surgery or as a preanesthetic for gas anesthesia.

Xylazine: This anesthetic is used in conjunction with ketamine (a common injectable anesthesia for cats) for short procedures. Because it causes bradycardia (slowing of the heart rate), it should not be used on older dogs or dogs with heart problems. This is a reversible type of anesthetic.

Telazol: Telazol is similar to ketamine and is a very safe anesthesia. It is used for minor surgery and short abdominal surgeries. This drug is excreted through the kidneys and should not be used for dogs with kidney problems.

InnovarVet: This drug does not provide a deep anesthesia plane. It is associated with side effects in certain breeds. This drug is not widely used and is not one I feel comfortable using.

INHALANT ANESTHESIA

Halothane: One of the most common anesthesias used; it is considered safe and effective and has a quick recovery time.

Methoxyflurane: This is an effective gas anesthesia requiring a longer recovery time.

Nitrous Oxide: Commonly known as laughing gas, you may have had this anesthetic yourself during a dental procedure. Nitrous oxide is usually combined with halothane or methoxyflurane as a mix for anesthesia, enabling the dog to be maintained on a lighter anesthesia plane.

Isoflurane: A newer gas anesthesia, this is one of the safest anesthesias available to veterinarians. Recovery is rapid and few problems are experienced with this gas. It is also an excellent anesthetic for older dogs.

Diuretics

A diuretic is used to increase urinary output. These drugs are often used for dogs, most commonly for treatment of congestive heart failure. There are several different types, and each is specific for a particular medical problem. The most common type of diuretic is furosomide (common trade name Lasix).

When diuretics are prescribed there is usually a good reason. However, the use of this type of drug should be tempered with some common sense. Remember, your dog will urinate more, drink more, and lose more of the body's electrolytes when given a diuretic. Be sure to provide plenty of fresh water and let your dog out more frequently.

To replace the electrolytes, a daily vitamin supplement is given as well as an electrolyte solution, which is added to the food or water. If you add electrolytes to the water, be sure your dog will drink the water, because it will have a different taste. If she doesn't want to drink it, add only a small amount and gradually increase to the recommended amount. In this way she will become accustomed to the different taste.

Electrolytes are available in a powder form and are easily mixed into food and water. Most veterinarians have electrolytes available, but if you have trouble obtaining them, check with a livestock feed store and buy horse electrolytes, reducing the dosage accordingly. Another alternative is to buy electrolytes for babies, which are now sold in supermarkets. One common brand is Pedialyte.

If you want a mild diuretic effect and want to avoid the problems of the pharmaceutical drugs, distilled water is usually very effective and works within a few hours. There are other herbal diuretics to choose from, but they also have side effects and should be used under the supervision of a veterinarian.

Steroids

Another category of drugs that is greatly overused is corticosteroids, or steroids. Steroids are synthetic drugs that are related to the adrenal hormone cortisone. This family of drugs is used primarily to treat dermatitis (skin problems), joint inflammation, and shock. They are prescribed through injections, pills, or topical creams. Steroids are considered by many to be a miracle drug because they can cause inflammations, skin disorders, and allergies to disappear almost overnight. Unfortunately, allopathic medicine does not recognize the dangers of steroids—probably because they have no other options. Steroids work because they suppress disease. At the same time, however, they are toxic, create dependencies, and weaken the immune system by suppressing the functioning of the thymus, lymph nodes, and white blood cells.[7] Additionally, steroids suppress the adrenal function and can lead to a degenerative joint problem when used in joints.

Occasionally steroids must be used; I'm certainly not condemning their use entirely. What I am saying is that steroids are overused and relied upon when they could (and should) be avoided. This sometimes means a more complex form of treatment, so to avoid the hassle and expense, it is easier to prescribe steroids. I particularly do not like the anabolic steroids (those that athletes use) because there are so many side effects and so few benefits.

Certainly shock is one of those unavoidable circumstances where the use of the proper steroid can mean life or death. The body is in serious trouble when shock sets in. In this type of emergency the body uses up the steroid almost immediately so side effects are rare.

The number-one reason that steroids are prescribed for dogs is to treat dermatitis. Most of these cases could be effectively treated with safer methods that deal with the causes of the skin problems rather than just suppressing the symptoms. Owners are starting to realize that there may be other answers to these problems. A few months ago a chocolate Labrador retriever was brought to my clinic with a skin problem. The owner was tired of endangering his dog with steroid use and wanted to know if there was another way to get rid of the dry, flaky skin that plagued the dog. In questioning the owner I found that the previous veterinarian had never discussed the dog's diet and the possibility that it might be contributing to the problem. I learned that the dog was being fed semimoist food. As mentioned in chapter 6, this type of food is never acceptable because of the high percentage of chemical preservatives, additives, and low-quality ingredients. The dog was placed on a soy-free food. I asked the owner to refrain from feeding table scraps so we could determine if the food was making a difference. Within four months his skin and hair were the picture of health, and no problems have recurred. Not all solutions are that simple. But to put a dog on steroids without investigating other causes is unfortunate, to say the least. Once steroids are

7. Andrew Weil, M.D., *Health and Healing*, Houghton Mifflin, 1990, p. 193.

being used, they mask the symptoms of the problem, making discovery of the cause much more difficult.

Acupuncture is very effective in reducing the stress and swelling associated with inflamed joints, even joints that have been injected with steroids in the past and are inflamed again. When steroids are used for joint inflammation, the joint surfaces can suffer serious side effects. When steroids are prescribed in such cases, the veterinarian should inform the owner about the possibilities of this consequence.

The bottom line with steroid use is to be sure that there are no other alternatives, because steroids can be very detrimental to your dog's health. Once steroids are started, they cannot be stopped cold turkey. The dosage must be decreased gradually to allow the adrenal and pituitary glands to begin working again. If you are planning to take your dog off steroids, I advise that you consult a holistic veterinarian to help your dog through this difficult period. There are homeopathics, herbs, and supplements that will support your dog's adjusting system and make the transition as problem-free as possible.

Surgery

Much like human medicine, veterinary surgery has advanced to the point that it is no longer practical for a general veterinarian to do every type of surgery possible. Techniques are changing and developing so quickly that it's almost impossible to keep up with all the latest surgery changes. In addition, some of the surgeries require special equipment that can be very expensive. There are now specialists, called Board Certified Surgeons, who do nothing but surgery. Like many veterinarians I do some types of surgery myself and refer more complicated cases to veterinary surgeons. If surgery is required, you will get state-of-the-art surgery from a specialist. But let's take first things first and look at the question of whether a particular surgery is necessary. If surgery has been recommended for your dog and you're not comfortable with the idea, get a second opinion. Veterinary medicine is following the example provided by human medical practices and second opinions are now commonplace. If your regular veterinarian has recommended a surgical procedure and you want a second opinion, you may be able to get a referral from the American Holistic Veterinary Medical Association (see Appendix) or a local chapter or organization of veterinarians. In many cities the latter is listed in the phone book. Also, most veterinary offices will have the number of such organizations available.

Some of my clients have sought second opinions for the most routine procedures, and I encourage them to do so if they have any doubts. This concern shows how much they care for and value their dogs. I would probably do the same thing in their place. As a matter of fact, I have done just that when I am not sure if there is a more advanced technique available for one of my own dogs. Although I enjoy doing surgery and keep fairly current, another veterinarian may look at the case from a different perspective, which is sometimes valuable.

There are two types of surgery—elective and required. Elective surgeries include spays and neuters and any other surgery that is not required because of a life-threatening situation. Spays and neuters are certainly necessary to control the pet population, and most veterinarians do them routinely with few problems. The majority of dogs who are spayed or neutered are young and vigorous, and they normally tolerate this surgery well. When elective surgery is considered for an older dog, a laboratory workup is usually done to ensure that the dog will be able to cope with the surgery.

If your veterinarian recommends surgery—either elective or required—you should ask these questions before making the commitment:

1. Will my dog safely tolerate this type of surgery?
2. Is this surgery in my dog's best interest?
3. Are there nonsurgical alternatives that we can consider?

If the answers to these questions satisfy you, then you should consider proceeding. If, however, they have brought up more questions, talk it over with your veterinarian or get a second opinion. Any surgery carries with it some risks.

If surgery is unavoidable, certain precautions can be taken to help your dog through it.

Precautions Before Surgery

1. Be sure the veterinarian does laboratory tests to determine that your dog's body is in shape for surgery. If the tests show abnormal values and the surgery must be performed anyway, at least the surgeon will be forewarned and prepared for possible complications.
2. The drug methocol should be given to help cleanse the liver, which is the organ that must detoxify the anesthesia.
3. Give the following homeopathic remedies:
    - Ferrum phosphoricum (tissue salt #4) to support the oxygen-carrying capacity of the blood and strengthen the blood prior to surgery.
    - Phosphorus 6X or 12X to help promote blood coagulation thereby reducing blood loss during surgery. Phosphorus can also be given during surgery if excessive bleeding is a problem.

Several years ago I agreed to perform a routine spay on my receptionist's golden retriever. While doing the surgery I noticed excessive bleeding. When the surgery was complete there was so much bleeding that I rechecked to make sure all ligatures (where suture is used to tie off a blood vessel) were tight and no major vessels were leaking. All the ligatures were in place and there was no leaking. Because there were no clots in the blood in the abdomen, I had to assume that this golden retriever was a hemophiliac. (Hemophilia is an inherited blood disease characterized by defective coagulation and an abnormal tendency to bleed.) I immediately gave her more phosphorus and, thankfully, the dog stopped bleeding about five minutes later. Without the phosphorus I'm not sure the bleeding would have stopped. This was a much closer call than I anticipated, and illustrates that even a routine spay can develop into unforeseen complications.

Vaccinations and Nosodes

The issue of vaccinating has become a highly controversial subject for holistic veterinarians and owners who want a natural approach to their dog's care. Many veterinarians are realizing just how detrimental some of the standard canine vaccinations are on the immune system. Have you ever noticed that your dog may seem less active and have a poor appetite after vaccinations? This lethargic period may continue for as long as two weeks and is particularly noticeable in older dogs. Some old dogs act as if they were suddenly affected with a case of generalized arthritis—stiff, painful movements that show up a day or two following the vaccination.

A vaccine utilizes the bacteria or a virus of a specific disease, which has been weakened and killed so it is no longer active. The vaccine is given with the intent that it will help the body develop an immunity to that particular disease. According to Dr. Richard Pitcairn, a veterinary specialist in immunology:

> There is an implicit assumption among many people that vaccines are 100 percent effective. This belief can be so strong that a veterinarian may tell you, "Your dog can't have distemper (parvovirus, hepatitis, or whatever) because he was vaccinated for it. It must be something else." But one thing I learned from my studies in immunology is that vaccines are far from 100 percent effective. Obviously it is not just the injection of the vaccine that confers immunity; the response of the individual animal is the critical and necessary factor. Several things can interfere with the ideal body response (production of antibodies and immunity). These include vaccinating when the animal is too young or is sick, weak or malnourished; using the wrong route or schedule of administration; and giving the vaccine to an animal with an immune system that has been depressed as a result of previous disease, inheritance or drug therapy.[8]

One alternative to vaccinations is to use nosodes. A nosode is similar to a homeopathic remedy. Nosodes are sometimes used instead of a vaccination as a more natural immunization, and they can also be used as an adjunct to conventional vaccines. They are used to boost the immune system against a specific disease, usually one that is vaccinated against. Nosodes, like homeopathics, have been diluted

8. Richard H. Pitcairn, D.V.M., Ph.D., and Susan Hubble Pitcairn, *Dr. Pitcairn's Complete Guide to Natural Health for Dogs and Cats,* Rodale Press, 1982, p. 250.

many times yet they are very effective in stimulating the immune system.

While nosodes can be very effective in some places, in the southern United States, where strong strains of virulent viruses flourish in the hot, humid climate, I have not found nosodes to be strong enough to prevent some forms of distemper and parvo. I have found that using the nosodes in addition to vaccinating strengthens the reactions of the immune system and decreases the side effects of the vaccines. Before I began using nosodes as an adjunct to vaccines, I found that some dogs I treated in kennels and pet stores would come down with a virus even though they had been vaccinated against it. When I started giving the nosodes as well the problem was diminished to the point that it rarely occurred. To decrease the side effects of vaccination, especially in older dogs or dogs that have previously had problems, I like to use nosodes following vaccination and once a month until the next vaccination. This may seem like a lot to some people and perhaps it is aggressive, but here in the South diseases like distemper are still all too common, so this approach seems warranted. (It is important to note that nosodes will not stop an allergic reaction to a vaccine.)

You will have to discuss the issue of vaccines with your holistic veterinarian, who will know the risks of specific diseases in your area.

Here are the diseases dogs are most often vaccinated for:

Distemper

As mentioned previously, this disease is still too common in many areas of the South. It is very contagious and it can be fatal. This vaccination is usually given starting at six weeks of age and is given every two to three weeks until 16 weeks of age to ensure immunity. For more on distemper, see "Viruses" in Part II of the book.

Parvovirus

This is a difficult disease because there are different strains of parvo in different areas. I have found that vaccinated dogs that were given the nosodes had fewer outbreaks when they were exposed to dogs with the parvovirus. This vaccination is usually given together with the distemper vaccine and in the same frequency. For more on parvovirus, see "Viruses" in Part II.

Rabies

Although rare in some parts of the country, this fatal disease is still diagnosed frequently in the eastern and southern states. Vaccination for rabies is required by law in most states. It is usually required beginning at 12 to 16 weeks (depending on the specific state law). For more on rabies see "Viruses" in Part II.

Kennel Cough

This disease is usually not serious. However, the long-term cough can last up to a month. Most boarding facilities require that all dogs be vaccinated for kennel cough because it is very contagious. The most effective vaccine for kennel cough is given internasally (in the nose).

When possible, it is best that vaccines be given separately so the immune system is not overburdened. Unfortunately, the current trend is to mix vaccines rather than separate them.

My own solution to the issue of vaccinations is to use them for the viruses that are prevalent and endanger a dog's health. I give individual vaccinations separately as often as possible, allowing at least one week between them, and then follow up with a nosode specific for that vaccine.

X Rays (Radiographs) and Radiation Therapy

X rays are sometimes necessary in the diagnostic process. However, questions arise concerning the safety of the procedure. Each time your dog is x-rayed, he is exposed to radiation. No amount of radiation is good for him, so X rays should not be done unless they are justified. Two to four X rays probably don't pose a threat to your dog's health, but you can practice preventive medicine and give additional vitamin C following the procedure. The dosage will vary depending on the size and weight of the dog, but 100 to 2,500 milligrams is the general range.

Radiation therapy, commonly used to treat various forms of cancer, is not a procedure I use or recommend. (For alternative holistic treatments, see "Cancer" in Part II.) If an animal who has undergone radiation therapy is presented to me, the therapy for overexposure to radiation is more complex. Each case is treated separately depending on the type of radiation that was used. A combination of supplements and dietary changes can help the dog's body eliminate some of the harmful radioisotopes.

11

Home Health Care

Sometimes you, as an owner, will have to make decisions regarding the care and treatment of your dog. Your decisions range from the brand of food to buy to a certain amount of self-prescribing of natural remedies such as Bach flowers and herbs. It's always best to consult your veterinarian on these questions, but if your veterinarian is not holistic, he or she may not be familiar with Bach flower remedies and may not be concerned about by-products and preservatives in food. Although it is safe for owners to prescribe some natural remedies such as Bach flowers themselves, many people need some guidance on this. Fortunately, there are a couple of diagnostic techniques that you can use to help. These techniques can also be used to decide on a particular food. In this chapter I'll share these diagnostic techniques, review the various methods of giving medications, and discuss fasting.

Diagnostic Options

Dog owners often ask me how I decide which medication to use. It's a good question. I'll review some of the thought processes a veterinarian goes through in making these decisions. Let's look at the criteria a veterinarian uses to select the proper prescription.

In reviewing the treatment for a patient, your veterinarian has a number of factors to consider. If the dog is being hospitalized, the staff will be able to administer medications by injection, if needed. But when the owner has to give the medications, the veterinarian must review the following variables:

- Is a medication absolutely necessary at this time?
- What are the exact reasons for giving a medication?
- What medications are available to choose from?
- Could the dog have any reactions to medication or is she allergic to any medication?
- Is the owner able to give the proposed medication? Does the dog take pills, liquids, or injections best?
- Will the owner be able to give the medication of choice exactly as prescribed? (Three or four times a day can be a problem if you work away from home.)

These are just some of the questions your veterinarian reviews when prescribing medications. They might seem somewhat simplistic to you, so here's a case scenario that will help you understand the reasoning behind the questions.

Sandy, a 36-pound pit bull terrier, was brought to my clinic, barely able to walk. She had white mucous membranes and was in congestive heart failure, which is the result of shock or severe blood loss. As a result her heart was failing to pump blood efficiently, which also led to fluid buildup in the lungs. After a thorough exam I was unable to find an exact cause for the blood loss. Further questioning of the owner revealed that Sandy was the product of a mother-son cross, leading me to believe the heart problem was congenital and caused by inbreeding. I also suspected she had a blood parasite such as Rocky Mountain spotted fever.

There were several problems with medicating Sandy. First, I wouldn't be sure about the diagnosis until the test results came back. But some of them took up to two weeks to complete and I knew Sandy wouldn't live that long. If she didn't receive immediate treatment, she would die. Her condition was already so precarious that she wasn't eating, so any medication given by pill would have to be manually put down her throat. Sandy was also upset, weak, and frightened. As a result she became aggressive and would try to bite anyone who attempted to give her a pill.

Additionally, I was concerned about the inbreeding because it frequently predisposes a dog to allergic reactions. In this situation we had no choice but to proceed with treatment; it was Sandy's only chance for survival. Although we used a long pilling gun to get the pills into her mouth to avoid getting bitten, I do *not* recommend this method unless you are very experienced. The liquid medication for her heart was given with a syringe between the teeth. She was muzzled with a soft nylon type of muzzle during this procedure. I gave her other medications by injection. Fortunately my diagnosis was on target and Sandy recovered. Because of the congenital problems, however, she will have to remain on the heart medication for the rest of her life.

Kinesiology (Muscle Testing) and Pulse Diagnosis

Two methods being widely used by holistic veterinarians have proven quite effective in diagnosis and prescribing. In both methods the body actually helps you to decide which medication to use. The methods—kinesiology (which I'll refer to by the commonly used term *muscle testing*) and pulse diagnosis—have one common denominator: both tap into the body's innate intelligence so it can guide you. Although these methods are not a substitute for scientific expertise, I have found them invaluable in diagnosing and prescribing all types of treatments, from allopathic to holistic.

The uses of these methods are innumerable. Within certain parameters, owners can also use these methods in a number of arenas, including determining the specific Bach flower remedy (or combination of remedies) to use, ascertaining the best homeopathic remedy (and the specific potency) to use, or making sure a new supplement or food will not cause a food allergy. This method is not infallible and only responds to the body's present needs. A long-range plan or slow-response medication may be the best choice but may not respond to muscle test or pulse diagnosis response. Do not rely solely on these methods.

Muscle Testing

A number of muscle testing methods are currently being used. An excellent book on this subject is *Your Body Doesn't Lie* (also published under the title *BK: Behavioral Kinesiology*) by Dr. John Diamond, who pioneered this field. Muscle testing utilizes a "muscle resistance" to determine whether a substance strengthens or weakens the body. When you are testing for an animal (or an infant), a second person must "stand in" for the animal as an intermediate or surrogate. Let's look first at how muscle testing is used for humans; then I'll discuss how we adapt it for animals with the intermediate person.

Stress expert Dr. Jerry Teplitz, gives the following step-by-step method for muscle testing. It is necessary to have a partner to do the following muscle testing procedure with you. Before you begin the actual muscle testing, you must test the normal level of resistance of your partner's arm muscles. If this method of testing is new to you, it will become clear as I proceed.

Finding Normal Resistance

STEP 1: Face your partner.

STEP 2: Your partner should raise one arm up from the side of the body so it is at a right angle to the body and level with the shoulder, with the thumb pointing toward the floor. Imagine a bird with a wing outstretched and you'll have the correct arm position. The other arm should remain at the side of the body.

STEP 3: Now place one of your hands on your partner's extended arm, just above the wrist. Place your other hand on your partner's opposite shoulder.

STEP 4: Instruct your partner to *resist* as you push down, firmly and steadily with a hard pressure, on the extended arm. Say out loud "ready—resist," as you are about to push down on your partner's arm. You are *not* trying to force her arm down; her arm should stay fairly level during the pressure; however, you want to place a hard steady pressure on the arm in order to measure her normal level of resistance. You should press firmly for several seconds, and then release.

When doing this testing method, do not look directly at your partner's face, because facial expressions can affect the outcome. (A

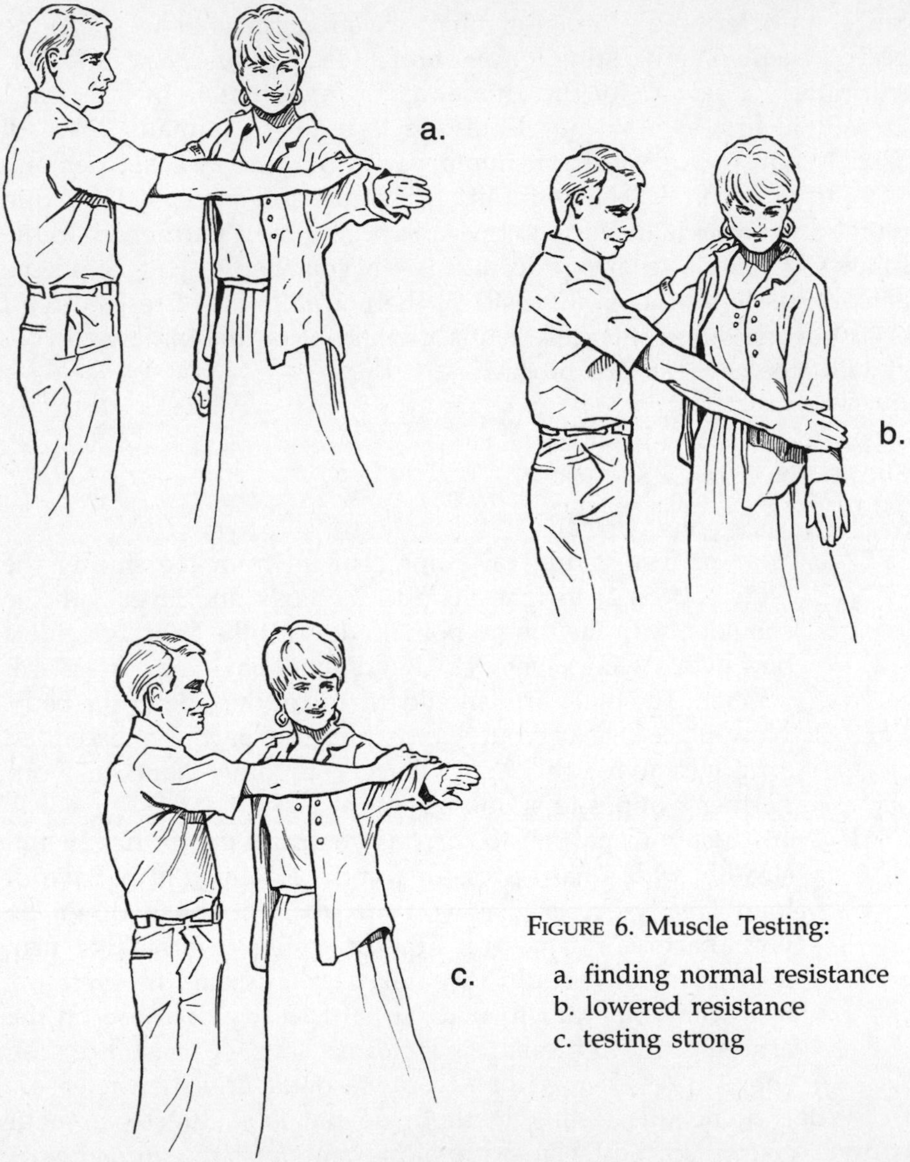

FIGURE 6. Muscle Testing:
a. finding normal resistance
b. lowered resistance
c. testing strong

smile is strengthening to your partner's resistance; a frown is weakening.) Also, remember that this will work only if you both understand that you are looking for a level of resistance in the arm muscles. This is not in any way like arm wrestling; you aren't trying to overcome your partner and, similarly, your partner should not try to resist the pressure to the extent that she recruits other muscles to "fight back." When the arm muscle starts to fade, your partner should allow it to do so.

Your partner is now the intermediary who will touch your dog while being muscle tested. When I use this method, I have the intermediary touch the acupuncture point that corresponds with the organ or the area being treated. If you are doing the muscle testing on your dog and don't know which area to have the intermediary touch, just ask her to touch the dog's back area with the palm of her hand. The intermediary will hold the medication, natural remedy, food, or supplement you are testing. A weakness in the intermediary's arm muscles will indicate that the item being tested is not the best; a strong arm will indicate that the item being tested is a good choice. Sometimes you will have more than one item that gives a positive response. In that case it is sometimes possible to discern that one tests somewhat stronger than the others, and is therefore the best choice.

Here's a step-by-step guide to test the possible medications or other items:

Muscle Test Using Intermediary

STEP 1: Face your partner.

STEP 2: Ask the intermediary to place one hand on the dog (on the acupuncture point or affected area if you know where that is) and place the medication or other item in her other hand. Your partner should not know what medication she is holding. Ask her to outstretch her arm as she did in step 2 of "Finding Normal Resistance."

STEP 3: Place your hand on your partner's outstretched arm, just above the wrist, and your other hand on her opposite shoulder.

STEP 4: As in step 4 of "Finding Normal Resistance," ask your partner to *resist* as you push firmly and steadily down on her arm. Press firmly for several seconds, and then release.

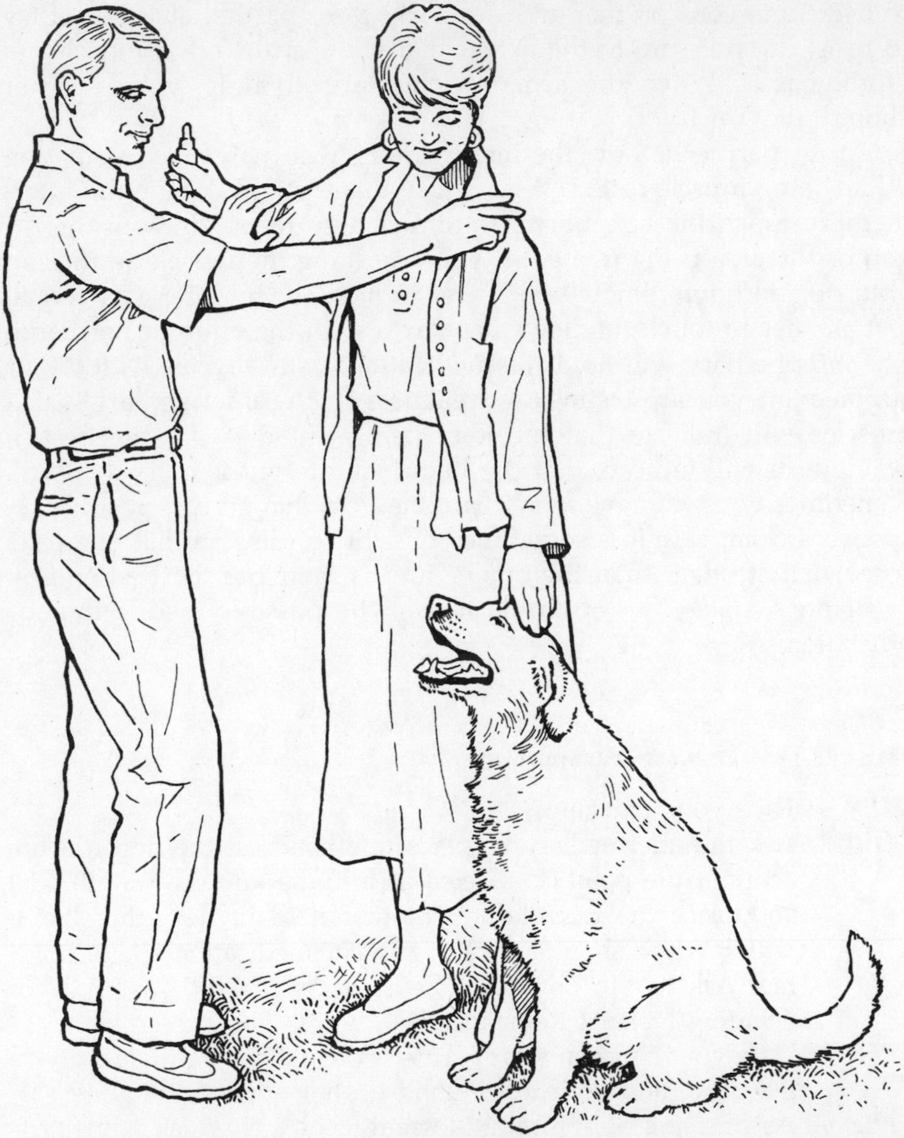

FIGURE 7. Muscle Testing Using Intermediary.

If the resistance of the arm is made stronger, this medication is a good choice. If the arm resistance is weaker and easily pushed down, this medication is a poor choice, ineffective or not agreeing with the dog's body. This may sound rather simplistic but it is surprisingly accurate. I have used kinesiology testing successfully on small animals and also in the field when testing horses for food allergies. I have found a remarkable degree of accuracy—the kinesiology testing almost always agrees with skin tests for allergies. This method has also identified supplements that contained substances an animal was allergic to. Without the muscle testing, the animal would have been given the supplements and we wouldn't have known there was a problem with them until it affected the health.

Pulse Diagnosis

Another method that can be useful in choosing a medication as well as diagnosing a problem is pulse diagnosis. In Chinese medicine and acupuncture, the pulses are used to help pinpoint exactly which energy meridian is deficient. This is an ancient Chinese system that has been used for thousands of years. In the Chinatown area of any large city there is usually an herb store and pharmacy where someone will take your pulse and prescribe the appropriate herbal tea or Chinese patent medicine for your condition.

Although pulse diagnosis requires practice to distinguish the individual pulses, it's not as difficult as you might imagine. Many people can master the basic pulses. At a recent conference of the American Holistic Veterinary Medical Association, Dr. Are Thorsen of Norway reported that he has taught many farmers this technique. Because some of the farms are more than 100 miles from the nearest veterinarian, the farmers' ability to take pulses on sick animals often means appropriate treatment can be started immediately, saving the lives of animals whose conditions are critical.

In this method, you first determine the pulse of the animal. Then hold the proposed medication in your hand or put it on the animal's body and recheck the pulse. If the medication is correct, a weakened pulse should return to near normal in the affected meridian; if the medication is not correct, the pulse will not react or it will get worse. This method has been found to be extremely accurate and very helpful in selecting treatments.

FIGURE 8. Pulse Diagnosis:

STEP 1. Take the pulse of the person who is acting as an intermediary by touching your fingertips to his or her wrist area, and determine if his or her normal pulse is strong, weak, or irregular.

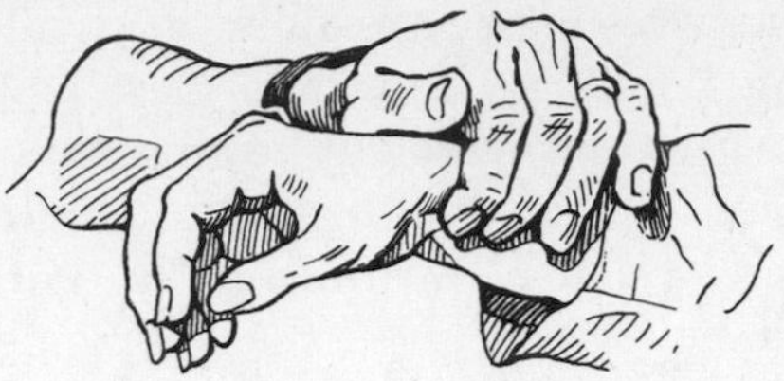

STEP 2. Ask the intermediary to place her hand on the dog's back, and check the intermediary's pulse again, noting any changes in the pulse at this point. This is considered the "dog's pulse."

STEP 3. Ask the intermediary to hold the medication you are considering in the same hand that is touching the dog's back and recheck the pulse. If the medication is appropriate, the intermediary's pulse will return to the dog's pulse as in step 2. If the medication is not appropriate, the intermediary's pulse will be the same as it was in step 1.

Taking the Temperature

If you suspect your dog has an elevated temperature, it can be very helpful to take his temperature yourself. Many owners have no trouble at all doing this. You may not want to attempt this procedure, however, if your dog is difficult to control. If you feel comfortable doing it yourself, it is wise to have another person's help in gently restraining the dog while you are taking the temperature.

This can be a stress-free experience *if* you are calm. It's a good idea to begin by giving your dog Rescue Remedy and taking some yourself (see "Bach Flower Remedies," p. 160). This will help to soothe the nerves. Also, talk to your dog during the procedure, explaining what you are doing and why. Your calm and loving voice will do much toward keeping your dog calm.

Use a rectal thermometer and coat the tip with petroleum jelly or K-Y jelly. Insert it into the rectum and leave it there for at least two to three minutes. Normal temperature for a dog varies from 101 to 102.5°F. A temperature of 103°F or higher is cause for concern and a signal to call your veterinarian as soon as possible. However, if your dog is excited about something or has gone through a traumatic experience, the temperature may be elevated as high as 103°F for a short time and will go back down to normal once the dog has calmed down.

Giving Tablets and Capsules

Note: The following information is for giving medications *other than homeopathics.* For instructions on giving homeopathics, see pages 165–168.

Tablets and capsules are the most common type of medications dispensed by veterinarians. There are several different ways to give pills—hiding the pill in food, forcing the pill down the dog's throat, using an instrument to help, or crushing the pill and mixing it with food or water.

Hiding the Pill in Food

In most cases you will be successful by simply hiding the pill in a small bit of food. This doesn't always work with the dog's regular food because some dogs are able to detect the pills in their food and refuse to eat it. In these cases it's best to hide the pill in a treat food. The best treat foods in which to hide pills are cheese, peanut butter, bratwurst, and liverwurst. If you choose peanut butter, be sure not to give too much at one time because it sticks to the roof of your dog's mouth just as it does to yours. One of the reasons I like to use bratwurst or liverwurst is that the flavor of these foods is so strong. Dogs are natural carrion or dead carcass eaters and seem to love the taste and strong odor of bratwurst and liverwurst. Although they are just about as far from natural as you can get, the small amount it takes to give a pill should not cause any problems.

The goal is to use a food that your dog likes and will eagerly gulp down. This can be difficult with smaller dogs; they tend to chew their food more because of the small size of their mouths. In this case, cut the pill into smaller pieces so the food treat can be smaller and the dog is less likely to chew it.

Once you have selected your food treat and the pill is the correct size for your dog, it's time to give it to your dog. If he or she is suspicious, I suggest that the first food treat offered have nothing in it—and possibly the second treat as well. Put the pill in the third treat; your dog should be so enthusiastic that the pill will go unnoticed.

Forcing the Pill Down the Throat

But what if food treats do not work, or what if your dog is too sick to eat? The next solution is to try forcing the pill down the throat. This method is fairly easy for small dogs and dogs who have shorter noses, such as the bulldog and the Pekingese. Your veterinarian can demonstrate how to pill your dog in this way. First, have the pill in your hand, open your dog's mouth, and place it all the way at the back of the throat. Close the mouth and massage the throat to encourage your dog to swallow. If that doesn't work, blow air on his nose, which will cause him to swallow. Be sure to talk to your dog in soothing tones before you begin. Start by explaining why you are giving him the pill and how you are going to give it. Dogs may not

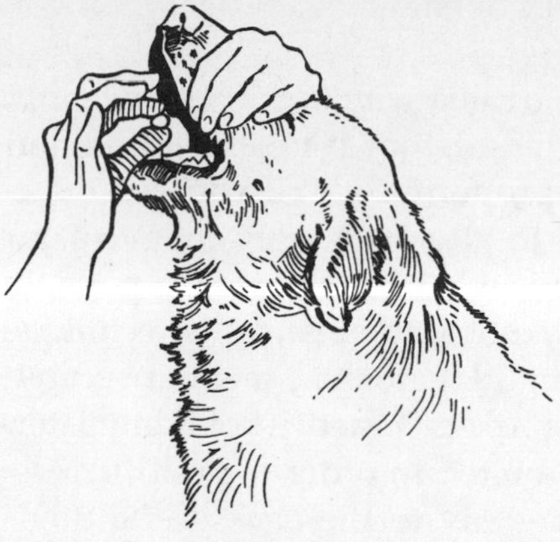

Step 1

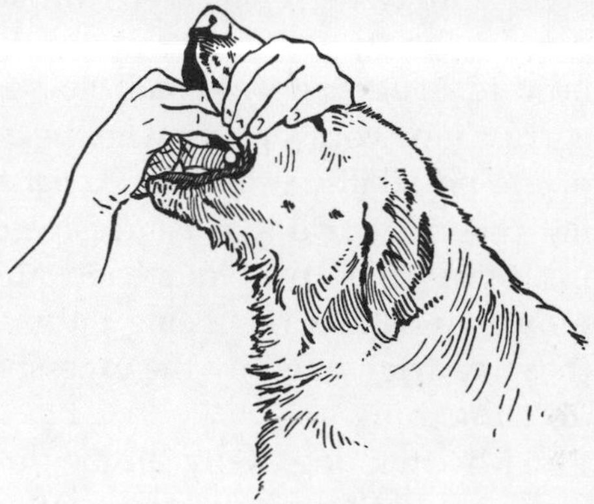

Step 2

FIGURE 9. Giving Pills:

STEP 1. With the pill in your hand, open the dog's mouth.

STEP 2. Place the pill all the way at the back of the throat.

STEP 3. Hold the mouth shut and massage the throat to encourage the dog to swallow.

Step 3

understand the words but they often understand a concept when you take the time to talk to them.

Forcing the pill down the throat in this way sounds simple, but there are several reasons you shouldn't attempt it unless your veterinarian has shown you how to do it properly. First, if you don't succeed, it may be much more difficult to attempt giving pills to your dog in the future since she will know what to expect and possibly how to evade you. Second, you may not understand the technique correctly or your dog may not be a candidate for this method because of the possibility of biting. *Do not* attempt this method of administering pills if your dog is aggressive or a biter. In order to do it successfully you must put your hand all the way to the back of the dog's mouth and thus risk being bitten. Some dogs may bite just because they are frightened by the excessive restraint and are being forced to do something.

My own dog, Kelly, bit me three times recently. She and Lily had come to work with me as usual and she had managed to get into a trash can where a chicken bone had been carelessly thrown by someone working in the clinic. Cooked chicken bones should always be disposed of in such a way that a dog cannot have access to them. They are extremely dangerous because they can splinter and a dog can easily choke on them. (Raw bones are safe because they don't splinter.)

When Kelly bit down on the bone, it wedged in the top of her mouth. Panic ensued and three veterinary technicians suddenly didn't know what to do. I heard the screaming and came running out to find Kelly frantically clawing at her mouth and resisting all attempts to help her. Examining her quickly, I accessed the situation and grabbed a pair of hemostats (a medical instrument used to hold things) and tried to dislodge the chicken bone. The hemostats didn't help so I used my fingers and jerked the chicken bone loose, getting bitten three times in the process. Kelly was frightened and she simply reacted without even realizing that it was me she was biting. Poor Kelly was terribly shaken and confused. It took an hour of holding and soothing to calm her down. This was unusual because Kelly doesn't like to be held under most circumstances. If I can get bitten so easily, it can happen to you as well. Don't take the chance of forcing a pill down the throat unless you're sure it is safe.

Using an Instrument to Give Pills

Using an instrument to put a pill in the dog's mouth is the third method of pill giving. But it is not a method I recommend unless you are very experienced. The soft tissue at the back of the dog's mouth can be injured very easily, potentially doing serious damage and, in the end, making cooperation even more of a problem in the future. Instruments for pill giving include pill guns, hemostats, and other homemade devices. Pill guns usually have a piece of rubber that the pill fits into and a plunger on the other end. The pill gun is inserted in the dog's mouth so the pill will be aimed at the very back of the dog's throat, and the plunger is then pushed. Hemostats are used in much the same way except that the instrument is held like a scissors.

Mixing the Pill with Water

The last way to give pills is to crush them up and combine the powder with water, using a syringe to administer the solution. If you are thinking of using this method, be sure to check with your veterinarian to see if the medication can be mixed with water. A problem with this method is taste. Some medications are bitter, and your dog may not tolerate the taste. Once you have added water to the pill be sure that the powder is completely dissolved and that none remains in the container after it is pulled up in a syringe. A dose syringe is used for this procedure. This type of syringe has a large opening at the end, which allows easy dispensing into the dog's mouth. For instructions on administering medication in a syringe, see the next section on giving liquid medications.

Giving Liquid Medications

To administer liquid medications it's best to use a syringe or eyedropper to prevent loss of medication and ensure an accurate dosage. Syringes are available in a variety of sizes, from 1 milliliter (the same as 1 cc) to 60 milliliters. If you need to give a medication that is marked in household measurements with a syringe that is marked in milliliters, here are some conversions to help you:

1 drop	=	1⁄20 ml
1 teaspoon	=	5 ml
1 tablespoon	=	15 ml
1 fluid ounce	=	29.57 ml
1 cup	=	250 ml

When liquid medications are prescribed, an allowance is usually made for a slight loss factor when administered. However, some medications require that the entire dosage be given very accurately. Be sure to check with your veterinarian to learn how accurate the dosage must be if you know that your dog is difficult and some medication may be lost. With most antibiotics it is okay to lose a tiny bit, but if you are using the heart medication digoxin, it's essential that the dosage be as accurate as possible.

When giving a liquid medication, hold your dog or place your dog in a position that will allow you to safely administer the medication. Sometimes it's best to have someone help you, at least the first few times, until your dog realizes that there is nothing to fear when being given medication.

1. Talk to your dog about what you are going to do. Always use a soothing tone to explain the procedure. Have the medication ready.
2. Tilt the dog's head back about 45 degrees. Do not tilt the head back any farther than this or you could put the medication down the dog's trachea (windpipe or entrance to the lungs), causing severe problems.
3. Open the dog's mouth and squirt the medication into the back of the mouth.
4. Once the medication is in the dog's mouth, close the mouth and rub the throat to encourage swallowing.

If the dog coughs a lot you may have gotten the medication into the trachea. If just a small amount went into the trachea, most dogs can cough it up, and you'll have to administer the medication again. If the dog continues to cough, it's possible that a large amount went into the trachea, so you should take the dog to a veterinarian right away.

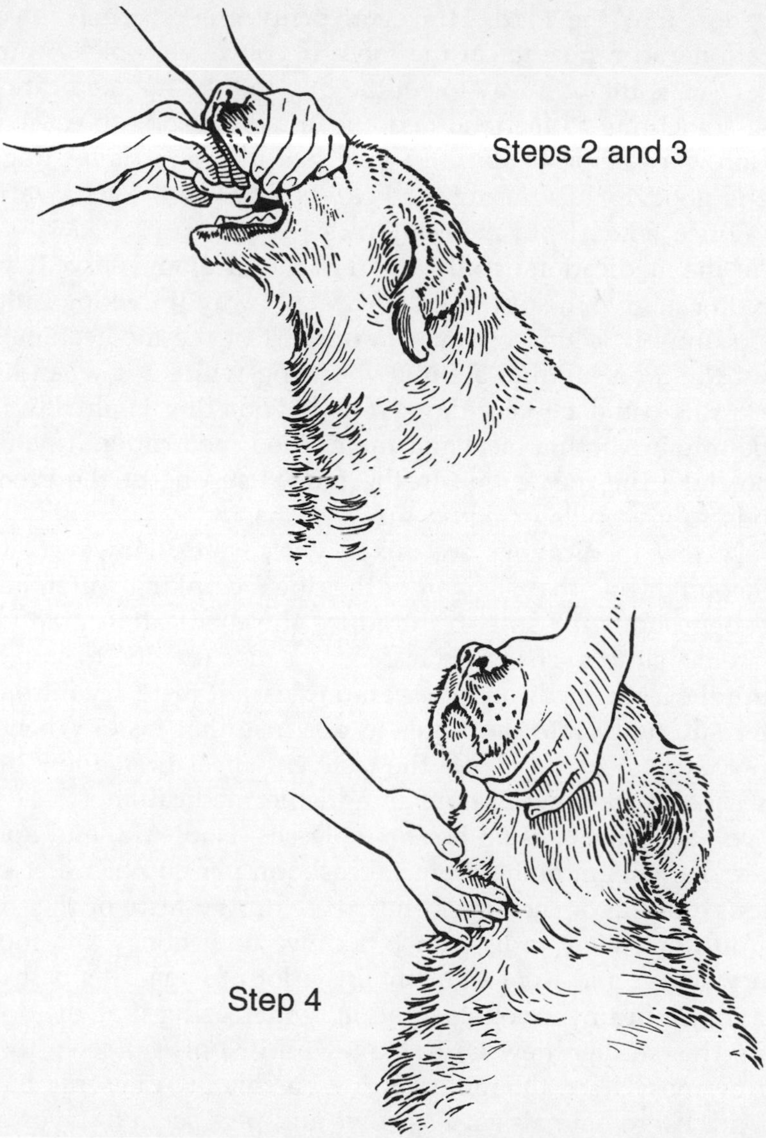

FIGURE 10. Giving Liquid Medications.

Mixing Medication into Food or Water

If your dog is an enthusiastic eater, you may be able to mix the medication into the food. However, picky eaters often detect the medication and refuse to eat the food. If you have a picky eater but still feel this is the best way to get the dog to take the medication, try adding something to the food and encourage the dog to eat it. I find that Nature's Recipe Rabbit and Rice has a strong flavor dogs like and it is good for disguising medication. My own dogs love it and never notice when I put medication in it.

Put the medication in only a part of the meal and serve that first. Then you can give the rest of the meal. That way if the dog isn't hungry you don't risk him missing out on part of the medication. Don't just put the food out and assume your dog will eat it when he gets hungry; this could be very dangerous if your dog is already ill. He may be missing both a meal and the needed medication. If your dog will not take the medication in the food, use one of the preceding methods to give pills or liquid medications.

Very few medications are mixed with water. However, in case you encounter one that is given in the dog's drinking water, here are some suggestions. Be sure to introduce the medication gradually to the water. A sudden change in taste may cause the dog to stop drinking entirely. If the medication has an unpleasant taste, try introducing another substance into the water to disguise that taste. When using this method it's easiest to add the taste enhancer first, allow the dog to get used to the new taste, then add the medication.

I've had success using honey, molasses, Kool-Aid, and apple cider. Use a small amount—about ½ teaspoon per cup of water should be enough to flavor the water and cover up the taste of the medication. You don't want to use much because both honey and molasses are very sweet, and Kool-Aid contains a lot of sugar. It's best to add the flavoring in tiny amounts, gradually increasing it as the dog gets used to this strange new taste. Honey and Kool-Aid seem to be favored by most dogs, though each dog has his own favorite flavor of Kool-Aid. Large animals such as cows and pigs seem to favor orange or cherry flavors, while horses like apple or cherry. My dogs prefer orange and pineapple, while other dogs like grape or orange.

It's very important to monitor the water supply to ensure that the dog is drinking enough and not becoming dehydrated. Remember, your dog's instinct tells him not to drink odd-tasting water so don't just assume that he will drink the medicated and flavored water. Try putting some in his mouth to taste. Another way to get him to try it is to pretend you like it by drinking a bit of the flavored water (before the medication has been added)—many dogs like "human food" and will consume anything if they think it's something you are going to eat.

Fasting

During fasting the body goes through a normal detoxification process as it expels wastes and cleanses organs, glands, and cells. Fasting is sometimes a normal response to illness; a dog instinctively stops eating while the body focuses its energy on recovery. Allowing a dog to fast on the first day or so of an illness can be a natural part of the healing process. And, of course, fasting is sometimes necessary in preparation for surgery or other procedures. Even a healthy dog can benefit from fasting. In any of these circumstances, fasting can be a very positive experience. Fasting is *not* recommended for dogs who suffer from diabetes or hypoglycemia, because their insulin and glucose levels must be maintained.

Owners often get unnecessarily upset as soon as their dog stops eating. It's natural for us to worry when a dog refuses to eat, but remember, it can be the most natural of occurrences. Carefully monitor the dog for symptoms of illness at this time, but don't panic about a missed meal unless there are other indications that something is wrong. If your dog misses a second meal, call your veterinarian.

It is vital that your dog drink plenty of fresh water with nutrients added to it during a fast so dehydration doesn't result. If you are imposing a fast on your dog, it's best to do so with the supervision of a veterinarian. Here are some important guidelines:

Fasting Guidelines

1. Without food only for 24 hours.
2. Supply plenty of fresh water. Add one of the following

sources of nutrients to the water in a ratio of 1 teaspoon per cup of water.

- Honey
- Gatorade (or similar electrolyte replacer)
- Pedialytes (electrolytes for babies, available in supermarkets)

(*Note:* If the dog will not drink the water with the nutrients in it, leave them out.) If the dog will not drink any water, give by syringe in the mouth. (Give as you would liquid medications. See "Giving Liquid Medications" earlier in this chapter.)

3. Give Kyolic garlic tablets or capsules (without yeast). Dosage should be one capsule for each 20 pounds of the dog's weight. (See page 97 for more on garlic.)

4. Keep your dog quiet. Exercise should be limited.

5. Give homeopathic nux vomica 6C three times a day. (See "Homeopathy," p. 165.)

Breaking a Fast

Slowly return to the standard diet and supplements. For the first day or two after a fast, feed boiled chicken (no fat or skin) with rice. Gradually add the other ingredients back into the diet. Be sure plenty of fresh water is available.

12

Dealing with Illness

The Power of Your Mind

Have you ever wondered how some people accomplish goals that seem nearly impossible and how others can overcome illnesses that are considered terminal or incurable? At one time or another all of us have had to cope with a difficult situation that seemed unsolvable at the time. Think back and remember your response to one of the challenges that you overcame. Did you get angry, frustrated, panicked, or begin a search for new answers? We all go through a range of emotions when faced with a trying situation.

Over the years I have been the bearer of bad news about a beloved animal's prognosis more times than I'd like to remember. In the face of this adversity I am always delightfully surprised by those rare individuals whose optimism kicks in and seems unstoppable. When told that impossible odds are against them, some people seem to tap into a deep well of faith, determination, and conviction.

An example is the case of Daisy, a 13-year-old golden retriever who came to me with tumors in the mammary glands. She had lost weight, the tumors were large, and a biopsy confirmed my diagnosis of cancer. Daisy's prognosis did not look good, and I painted a rather bleak but truthful picture for her owner. This particular type of tumor usually spreads rapidly; sometimes the tumors become so large that they break through the skin, and often spread to the lungs or other parts of the body.

Following my advice Daisy's owner declined a full mastectomy. I was relieved, because I did not think she would have recovered well from the surgery due to her age. Instead, we decided on more conservative surgery to remove the worst lumps, followed by a series of special acupuncture treatments that work against cancer. I also prescribed an injectable form of homeopathic. In addition, I altered Daisy's diet to one with less protein, more digestible carbohydrates, and no preservatives. Digestive enzymes were included in each meal to ensure all the nutrients were thoroughly digested and utilized.

Daisy healed quickly from her surgery and responded well to the acupuncture, homeopathy, and dietary improvements. In cases like this the best we could have hoped for was to eliminate some of the pain and prolong her life a little. But, amazingly, Daisy's recovery was complete. The tumors did not return and Daisy regained her weight, returning to top condition with a glossy coat and plenty of energy. I was delighted that the treatments I recommended, including the more conservative surgery, were successful in this life-threatening case. However, I believe the owner was also a major factor in Daisy's recovery. Throughout the surgery and recovery Daisy's owner maintained an extremely optimistic attitude.

Daisy is not an isolated case. I've seen many cases like hers that defy the odds and recover completely. The power of your mind and its influence on your dog is very strong. When dealing with illness, try to keep a strong positive attitude to encourage your dog to recover.

One of my favorite examples of this kind of determination is the true-life story of Bob Champion, which was made into the movie, *Champions*. Bob Champion was a steeplechase jockey at the top of his career when he was diagnosed with cancer and given little chance to live. About the same time as Bob's diagnosis the horse that he had ridden to many victories was severely injured and not expected to ever race again. After a series of radiation treatments Bob tried to return to racing, but found that he was too weak and had no feeling in his hands and feet. But Bob refused to give up and continued to recuperate until eventually he was able to go back to work. Meanwhile, the injured horse also triumphed over his leg injury and was able to return to the track. They once again became a team, winning England's Grand National, one of the world's toughest races. Together they overcame immense odds and gave new meaning to the word *determination.*

It's hard to fathom how powerful the mind can be—particularly when it comes to influencing your dog. Dogs have a strong desire to please their owners and this goal often overshadows other seemingly more powerful forces. An example of the power of a dog's desire to please was published in *DVM,* the veterinary magazine. In a column that often discusses the practice of veterinary medicine in a humorous light the following story was told. A client brought her dog to the veterinarian to be euthanized (put to sleep). The dog was very old and in the last stages of cancer. Despite the seriousness of the disease, the dog seemed happy and not in pain, but it was severely debilitated.

The veterinarian complied with the owner's wishes and, while the client held her dog, administered the injection. To make sure the dog would go quietly and quickly the veterinarian overdosed the medication slightly, as most of us do. However, the dog had absolutely no reaction. He just sat there and did nothing; he didn't even lie down. This was extremely unusual, because the dose administered was more than sufficient to end the dog's life. A second injection was given and again the dog just sat there. Finally the owner suggested that she might be the cause of the problem. She told the veterinarian that she is a psychic and she had focused her energy to keep the dog free from pain during his illness. In an attempt to reverse the effect she had, she said a few words to the dog and then asked the veterinarian to try again. This time the dog died immediately following the injection. This true story shows to what an extreme an owner can influence and control a dog.

You may possess similar abilities to that of the woman just mentioned, whether you know it or not. Each of us has more power than we realize. I know my dogs often mirror my moods and stresses and I try to maintain a watchful eye on them when I'm going through a difficult period. When I was in veterinary school I studied constantly and faced many nerve-racking exams. My miniature poodle, Kelly, was always next to my chair and at final exam time she seemed to worry as much as I did. She would lose weight and be less interested in play until exams were over. When your dog is ill or injured, your attitude can influence your dog's recovery just as easily as my stress influenced Kelly's behavior.

There is another way in which an owner's state of mind and energy can influence an animal's well-being. It is not unusual to see dogs who mirror their owner's problems, whether physical or emotional. You've probably heard it said that dogs often look like their owners. I haven't found that to be especially true but I do find that dogs often *act* like their owners. This can occur in all species, but it is seen often in dogs because they are so emotionally close to their owners.

Of all the cases I've seen of this type of human/animal bond, I will relate an experience I had with an owner and her horse, because it has been one of the most amazing I have witnessed. The owner, Beth, had called me to her farm to do a veterinary check on a horse she was planning to purchase. The mare passed the veterinary check with flying colors, and I noted no problems. As we talked during the exam Beth told me about her other horses. Two had died, one was permanently lame, and they had all suffered neck problems. I was surprised that Beth, a woman in her early thirties, had so many problems with horses in a short time period, because most horses are healthy for a great many years. I made some notes about the other horses' histories on the chart and left the farm.

Two weeks later I was called back to Beth's farm to treat the newly purchased mare. She now had a severe inflammation on her neck and was on the verge of becoming seriously ill. I initiated treatment immediately and the mare responded well. Within two weeks she was completely healed. In referring to my earlier notes, however, I was reminded that each previously owned horse had incurred neck injuries. It seemed too much for coincidence, so I spoke to Beth about it. It turned out that she had been wondering about the same thing. When I suggested that she have a medical checkup to see if there were any problems with her own health that were influencing the horses, she admitted to having frequent headaches and pain in the neck area. A medical exam revealed that Beth's cervical (neck) vertebrae were degenerating and misaligned. After receiving treatment for her neck Beth is doing much better. And, interestingly, her horses have not had neck problems since then.

By increasing your awareness you will be able to see how your attitude, energy, and even your own health can influence your dog.

So be vigilant. When your dog has a recurring illness or a sudden and unexplained illness it may be beneficial to consider what is going on in your own life.

A Healing Environment

When your dog has suffered an illness, injury, or surgery, the environment you provide will influence the rate of recovery. An extra dose of tender loving care will go a long way. Always be sure your dog is comfortable. Your sick dog may gravitate to a special area in the house because she is seeking warmth or coolness. Perhaps an extra towel or blanket will help—a hard, cold floor isn't conducive to healing.

Here are a few considerations when caring for an ailing dog:

- Check the bedding to make sure there is enough padding and support. Dogs who are recovering from injuries such as a fractured leg may not be able to move about easily, so the mattress you provide must be thick and supportive enough to guard against bedsores.
- If your dog has difficulty rising and walking, make sure the food and water are within his reach.
- Check the diet to make sure it is high quality and that the nutrients are digestible. During illness a homemade meal with chicken and rice as the main ingredients may entice a sick dog to eat. Avoid foods that overstress the digestive tract, such as high-fat items, including bacon and ham. (See chapter 6, "A Healthy Diet.")
- Find a quiet and restful place for your dog to recuperate. Do not allow children or other pets to overtax your dog during an illness.
- Do not expect your dog to play or carry out normal activities when ill. Sometimes house training cannot be adhered to by a sick animal. Often the dog is as upset as the owner when accidents occur. Try to help out by taking him outside often and providing newspaper for unavoidable accidents.
- Avoid taking your dog on extended car trips when ill. They can be very stressful on a sick animal.

Treat your dog with every bit of respect that you would want if you were ill or injured. Remember that just because dogs can't talk and tell us about the pain they are experiencing, doesn't mean they don't feel it. I've encountered owners who expected their dogs to be completely normal three days after a major surgery. Having experienced major surgery and the gradual recovery afterward, I empathize with a dog going through this experience. Most dogs do recover much more quickly than people and are okay within two weeks—but each case is unique. Watch your dog for signs of excessive discomfort, including lack of appetite, lack of movement, or irritable behavior such as growling and biting.

If you suspect your dog is in pain *do not* jump to the conclusion that medication must be administered immediately. There are times when it is best that your dog experience some pain, however distressing, so she will limit her movement and allow healing to take place. If we medicate a dog who should not be moving around, she will be without pain and may exercise more than she should, possibly doing *more* damage to her body. Consult your veterinarian about what is best for your dog.

Following a spay small dogs are often very sensitive to the discomfort. The best medication to relieve this pain is arnica, a homeopathic remedy that decreases inflammation and pain. It is very effective and is my treatment of choice both for dogs and myself for many types of pain. When used to alleviate pain from surgery, I suggest lower potencies such as 6X, 12X, or 6C (see "Homeopathy," p. 165). Another alternative is to give a small amount of baby aspirin. (Always consult your veterinarian about dosage.) Whenever using aspirin be sure to use the buffered type. Aspirin acts as an anti-inflammatory, helps control pain, and reduces any rise in body temperature.

If your dog is recovering from mental stress such as a traumatic accident or a history that included abuse and mistreatment, a healing and supportive environment is even more important. Your own consistency in behavior patterns and patience will contribute greatly to your dog's emotional healing. Having adopted abused animals in the past, I have experienced both the frustration and the rewards of rehabilitating an animal. Some are more challenging than others; it can be difficult to understand their exact needs, especially the ones whose backgrounds are unknown.

If your dog must stay at the animal hospital during the recuperation period, you can provide therapeutic support in several ways. Dogs always recover faster when their owners visit regularly, bringing along reminders from home to let them know they have not been forgotten. A favorite blanket or towel, or a familiar toy often cheers up a hospitalized dog.

I have worked in many animal clinics, but one became a model for me because the staff lavished such tender loving care on the animals. I had never before seen such a loving attitude as the one displayed there—nothing was too much to do for the pets in that clinic. Because this loving care was communicated to the animals, I saw many borderline cases recover due to their diligent care.

I was particularly impressed with the many aggressive dogs that the staff was able to handle without problem. When a staff member was successful with a difficult dog, a special record was made so that person could be assigned to the dog on future visits. They also did a great deal of boarding at that clinic and the dogs always seemed to thoroughly enjoy their stay. The special care and daily walks in the surrounding woods provided the very best of care. The hospital environment should be conducive to healing—from the attitude of the veterinarian and staff to the lighting, colors, and sounds.

Dealing with Death and Dying

We all have to face the death of our beloved companions at some point. Preparing for it is a very difficult thing to do. The death of a dog is the loss of a member of the family. As owners we face life knowing that one day our friend will no longer be with us. Often we try not to notice that a dog is aging. The loss of sight, hearing, and teeth problems are all signs of advancing age.

I always become very close to my dogs and the thought of losing them fills me with great sorrow. However, we all know Mother Nature did not design dogs to live as long as humans. Their inevitable death must be faced. My goal is to make my dogs as comfortable as possible in their old age, giving them every advantage of health management such as acupuncture, chiropractic, and proper nutrition. When I have done as much as I can, it's the dog's turn to live the best life possible.

I have lost a couple of dogs to old age. Toward the end of their lives they have always let me know when their time was drawing to a close by refusing treatment and becoming reclusive. Most owners are well aware of their dog's behavior and can detect subtle changes that occur when a dog knows that life is coming to an end. The behavior of other animals in the family also may change at this time. If the dog is a senior, one of the other dogs usually assumes the leadership role. It may be subtle in many instances. In one case, I noticed that the younger dog started taking care of the older dog. No longer did the older dog get up to bark first or check out noises first. If something really important was happening, the young dog went to get the older dog. These changes can take place gradually or suddenly, depending on the health problems the older dog is facing.

I hope your dog lives to a ripe old age—but sometimes it's the sad truth that young dogs become injured or sick and we must face their death too. Whatever the dog's age, the way you handle the situation can assist the animal when death comes. As I discussed at the beginning of this chapter, the power of your mind can have a great influence on your dog.

When it comes time to die it is important that you let your dog go willingly. If you persist and hang on, the incredible faithful nature of a canine will often cause the dog to try against all odds to prevent death. Most veterinarians have witnessed this. I encourage owners to assure their dog that it is okay to die. Even in cases where severe debilitation has occurred and the death is going to be assisted by euthanasia, if the owner has not emotionally let the dog go, the death is more difficult and the dog will often fight to stay. Witnessing such a struggle is very sad, but can be avoided if you are properly prepared and have said your good-byes and mentally let your dog go. When I sense that the owner has not let a dog go and euthanasia is necessary, I tranquilize the dog before the euthanasia so this struggle can be avoided.

Euthanasia is always a difficult question. I have clients who do not believe in euthanasia except in extreme circumstances. Everyone has their own beliefs on this subject and when you own a dog it's best to consider what you would do if the situation ever arises. Unfortunately, due to indiscriminate breeding, euthanasia has become a form of population control to many breeders. This is a very sad commentary on how some people value the life of their animals. Euthanasia is not the answer for controlling population or to replace responsible breeding practices.

If you are considering euthanasia for your dog due to a severe illness or injury, it's best to know what to expect. Owners often wonder if their dog will feel any pain and if death will be instantaneous. The solutions now used to euthanize animals work very quickly, usually before the injection is finished. Consciousness goes first so the dog is unaware of what is happening and slips into a sleeplike state, then death. This all happens in a matter of seconds with no pain or struggling. For dogs who are difficult to handle and normally struggle during medical procedures, I suggest a tranquilizer before the euthanasia solution is administered.

To assist you and your dog emotionally I recommend using Rescue Remedy (see "Bach Flower Remedies," p. 160). Some dogs are very calm throughout, whereas others are helped by Rescue Remedy. I also suggest that owners take it both before and after the procedure.

Because emotion is a natural part of losing a beloved friend, I do not discourage my clients from showing their grief. If you know that you must have your dog euthanized and are going to the hospital for that purpose, I recommend that you bring a friend along to help you. Not only will your friend be there to console you, but that friend can also drive you home. Feeling a strong sense of loss is normal and nothing to be ashamed of.

I also suggest that owners observe whatever customs or rituals they are comfortable with when their dog is dying. I have had clients perform religious ceremonies during the procedure, and one owner even brought a priest along to stand by while her dog was euthanized.

Although owners often hold their dogs during the procedure, it is not necessary to do so unless you want to. My best advice is to do whatever you are comfortable doing. Helping your beloved companion through this experience is one of the most selfless acts you will ever do.

When a Child Loses a Pet

As hard as it is for us to deal with the death of a pet, it can be even more difficult for a child. The concept of death can be strange and terrifying for a child who has never before dealt with it. Rather than trying to shield the child from this experience, I find that involving the child is best.

If the dog is dying of a long illness, try to explain this to the child. Obviously the age of the child is a major factor here, but remember that even a very young child has some awareness of what's going on.

The child must deal with the same range of emotions that adults go through, from denial to guilt, anger, despair and, finally, acceptance. Ask the child what he is feeling and discuss these emotions with him. Above all, let him know that his feelings are normal. Over the next days and weeks, continue to ask the child from time to time what he is feeling about the loss of the pet. He may have gone from denial of the experience to guilt. Children often feel that they are the cause of a bad thing that happens in their lives. The child may remember a time when he did something wrong such as hitting the dog and feel that this is the reason the dog has died. This guilt must also be discussed so you can explain that his actions had nothing to do with the dog's death.

Asking the child to talk about these feelings is the only way to know how the child is dealing with the death. It may be difficult for you to talk about the death because you are grieving too. However, your grief is a wonderful example to your child, showing him that it is okay to display your emotions and share them with others. If the child has lost a human friend or family member, it may be appropriate to mention that loss as a reference point.

If possible, allow the child to help you bury the animal. It can also help to perform a little ceremony, involving the child to whatever extent is appropriate for his or her age.

A number of books are available to help all of us deal with death and dying, including those by Elisabeth Kübler-Ross, the leading expert on this subject. *The Fall of Freddie the Leaf* by Leo Buscaglia is an excellent book that helps to explain the concept to young children.

13
The Aging Dog

When is a dog old? The answer to this question is highly individualized. Signs of aging are related to a host of factors, including the dog's care (including diet and grooming), exercise, genetics, and the owner's attitude. These factors are much more significant to the aging process than the actual chronological age of the dog. Many large dogs begin showing signs of old age earlier than small breeds. However, these rules of thumb are made to be broken. I have seen many large breed dogs live well into their teens. When questioning the owners of these dogs I generally find that they *expect* their dogs to live to a ripe old age.

Whether you are aware of it or not, you have a tremendous influence on your dog's aging. Owners who expect their dogs to act "old" often regard signs of aging such as cataracts and arthritis as inevitable. They don't have to be. Just as many senior citizens today are healthy and energetic, your dog's golden years can be too. Some adjustments are warranted as your dog gets older, but not all dogs suffer the infirmities associated with age. If an age-related health problem does arise, this chapter will help you better understand how to deal with it and meet your dog's special needs.

An example of the owner's attitude about aging was brought home to me one day when I was walking my dogs. At the time my dogs were 14 and 15 years old and still in good condition, running around me as I exercised them and, at the same time, trying to chase the neighbor's cat. Another dog walker approached. Her dog was walking slowly and without any enthusiasm. Noticing the fun my dogs were having as they frolicked together, the woman commented that it must be nice to have young, energetic dogs who can still enjoy life. She explained that her dog was 10 years old—obviously ancient by her standards—and that she didn't expect him to live much longer. You can imagine her surprise when I told her my dogs were 14 and 15. I gave her some suggestions that might improve her dog's health and overall condition.

It turned out that this owner had no idea that the signs of age she was seeing could be improved upon. In fact, she had been told that dogs were old after the age of eight, so she had decreased his exercise and eliminated much of his regular health care, because she expected him to die soon. I told her that it's never too late to make improvements in her dog's care and that she will undoubtedly see noticeable results with increased vitality and health.

While I've seen many older dogs make miraculous turnarounds in their condition, Elsa stands out as an exemplary illustration of my point. Elsa was a 13-year-old yellow Labrador with a number of health problems. I first met her after working on her owner's horse. The owner was so impressed with the horse's progress using holistic medicine that she brought Elsa to me. Due to her excess weight and arthritis it was difficult for Elsa to get up and walk around. Her owner had to carry her into my clinic. Her hormones were out of balance and her teeth were causing problems. Within a month or so, a combination of acupuncture, homeopathy, diet changes, and herbs made Elsa look like a new dog! She was able to walk around without pain, and the dental care and new diet helped her to lose weight. I was gratified that Elsa lived out her remaining years as a fully functioning, happy dog.

So, when is your dog old? Well, each dog ages differently. You should approach each individual dog with the idea of providing as much care as possible to delay the health problems associated with old age.

Special Considerations and Requirements of the Aging Dog

All dogs, as they age, have some special problems just as older people do. If we know this and watch for these problems, giving them special consideration when they first occur, many of them can be forestalled or avoided altogether, making your life with your dog much more enjoyable. These special considerations and requirements of older dogs include exercise needs, diet changes, more frequent health checkups, and habit changes. Let's look at them one by one.

Exercise Needs

Older dogs must continue to get exercise on a daily basis so they remain in good physical shape. When a dog does not get enough exercise, the overall health is affected, influencing all the bodily functions—from digestion to the flexibility of joints. As the dog ages, he will not pursue as much strenuous exercise as he did when he was younger. A walk may take the place of a game of Frisbee. That's all normal and appropriate. Allow the older dog to slow down—but make sure he continues to get an acceptable amount of exercise, albeit at this slower pace.

Make special adjustments if your dog is no longer able to make certain physical movements. If you find that a particular type of exercise, such as jumping, aggravates your dog in any way, avoid that type of exercise in the future. For instance, as she ages, a tiny dog may no longer be able to jump up into a car or truck seat. Be aware of these problems to help her overcome the confusion of not being able to do something she has done easily for years.

Diet Changes

As dogs age their bodies require less protein and more carbohydrates; their food also needs to be more easily digestible. Feeding a dog food specifically designed for older dogs will help meet these needs. Feed the more digestible homemade Restricted Protein Diet in chapter 6 or buy one of the senior diets made by a natural pet food company. As they age, dogs require fewer calories. You may have noticed that your older dog has gained weight as he ages, even though he is eating the same amount of food. Each dog's metabolism will slow down at a different rate, so you need to be observant. If you notice a gradual weight gain, reduce the amount of food you are feeding. If slightly reducing the quantity of food does not result in weight loss, take your dog for a checkup to make sure a metabolic problem isn't the cause. Care should be taken not to overfeed any dog; this is even more important for an aging dog.

It's okay to feed your older dog some table scraps, but you will need to be more aware of what he will be able to digest and tolerate. He probably won't be able to eat every food as he once did. Do not feed older dogs strongly spiced, fatty, or oily foods; they strain the digestive system and can create health problems. Flatulence or gas can also be a problem as the dog ages. In addition to the special diet, add acidophilus to the diet to supply the necessary normal digestive bacteria. (See "Garlic, Acidophilus, and Yogurt" on page 97.)

More Frequent Medical Checkups

The dog's body will experience changes as it ages. Sight problems and tooth decay are among the common problems of older dogs. Increased tartar buildup on teeth can eventually develop into a gum infection or tooth abscess. Regular cleaning of the teeth can prevent many of these problems. In general, regular checkups can catch many health problems at an early stage, which is even more important for the older dog. Preventive maintenance will help you avoid the further progression of a problem, hopefully catching it before it becomes a major medical emergency. I recommend an annual laboratory workup for older dogs to detect any changes in internal organs and to provide a normal comparison for future reference.

Habit Changes

Just because your dog has always done something a certain way does not mean that she will be able to continue with that habit the rest of her life. Be observant. If you notice a behavior change in your dog, such as urinating in the house, don't jump to the conclusion that she is suddenly misbehaving and needs to be disciplined. As a dog ages there are a variety of influences that might cause her to be unable to hold her urine as long as she once did. She may be as surprised as you when an accident occurs. It could be caused by a problem with the sphincter muscle of the bladder, a urinary tract infection, developing diabetes, or a number of other health problems. I'll discuss these problems in more detail later in this chapter. Check with your veterinarian when you notice any significant behavior changes. You may be able to avoid a major problem by catching it early.

Both you and your dog may have to change some well-established habits as the dog's body ages. However, attention to these concerns with a watchful eye will allow you both to deal with these changes more easily.

Common Health Problems of the Aging Dog

What health problems do you need to watch for as your dog ages? Most of the medical difficulties your dog may experience with age are similar to people problems, so that will give you some guidelines. The main problems facing older dogs are arthritis, eyesight problems, deafness, urinary incontinence, confusion, lack of energy, and decreased appetite. Let's look at these problems and what you can do about them.

Arthritis

If your dog begins to have difficulty rising, seems to stumble and fall easily, or just doesn't move as fast as he once did, he may be suffering from arthritis. The condition can develop gradually and you may not be aware that anything is wrong until very blatant signs are evident. Because you see your dog every day you may not notice the gradual slowdown until one day when he has trouble rising or reaching down to eat his food. Try to be observant as your dog ages to detect the earliest changes in the range of his movement so arthritis can be diagnosed and treated in its early stages.

There are many types of treatment for arthritis, ranging from aspirin to acupuncture, each specific to the individual dog's needs. I use acupuncture, chiropractic, homeopathy, diet changes, and herbs in various combinations to treat arthritis. What works for one dog may not be the correct treatment for another, because arthritis has a variety of causes and they must be specifically addressed.

Arthritis is a thickening of the bone or added areas of bone that develop as the body's response to an injury, an insult to the tissue, a bacterial infection, an instability, or as a result of disease. Whatever the cause, extra bony tissue develops where it shouldn't be and the result is pain. Often the pain will be worse when the dog is exposed to damp, cold weather. For that reason, dogs seem to suffer more arthritis pain in the fall and winter.

How can you help your arthritic dog? Don't just give him aspirin and think that easing the pain is enough. You can also decrease the discomfort of arthritis by addressing his environment to be sure he is warm enough in cold weather. Also check your dog's diet to be sure it fits his needs and is properly balanced. A poor diet can speed the development of arthritis, whereas a high-quality diet will decrease the toxin load that can influence arthritis.

Acupuncture has proven to be extremely effective in treating arthritis. It has also been one of the most rewarding modalities of treatment I have used. Surprisingly, most dogs actually enjoy the treatments and associate good feelings with acupuncture. I almost always combine acupuncture with homeopathy, because these modalities always seem to complement each other well. There are a variety of homeopathies that can be effective in relieving the symptoms. Herbs and natural products such as various forms of seaweed and shark cartilage can also help in managing arthritis. As I mentioned earlier, each case must be considered individually and a management program developed. Some dogs do well with moderate exercise, whereas others do best with regular but less exercise. You have to work with your dog and your veterinarian to determine the right combination for him.

(Also see "Arthritis" in Part II of this book.)

Eyesight

Eye problems are one of the most challenging health problems to deal with in older dogs. Diagnosis and treatment are difficult, because there are a variety of eye problems that can develop. The most common are cataracts and glaucoma. Cataracts occur gradually as the dog ages, and involve the lens of the eye. There is now a surgery that can be performed to remove cataracts in dogs much like the one that is used with humans. This type of surgery is offered by veterinary ophthalmologists, a growing specialty in veterinary medicine. It is most successful with dogs who are diagnosed in the early stages of cataracts, but I'm sure as this type of surgery is further refined it will be more helpful for the very advanced cases as well. If your dog needs to have cataract surgery, either you or your veterinarian should contact a veterinary ophthalmologist or veterinary school for information, and to see if your dog is a candidate.

If surgery is not an option for your dog, a few other forms of treatment can be considered. Cataracts can be very frustrating to treat because the lens resides inside the eye. It's difficult to get adequate medication to the area because the topical medications that are applied to the eye are not well absorbed through the cornea, making treatment of the cataract difficult. Vitamin C in eyedrop form has been used with some success in treating cataracts. The drops must be applied daily, but it often takes a month or two before results can be seen. When I've used vitamin C drops for cataracts each experience has been a little different. However, I have seen a significant decrease in further development of the cataracts. In other words, the cataract does not seem to get worse. In a few cases, the cataracts have actually improved, with fewer cloudy areas present in the eye.

Glaucoma is a condition that occurs when the pressure in the eye increases due to a malfunction in the eye's physiological system. It is more commonly seen in dogs with protruding eyes such as Pekingese, but it can occur in any breed. Glaucoma can occur as a result of an injury or just appear without a known reason. It's important to diagnose the problem quickly, because the excessive pressure can cause permanent damage to the eye's sensitive structures. Medications are now available that can control glaucoma and prevent the eye from being damaged. The change you will notice is the excessive protrusion of one eye. Sometimes the affected eye will have a discharge as well.

Deafness

Deafness is often a problem for aging dogs. My own dog, Kelly, has been deaf for several years now and gets along fine. However, there are several considerations that must be made when living with a deaf dog. First, when diagnosing a deaf dog I prefer to check all possible reasons for the dog's deafness, such as infection or excessive ear wax. If the commonly known medical reasons for deafness are not present, I use acupuncture to help stimulate the nerves to the ears. Acupuncture can sometimes help give the dog some of hearing back. The cervical or neck vertebrae should also be checked to make sure they are properly aligned. If they are out of alignment, a chiropractic adjustment of these vertebrae can help with hearing problems.

If your dog is unable to be helped, here are some guidelines to help you with deaf dogs:

- Keep deaf dogs confined to a fenced area, or exercise in an area where there is no traffic or hazards that would require hearing to warn the dog of danger.
- Teach your dog hand signals for the basic commands. They can be learned from a dog trainer, or look for a book on obedience that also includes hand signals.
- Try to avoid situations that will require a warning yell by keeping your dog leashed when in unfamiliar areas.
- Do not ignore your dog just because she can't hear. Deaf dogs still need affection and care just like hearing dogs.

My own dog, Kelly, copes well with her hearing loss. Years ago she learned hand signals, so I revived the training when she began to lose her hearing. At 15 she even learned a new hand signal—be quiet. Kelly has always prided herself on being an excellent watchdog. As her hearing failed, she learned to rely on her sense of smell to detect trespassers. However, once she notified me of an approaching vehicle or person, she couldn't hear me give the command to stop barking. She's a great barker but she sometimes overdid it. So I taught her to look at me occasionally to see if she should be quiet. I would give her the appropriate hand signal and peace would again reign! If Kelly can learn new tricks at 15 years, your dog can start learning, too.

(Also see "Deafness," p. 251, in the "Ear Problems" section in Part II of this book.)

Urinary Incontinence

Urinary incontinence is usually associated with female dogs, but it can occur in males as well. There are a variety of possible causes for leakage of urine. If your older dog exhibits this problem, a veterinary exam may determine the cause.

Females often have a deficiency of estrogen that affects their ability to hold urine. In traditional allopathic medicine, an estrogen replacement is prescribed. However, I often find that a complete holistic workup sometimes reveals the cause of the estrogen deficiency and a treatment for the root cause can then be carried out. If estrogen replacement is deemed the only recourse, the dog should be monitored closely to ensure other hormones do not go out of balance due to the excess estrogen in the system. The thyroid hormones in particular are sensitive to excess estrogen and can become low if extreme amounts are in the system.

A poorly functioning bladder sphincter muscle is another common cause of incontinence. This muscle controls the bladder's ability to empty the urine out; after urination it should be tight to prevent leakage. But sometimes in older dogs this muscle does not tighten up or stay tight, resulting in urine leakage. Acupuncture can sometimes help to stimulate the nerves to this area and decrease the problem. There is also an enzyme that can be prescribed to prevent leakage, which is effective in some cases.

A bladder infection could also be the cause of incontinence. A urine sample can be dropped off at your veterinarian's office so a check can be performed to make sure an infection is not the problem. Bladder infections are usually treated with antibiotics because they work quickly and are very effective. Chinese herbs can also assist in the treatment. If a bladder infection is diagnosed, however, I recommend that a complete physical exam be performed so I can be sure there is no other problem causing the dog to be more susceptible to infections.

Whenever a dog is suffering from incontinence problems a complete exam is important. This is something to act on as soon as you first observe the problem, because incontinence can also be the forerunner to a serious health problem. As always, catching it early can make a big difference.

While the older dog has an incontinence problem, do whatever you can to help minimize the stress of this experience. Remember, he's upset by it too. House training and doggy diapers are two ways to handle it until the problem is cleared up.

(Also see "Urinary Tract Problems," in Part II of this book.)

Confusion

As some dogs age they seem to become confused. Your dog may suddenly panic for no reason or wander off and not be able to find her way home. These are all common scenarios of confusion. Your dog may have this problem only occasionally or quite often. It's a difficult problem to treat because we usually don't know what caused the confusion in the first place. There are theories that some of the neurotransmitters in the brain are no longer functioning properly, but we don't yet know enough about how a dog's neurotransmitters work to be able to solve this problem.

I have had some success treating dogs suffering from confusion with acupuncture and homeopathics. However, not all dogs respond to treatment so each case must be dealt with individually. When treating with homeopathics each case is unique because of other factors that influence the brain's chemistry. For instance, a dog with liver disease can also show the same signs as a dog who is acting confused but has no other organ problems. Or a dog with a cervical (neck) vertebrae instability may also seem disoriented.

A confused dog can panic very quickly. Often panicked dogs will run and, because they are so upset, they usually don't hear an owner's commands. I've lived with several older dogs who suffered occasional bouts of confusion and found that once panic has set in the dog often goes in the wrong direction. One of my worst memories is of chasing my two older poodles when they both panicked at the same time and ran in opposite directions toward potentially dangerous places. I had never seen either of them panic so drastically. Thankfully, I was able to rescue both of them before an accident happened. But that was my sign that they would both need to be on leashes from that point onward.

If your dog gets confused occasionally, keep a leash on when in an unfamiliar area or a potentially dangerous situation. Take particular caution if your dog has additional problems that might further diminish his ability to respond, such as deafness or cataracts.

If you move to a new home it is especially important that you help an older dog become familiar with the location of the door and understand the new boundaries. I have seen some sad cases where a dog got lost in a yard and became exhausted trying to find a way into the house.

Lack of Energy

Many older dogs experience a decrease in energy. Don't just assume that a vitamin supplement will restore your dog's missing pep. If you notice a sudden decrease in energy, call your veterinarian right away to schedule an exam. Usually this lack of energy is a combination of a slower metabolism and medical conditions. For example, both arthritis and heart conditions can slow a dog down.

If the veterinarian does not find a medical problem, a diet and exercise program should be instituted. Although it is normal to slow down somewhat in old age, don't allow your dog to sleep all the time. Even a short walk can help the body to function in a more healthy manner. A high-quality diet of easily digestible food and appropriate supplements will provide the nutrients necessary for energy production. Additionally, special supplements such as yucca, kelp, and shark cartilage can be effective for older dogs. However, it is important to select the correct supplements for your dog in order to achieve the desired results.

Decreased Appetite

Some older dogs show a decreased appetite, even tapering off to very small amounts of food. This is not a normal occurrence. Many times when a dog stops eating, owners assume that it is because of an aversion to the current diet being fed. On changing to another food, the dog may be a little more interested in food but then the appetite decreases again. When you notice a decrease in appetite, suspect a medical problem and have your dog checked as soon as possible.

Decreased appetite can be a sign of several different diseases, the most common of which are liver and kidney disease. If caught early, these diseases can often be controlled. Another problem that can cause decreased appetite is a buildup of tartar on the teeth, which can actually cause abrasions and tears on the inside of the mouth. When this occurs, chewing and eating are uncomfortable or even painful.

PART TWO

Common Health Problems

Allergies

Allergies have become more common in recent years and are one of the most challenging aspects of veterinary medicine. There are several known causes of allergies and some proposed theories to explain this upsurge in cases.

The most difficult part of treating an allergy is figuring out what's causing the reaction. Is it an insect bite, a specific food, a plant or fiber sensitivity? Allergy testing is available to help determine what is causing the reaction, but this does not answer the most important question: Why did this allergy occur in the first place? Was the dog inbred and therefore predisposed with a poor immune system? Are there harmful chemicals in the dog's environment? Is the dog reacting to a stressful household? Have so many vaccinations been given that the immune system is affected? Is a diet of processed dog food affecting the overall health of the dog? These are all questions that we are searching to answer. As we deal with individual cases, however, we find that each case has unique aspects.

The problem of allergies has been around for a long time but seems to have increased dramatically in recent years. Research as well as observation have given us some answers and guidance; however, the more difficult aspect—relieving the dog of symptoms—can still be a problem. That is why diagnosis is a major piece of the puzzle. Occasionally your dog may be allergic to more than one thing, which makes it crucial that we understand the interaction of the various allergy-producing substances.

What is your role as an owner in combatting the allergy problem? Many owners feel that their responsibility stops when they take their dog to the veterinarian, but actually, it's just beginning. As the main authority in your dog's life, you have a great deal of influence on your dog's health. Excessive stress in the owner's life can be reflected in the dog, and some veterinarians believe that allergies flare up when the dog is exposed to additional stress.

One client who owns a young German shepherd started having allergy problems with her dog. The hair was falling out, the dog itched constantly, and nothing, except a steroid injection, seemed to help. Allergy testing of the skin revealed the main cause as insect bites. This same owner has other pets with the exact same problem, which didn't surface until a move to a new house a year ago. The owner was married, moved, and became pregnant within a very short time span. Interestingly, it was around this time the allergic reactions began in the animals. The owner was also extremely allergic to insect bites herself. After reviewing this case, I felt the owner was the root of the problem due to the stresses that accompanied this rapid set of changes in her life. On my recommendation, the owner saw a homeopathic practitioner who prescribed homeopathic and Bach flower remedies. I also suggested that she keep the dog as insect-free as possible while being desensitized. The program was successful for both the owner and dog. This is just one of numerous cases where it is so apparent that the owner plays a significant role in the dog's health.

The dog's environment can also play a major role in causing allergies. Owners who have had a succession of dogs with allergy problems want to know why every dog they get has developed these problems. That is when we start looking at the home environment and try to identify the root causes.

Skin testing is the most frequently used type of allergy test to identify specific allergies, because it is reliable and specific. However, this method requires each potential allergen to be tested individually, which can be cost prohibitive for many people. For that reason I often use kinesiology muscle testing as an alternative. (See "Muscle

Testing," p. 191.) Although kinesiology works well, it is sometimes difficult to test all the substances that might be causing the allergy.

CAUSES OF ALLERGIES

Diet

If you suspect a dietary allergy, then work with your veterinarian to eliminate from the diet as many ingredients as possible that may be causing the allergic reaction (i.e., beef, soy, yeast, wheat, etc.). If you notice an improvement in the dog's condition, you can gradually add foods back one by one to identify which foods have been causing the allergic reactions.

For many dogs who are allergy prone, diet may not be the main problem, but you can support the immune system and decrease stress on the body by keeping the diet as high quality as possible. When a dog is suffering from any type of allergy, I recommend a homemade diet. It often helps allergy-prone dogs because a high-quality diet gives the dog an edge in dealing with any health problem. An alternative is a food from a natural pet food manufacturer with lamb and rice, venison and rice, or rabbit and rice. These specific meats reduce possible allergens in the system. Be sure the food contains no chemical preservatives. (See chapter 6, "A Healthy Diet.")

Environment

There are some influences that we cannot see and therefore often fail to take into consideration when evaluating allergies. Take a close look at your dog's immediate environment to search for unseen or unnoticed allergens. Things to look for include Scotchgard on the carpet or furniture, carpet freshener powder (particularly the scented type), insecticides sprayed in the house and yard, air freshener, pollen, and smog. I had never considered smog as an allergen until living in Los Angeles, where I experienced a smog-related allergy with one of my own dogs. Often smog allergies are identified by simply removing the dog from the smog-filled environment to a smog-free area and noticing an improvement. (For more on chemical and pollutant stresses see chapter 9, "A New Standard for Your Dog's Health.")

If your dog is allergy prone, launder the dog bedding frequently using a soap with as few additives as possible. Decrease the use of chemicals in the dog's area whether it is inside or outside. Pesticides can stress a dog's system and should be avoided. If this is not possible try to remove the dog from the area being treated for at least 24 hours. Borax (as in soap powder) is a natural alternative to chemical flea-control products and is discussed in more detail in the flea section that starts on page 260.

If your dog stays in the house most of the time, change the filters in the air conditioner and heater at least once a month. This has been effective for dogs who have inhalant dermatitis problems (allergic to pollen, smog, or other breathable substances).

Immune System Deficiencies

Some breeds are very prone to immune system deficiencies. You must recognize this and do as much as possible to correct the problem. The most well-known breeds with immune system problems are Shar-Peis, West Highland terriers, Scotties, and Akitas. Each of these breeds has a different genetic makeup that contributes to immune deficiencies and becomes manifested as skin problems. As an example, Shar-Peis have a wrinkled skin and short bristly hair. They also have some unique skin problems. Because owners often come to a holistic practitioner after traditional treatment has failed them, my clinic is often the last hope for desperate Shar-Pei owners. This breed often tests to be low thyroid (hypothyroidism) and in many cases is nonresponsive to thyroid therapy. The reason for nonresponsiveness is that hypothyroidism is not the root of the problem, only a symptom. Many of these dogs have pituitary and/or thyroid insufficiencies, a necessary component in the stimulation of the adrenal gland. I have used a combination of homeopathy, herbs, supplements, and acupuncture to stimulate the adrenals and pituitary, which in turn stimulate the thyroid to function normally, causing the skin problems to disappear. Some breeds are not as responsive to therapy as Shar-Peis, but it is essential to understand the cause of the problem to treat or manage an allergy or immune-system deficiency effectively.

Symptoms

- Itching and biting the skin; red, irritated skin
- Sneezing
- Hair loss

Recommendations

- Determine cause of allergy.
- Eliminate the cause if possible and select the type of treatment that will work best for your dog.
- Decrease stress as much as possible.
- Feed a high-quality diet—homemade if possible. (See chapter 6.)
- Keep the dog's environment as clean as possible.

Animal Bites

(see Injuries)

Arthritis

Arthritis is a disease that is usually associated with older dogs, but may affect any dog at any age, particularly those dogs who fractured a bone at some time. Additionally, certain dogs have a genetic predisposition to this disease. Usually we do not realize that this is a possibility until there are generations of affected offspring. Arthritis results from the buildup of excessive bonelike material in areas where it should not be. It can occur on a bone surface or a joint surface and is usually the result of excessive wear and tear. Arthritis can also form when an area is unstable and the body attempts to strengthen the bone by adding more bone to it. There are many causes, including diet, that can contribute to the occurrence of arthritis.

If you suspect your dog suffers from arthritis, X rays are the best way to confirm its presence. Sometimes you can even feel a gritty, sandlike substance when an arthritic joint is flexed, or feel extra bone formation where it is not supposed to be. Once the diagnosis is confirmed, it's time to decide what can be done to alleviate the dog's discomfort. Each case depends on where the arthritis lesions are located and how much less movement has resulted in that area.

First, let's look at what problems have been caused by the arthritis. Pain is the most obvious, followed by loss of movement. Many other more specific problems are also possible, depending on the location of the arthritis. In Oriental medicine the decreased movement of *chi,* or energy around arthritic areas, is considered one of the main reasons for the pain.

To alleviate symptoms we must find what treatment works best for each individual dog. I like to start with an overview of the dog's lifestyle, including diet, exercise, environment, and medication that has been prescribed in the past.

First, let's look at the diet. Is this an old or young dog? Is the protein level excessive or not enough? What is the mineral balance in the diet? All these questions and more must be considered to properly evaluate the diet of an arthritic dog. Even genetically affected dogs can be aided through dietary changes.

Remember that Mother Nature designed dogs as carnivores, so their amino acid requirements (essential proteins) are best supplied through a meat-based diet. The dog's digestive system breaks down and utilizes meat-source protein most efficiently, so meat should be the base for the dog's diet. Occasionally dogs may be intolerant to meat in their diets—either incapable of digesting it or allergic to it. When this problem arises a vegetarian diet can be used with supplemental amino acids in capsule form. If a dog's diet is incomplete in amino acids, that alone can be a major contributing factor in arthritis formation, although it may take many years to see this result.

The mineral balance and source of minerals are also important. The dog's system must be able to break down and absorb the minerals in the diet in order for them to be properly utilized by the body. Oversupplementing the diet with one or more minerals can imbalance the system, also predisposing the dog to arthritic lesions. The mineral that is most often the culprit is calcium. Calcium must be balanced with other minerals, particularly phosphorus, when added to the diet. Most dogs do not require extra calcium supplementation, because their bodies take what they need out of their diet. Some of the most serious cases of arthritis I have seen are in giant breed dogs who have been given excessive amounts of calcium as puppies.

Many giant breeds cannot tolerate this excessive calcium and the result is a dog with permanent bone lesions at an early age. In other words, certain parts of the dog's body have developed faster than the rest of the body, and the body has tried to compensate by changing the shape of the bones. Mother Nature designed these giant breed dogs to develop at a certain rate and when this rate is manipulated, the results are often disastrous.

Once the diet has been checked and corrections made, it's time to look at exercise. Is the dog getting adequate exercise on her own? If your dog depends on you to walk her daily, then you must be sure to provide enough running as well as walking exercise. Even arthritic dogs require exercise to maintain their flexibility.

Aspects of the dog's environment are also important in specific cases, because it could be a contributory factor in the case of traumatic damage to a joint or bone. For instance, if a dog must jump down an enormous height every day, that repetitive motion could do damage and may eventually lead to arthritis.

Symptoms

- Painful, stiff movements or limping
- Pain and stiffness worse in cold weather

Recommendations

- Feed a high-quality diet as outlined previously and in Chapter 6.
- Vitamin C can provide relief of many of the movement symptoms of arthritis. Start with 125 mg and increase the dosage gradually. Most dogs can tolerate between 500 mg and 2,500 mg daily, depending on their size. Indications that you have exceeded the right dosage are loose stool and upset stomach. Be sure to feed vitamin C with the regular meal to avoid excessive acid in the stomach (vitamin C is ascorbic acid). Decrease the dosage if loose stool occurs.
- Homeopathic remedies. Consult your veterinarian to choose a homeopathic remedy from the following list, to help relieve pain and inflammation:

—*Arnica:* Give potency of 6C, 12C, or 30C four times a day
—*Rhus Tox:* Give potency of 3C or 6C two to three times a day.
—*BHI Arthritis:* Give three times a day
—*Zeel:* Give as directed on label

- Topical ointments and creams:

Note: Avoid counterirritants such as HEET, Ben-Gay, and linaments. Long-term use causes skin irritation and results are very transient.

—*DMSO:* Use only medical grade from the veterinarian; others have impurities that can be carried into the body with the DMSO. Skin must be very clean when used. Can be used after arnica lotion. Best results with DMSO are obtained with joint arthritis.
—*Arnica lotion:* A strong tincture of arnica in an alcohol base, which is rubbed on the affected areas. Decreases inflammation. Use on trauma areas and bruises.
—*Trameel:* An ointment that is anti-inflammatory. Extremely effective, particularly for acute flare-ups.

- Heat: When applying heat use a heating pad or hot pack. Heating pads should be the type with continuous water circulation to prevent burning the skin. (Regular heating pads can cause up to third-degree burns.) Use a towel or blanket between the dog and the pad and change positions frequently. Effects are only transient but can give considerable relief and relaxation.

Birth-Related Problems
(see Pregnancy, Birth, and Reproductive Problems)

Bites

(see Injuries)

Bladder Stones

(see Urinary Tract Problems)

Broken Bones

(see Injuries)

Cancer

There are many types of cancers known in dogs. I will review some general guidelines on this subject. Allopathic veterinary medicine has approached treating cancer in dogs much like it does with people—primarily with surgery and chemotherapy. Recently more alternatives have been available with holistic medicine. However, whenever you are dealing with cancer you must consider the complex nature of the disease. It's not just an isolated tumor or an affected type of cells (such as leukemia), but an entire body system that has allowed these cells to occur. Treating cancer successfully and keeping it in remission involves controlling the cancer and trying to support a failing body system, which is quite a challenge. In some cases it's difficult to comprehend that the body is failing when there is only an isolated tumor present. But that one tumor is the body's way of saying that something is very wrong, and it can't prevent these damaged cells from multiplying.

There are many approaches to cancer treatment and certainly many differing opinions. I'll give you some options and the reasons behind them to help you make your decisions. First I would advise becoming familiar with all the possibilities, then making your treatment choices in conjunction with your veterinarian's recommendations.

First you need as complete a diagnosis as possible. Some tumors can be easily identified as cancerous, whereas others require a biopsy.

Cancers such as lymphosarcoma can sometimes be diagnosed by symptoms and confirmed with blood work (laboratory tests).

In addition to identifying the type of cancer, the body's condition should be evaluated. A complete blood screen or laboratory profile will show how the body is handling the disease. This also alerts the veterinarian to any other problem areas that might require special attention. Radiographs (X rays) may be necessary if your veterinarian suspects metastasis (the spreading of malignant cells to other organs or parts of the body).

When all your dog's results are compiled, the veterinarian will make suggestions about specific cancer treatment. Here again you have several options: (1) to treat the dog, (2) not to treat the dog, and (3) to euthanize the dog if the disease is advanced and painful and the prognosis is poor. Sometimes when the disease has spread throughout the body and treatment is not an option, an owner can elect not to treat. In these cases the dog is kept as comfortable as possible with a high-quality diet and nutritional supplements. Nontreatment is chosen more often with older dogs that would not withstand the side effects of treatment.

I advise not rushing into any decisions until all the facts have been collected. Panicking and making hasty decisions can sometimes have unfortunate results. Cancers like osteosarcoma, a type of bone cancer, are difficult to distinguish from osteomyelitis, an infection of the bone. Osteomyelitis can sometimes be treated and possible amputation of the limb avoided. Sometimes just the presence of a tumor is enough to frighten many owners, and some decide to consider euthanasia immediately so their dog will not suffer. One case I remember was just that situation. A beagle named Snoopy had a large lump on his rear leg. The exam revealed a mass that was firmly attached and seemed to be part of the leg muscle. The owner did not want to pursue treatment and requested euthanasia. After much discussion, an exploratory surgery was agreed on and I performed it immediately. The mass turned out to be a granuloma, a thick fibrous material used by the body to wall off an unwanted area. Inside the granuloma was a 22-caliber bullet that evidently had been in the leg for quite a while. Although the lump could have been cancerous, it turned out to be benign, and the owner was extremely glad that he had agreed to the exploratory surgery.

Once the diagnosis of cancer is confirmed, the dog is evaluated for other health problems using blood work and a thorough exam.

At this point the entire case is reviewed for treatment options. Some considerations the veterinarian will review with you are the dog's age, current health condition, the time frame of possible treatments, and the cost of treatment options. Although the last thing to consider—money—seems difficult, often it's the bottom line. There are some outstanding treatment regimens available for cancer today, but not everyone can afford them. Time can be an important factor, because some treatments require a lot of owner care and many people are not comfortable with this. The condition of the dog's health is also extremely important, because it is the major factor in deciding which treatment to pursue or even if you are going to pursue treatment at all.

Many dogs with cancer are old and consideration must be given to this factor. The owner must discuss the following questions with the veterinarian: Are there other serious health problems? What would be the quality of life for my dog if treatment is pursued? Would the treatment substantially prolong my dog's life? Although these considerations are all on the negative side, the positive aspect is that there are many new successful treatments for cancer. The holistic approach suggests not only alternative treatment modalities but also relies on nutrition and a positive outlook. What could a positive outlook do for a dog with cancer? Remember, your dog is often a reflection of your feeling and therefore you can sometimes influence the recovery process.

One cancer case I remember from years ago involved a young pit bull named Molly. Detailed lab work sent to a special cancer treatment center revealed a lack of every immune response required to fight cancer. Her owner, Betty, had recently beat all odds and recovered from a near-fatal illness. Betty wasn't ready to give up on Molly, and her strong positive outlook seemed to have a clear impact on Molly. Surgery was performed to remove Molly's tumors, but the cancer had spread. If all of the cancer was removed Molly would have serious digestive problems. Betty decided to go for quality of life so only the major masses were removed, leaving Molly to function normally. After the surgery Molly did well on a combination of holistic treatments and Dr. Lawrence Burton's immunological augmentation treatment. The cancer was monitored with ultrasound.

During the two years I followed the case, it never got any worse. Molly didn't lose weight and when she seemed lethargic an acupuncture treatment would return her energy level to normal. So, despite the incredible odds against her, Molly survived and had a happy, quality life. Always strong in my impressions of Molly and Betty was that positive, happy attitude. I looked forward to their visits and my staff enjoyed them as well.

Many alternative cancer treatments are still being perfected. Holistic medicine bases its approach on supporting and healing the failing body, which allows the body to respond. In any type of cancer it comes down to the state of the body and what will help it prevent cancer cells from continuing to form. Acupuncture will stimulate the immune system and balance the body's energy so it can function. Homeopathy can be used to stimulate the immune system specifically against cancer and is also a good supportive measure. There are also a wide variety of herbs that have been touted to help combat cancer. My experience with herbs is that they can be very helpful, but each case must be carefully evaluated. Sometimes I use kinesiology muscle testing to help to make these choices. (See page 190.)

Symptoms

There are no specific symptoms for cancer.

Recommendations

- A high-quality diet—homemade is best. (See chapter 6.)
- Nutritional supplements:

  —Shark cartilage is a more recent form of treatment that shows great promise. Response depends on the purity of the product, so check with your holistic veterinarian to order it. Follow label directions.

- Upgrade diet and be sure to include a vitamin and mineral supplement from a natural pet food manufacturer.
- Increase vitamin C. While dosage varies, as a general guideline, give 250 to 500 mg daily for small dogs and 500 to 2,000 mg daily for large dogs.

- Give an antioxidant supplement such as Bioguard for Pets.
- Homeopathic remedies. Choose one of the following:

  —Cancerinum 6C. Give three times a day.
  —Nux vomica 6C. Give three times a day.

- Dr. Lawrence Burton's Immunoaugmentive Therapy: This therapy is basically homeopathic in nature. It is based on a very comprehensive set of lab work and involves a series of injections given by the owner. This program has a remarkable record and I have had good results utilizing it. It works well with other holistic treatments. The main drawback is the owner-intensive requirement. There are three to four injections given daily plus rechecks and follow-up lab work, which can go on for six months. Nutritional supplement recommendations and nutritional advice are included in this program.
- Electrical therapy: This program was developed in Sweden for human cancer patients. To date this therapy has been used successfully to treat animals who have external tumors.

Constipation

Constipation results when waste material does not move normally through the large bowel and bowel movements become irregular, difficult, or sluggish. This common problem often affects older dogs. Many less active dogs are prone to it as well. Constipation slows or halts the digestive process, causing stagnation and eventual putrification of food in the system, which leads to a buildup of toxins.

To prevent constipation use a homemade diet or a natural brand of dog food with adequate roughage. Dry food can help to add roughage to the diet or you can add cooked brown rice to the canned food you are using. For cases that need more of a laxative effect, add psyllium seed husks to the food; they mix easily with food and don't add any taste. Psyllium seed husks are commonly marketed as Metamucil but can be found in pure form in most natural foods stores and pet stores. Wheat bran is often added to the diet for constipation, but I prefer psyllium because it is more effective. Although mineral oil is also commonly used to treat constipation, I do not recommend it because it coats the digestive tract and decreases the body's ability to digest and absorb food.

In severe cases of constipation enemas are used to relieve the problem. I do not advise that you give an enema on your own unless you first talk to your veterinarian to be alerted to problems that might arise. The veterinarian can also advise you if giving an enema is contraindicated. For instance, if your dog was constipated, was showing signs of abdominal pain, and ate chicken bones the night before, an enema would not be the correct treatment because it could cause intestinal damage. Giving more than one enema within the same day can cause depletion of body electrolytes.

Symptoms

- Straining to have a bowel movement
- Passing only a tiny amount of fecal matter
- Feces are very small and hard

Recommendations

- Dietary changes to increase fiber and roughage: Feed brown rice (add one-quarter to one-half cup for small dogs and one to two cups for large dogs), dry kibble-type food, more fresh vegetables and fruits. (See chapter 6.)
- Add psiyllum seed husks to the food. Give 1 teaspoon mixed in the food for every 20 pounds of the dog's weight once a day. If using Metamucil, add a teaspoon and a half to the food once a day for every 20 pounds of the dog's weight. You can continue giving psyllium or Metamucil for five to seven days. If the stool is still hard at that point, consult your veterinarian.
- Increase exercise through regular daily walks and, if possible, swimming.
- Homeopathic remedies—choose from:

  —Aesculus Hippocastanum 6C. Give twice a day.
  —Aloe Socotrina 6C. Give twice a day.

—Nux vomica 6C. Give twice a day.
—Opium 3C. Give one to two times a day.

Cuts

(see Injuries)

Dandruff

Dry, flaky skin is another problem that is more common today, primarily due to poor diets. The hard part is to determine why this condition exists in your dog. Contrary to what we're led to believe in TV commercials, it's *not* just a matter of finding the right shampoo. Dandruff in dogs is an indication that there is a problem in the dog's body—something that requires more than shampoo to correct.

One of the breeds I see most often for scaly skin is Labradors, particularly chocolates. These dogs have a high sensitivity level to soy and do not tolerate it well in their diets. Because soy is a common ingredient in commercial foods, owners often don't realize their dog is getting soy in the diet until I point it out. Often just a diet change will clear up a dandruff problem. With dog foods you get what you pay for and cheap dog food means cheap ingredients. Poor-quality ingredients result in less digestible food for your dog. There is no rule that says dog food must be digestible, and often a dog with dandruff simply isn't getting proper nutrition.

In addition to changing the diet, I like to add nutritional supplements to improve the skin as quickly as possible. Adding a fatty acid supplement as well as a vitamin and mineral supplement will help ensure that a dog with dandruff is getting her nutritional needs met. Be sure that the supplement you choose contains zinc, silica, and sulfur, three minerals that have been found to help skin problems.

Symptoms

- Dry, flaky areas on the skin

Recommendations

- Upgrade the diet. Choose a diet that contains *no* preservatives, dyes, soy, or eggs. Good choices include lamb and rice (or barley), rabbit and rice, venison and rice, or, of course, a homemade food.
- Choose a natural vitamin and mineral supplement (such as Body Guard by Pro-Tec), which contains zinc, silica, and sulfur.
- Exercise should include daily walking and, if possible, swimming. If your dog goes into a pool, wash off the pool water after the swim.

Deafness

(see Ear Problems)

Demodectic Mange

(see Parasites)

Diabetes

Diabetes is a serious disease caused by an insufficient amount of insulin being produced by the pancreas. The body needs insulin to utilize glucose, the prime source of energy for the body, which is manufactured mainly in the metabolism of carbohydrates. Once diagnosed, a dog with diabetes must be continually under medical care and carefully monitored. Many dogs are medicated for diabetes and receive insulin injections just like humans.

If you have a diabetic dog, much can be done to decrease the amount of insulin required to control the blood sugar levels. The blood sugar level can be influenced by the diet, the type of insulin used, the number of injections of insulin given per day, and the home environment. The type of insulin used and the number of injections given daily are highly individualized so it will not be addressed here. However, the diet and environment can also be major factors in controlling insulin levels, and you can monitor these aspects of your dog's care as a diabetic patient.

The diet should be chosen carefully. It's important to feed a diet that is easy to digest so the dog will receive all of the necessary nutrients. Digestive enzymes should be used to reduce the effects of stress on the pancreas, an organ already compromised in a diabetic. A homemade diet is the very best choice; if you're able to, do prepare it. Special emphasis should be put on selecting a carbohydrate that your dog can readily absorb. Whether you make the food yourself or choose one of the natural pet foods, be selective about the grain that is used. Rice is often the best choice, but barley and oats are also among the most compatible and digestible for diabetic dogs. If you're not sure which grain works best for your dog, try using kinesiology muscle testing to check the various grains and use whatever tests strongest. (See "Muscle Testing," p. 191.) Do not use a dog food containing sugar or sugar products such as corn syrup. Any type of sugar will make it more difficult to regulate the insulin, so it's important to avoid it.

The home environment is important to a diabetic because stress is a big factor with this illness. The stress level in the home must be kept to a minimum to help stabilize the blood sugar. That means that all family members will have to cooperate. Review chapters 9 and 12, which deal with various issues of coping with stress.

Homeopathics can aid in stimulating the pancreas as well as the other digestive organs. The homeopathics work in many ways, and the use of more than one may be required depending on the case. Some dogs may have had other specific organs or glands that are overworked due to the failure of the pancreas, in which case the affected organ or gland must also be supported.

Acupuncture can help stimulate the pancreas and balance the rest of the body's organs and energy. I consider acupuncture an integral part of treating a diabetic, particularly in the early stages when the body is going through an adjustment due to the lack of insulin and must deal with accepting an outside source of insulin instead. After the dog is stabilized on insulin and eating a balanced diet, I recommend acupuncture about once a month, depending on the case, to help keep the correct energy balance in the body.

Symptoms

- Excessive urination; increased frequency of urination.
- Lack of energy
- Excessive water intake
- Loss of weight on normal diet

Recommendations

- Feed a high-quality diet—either homemade or from a natural pet food manufacturer. Make sure it contains no dyes, preservatives, or sugars. Check to be sure your dog's system can digest the grain used in the food. Rice, barley, and oats are generally easiest, but muscle testing can help make that determination (see page 191). (Also see chapter 6, "A Healthy Diet.")
- Specialty diets: Use the homemade Restricted Protein Diet on page 118 or a low protein or senior diet from a natural pet food company.
- Exercise should be moderate. Walking is best, but let your dog make these decisions.
- Homeopathic remedy: Iris versicolor 3C. Give three times daily.

Diarrhea

Diarrhea seems to be an ever-increasing malady among dogs. Why is there such an increase? The answer is not just due to one reason but several. First there has been a steady increase in the number of dogs in more densely populated cities. This has meant an increased exposure to many viruses that their immune systems are unable to fight off. And, unfortunately, there has been very little concurrent improvement in general health care. As a result, the spread of infectious diseases that can cause diarrhea has increased. While not all infectious diseases that cause diarrhea are as serious and potentially fatal as parvovirus or corona virus, there are many viruses that can cause just a few days of illness. Many of them are similar to the flu viruses that infect humans.

Another source of diarrhea is dog food. As I related in chapter 6, a common scenario at my clinic is a rash of diarrhea outbreaks following a new shipment of one of the less expensive or generic brands of dog food into one of the large grocery or discount stores. A slight change in the formulation or a substituted ingredient can wreak havoc with your dog's digestive system. A homemade diet or a reliable, well-formulated dog food can help avoid this problem.

Another common source of diarrhea is internal parasites. Whenever your dog has diarrhea, a check for parasites is always in order. Internal parasites such as roundworms or hookworms can cause diarrhea, particularly in puppies. Sometimes roundworms can be seen in the stool or are occasionally vomited. Lesser known internal parasites that can cause both diarrhea and blood in the stool are coccidia and giardia, both of which are microscopic. They are sometimes difficult to diagnose, because the eggs or organisms may not be shed in stool on a regular basis. Both parasites are highly contagious, so if one of your pets is diagnosed with one of these parasites, it is advisable to have all your other pets tested as well.

Stress can also cause diarrhea. I have seen many cases of diarrhea that were traced to the addition of a new pet or other change or stress in the household.

Now that you understand some of the possible causes of diarrhea, the next question is what can you do about it. If your dog is extremely ill or old, I advise that you take him to the veterinarian as soon as you detect diarrhea. The quicker the treatment is begun in serious viral-caused diarrhea, the higher your dog's chances are of surviving the disease.

For less serious cases—or cases where you are fairly sure you know the cause (such as a sudden food change)—there are some steps you can take to help your dog. First, understand that diarrhea is the body's way of coping with an illness, or trying to get it out of the body. If your dog is in reasonably good health and condition, and not a puppy or geriatric dog, I recommend withholding food for 24 hours. This rests the digestive system and allows the body to heal itself without the added burden of digesting food.

Before you decide to withhold food, check your dog's hydration level to make sure the body water has not dropped too much. Dehydration is serious and can endanger your dog's life. To check for hydration pull up the skin on the back of your dog's neck. If the skin returns immediately to its normal position, there are sufficient fluids in the system. If the skin stands up and does not quickly return to normal position, your dog is already dehydrated and should see a veterinarian immediately.

Symptoms

- Stool is loose and mushy or watery

Recommendations

- If your dog is in reasonably good health (not a puppy or geriatric dog) follow the directions for fasting on page 205. Fast the dog for 24 hours. When you start giving food again, or for dogs with diarrhea who cannot fast, feed boiled chicken (no fat or skin) with rice.
- Supplement the diet with garlic. Add one clove of crushed raw garlic to the food daily for each 10 pounds of body weight or give one capsule or tablet of Kyolic garlic (without yeast) for each 10 pounds of body weight. (Kyolic is also available in a liquid form.)
- Exercise should be limited while your dog has diarrhea.
- Homeopathic remedy: Ipecac 3C. Give three times daily.

Distemper
(see Viruses)

Ear Infections
(see Ear Problems)

Ear Mites
(see Ear Problems)

Ear Problems

There are a number of ear problems that can affect dogs, including deafness, ear infections, ear mites, and fly strikes.

DEAFNESS

Deafness is encountered occasionally in dogs. However, it is not genetically associated with white-haired dogs as it is with white-furred cats. I have noticed deafness more in inbred dogs—but it does not seem more common in any specific breed. It's difficult to diagnose a deaf dog, because most have developed their other senses extremely well in order to survive. For this reason, owners are often unaware that their dog is actually deaf.

I usually come across deafness accidentally during an examination. This happened when a dog trainer brought in a German shepherd who was difficult to train. The dog had been in training for two weeks and had progressed at a slow rate. While listening to the trainer, I noticed that the dog paid no attention to what was going on around her and overreacted when someone accidentally touched her or went near her. The trainer got the dog's attention by pulling on the leash, because the dog did not respond to voice command. When I inquired about the dog's lack of responsiveness, the trainer felt that it was due to lack of intelligence. Suspicious, I took two heavy metal trays and held them several feet over her head, banging them together slowly to avoid an air current. The dog never moved. Even when the test was repeated closer to her head and louder, she did not respond. After a few other tests and an extensive ear exam I diagnosed her deafness.

Deafness does not mean that the dog cannot be a good pet, but allowances must be made to accommodate deaf dogs. Do not allow a deaf dog anywhere near traffic. Be sure the dog knows when her food has been put down and where it is. Many dogs become deaf with age and since they already have a routine they are accustomed to, it is easier for them to adapt to deafness.

My own 17-year-old poodle, Kelly, has been deaf for several years and has adjusted well to the change. Years ago she learned hand signals when accompanying me horseback riding. Prior to her deafness, she would always range ahead and check back for a change in direction by these hand signals when she was out of hearing range. Remembering this, I began using hand signals with her again when I noticed the gradual loss of hearing, and she continues to function very well with them. You can learn hand signals from a dog trainer or from a book on training.

Symptoms

- Unresponsive to training; doesn't answer when name is called; doesn't respond to loud noises
- Overreacts when touched

Recommendations

- A complete ear exam is required.

EAR INFECTIONS

Ear infections are one of the most common problems presented to veterinarians—and one of the most frustrating to treat. There are two basic types of ear infections—bacterial and yeast. Bacteria and yeast make up the normal flora in a dog's ear canal, each keeping the other's growth in check. Ideally, a balance is maintained between them. If something happens to alter the conditions in the ear, however, either the bacteria or yeast might have more favorable conditions and multiply at a greater rate. In this way one of the organisms predominates and grows out of control. Then the ear is "infected" and causes the dog discomfort.

Several different types of bacteria and yeast can grow in the dog's ear, and the challenge is to select the correct medication to control the condition. Dogs with ears that hang over the ear canal and floppy-eared dogs are more prone to ear infections. The ear that hangs over the ear canal entrance does not allow for normal ventilation, trapping heat and moisture in the ear. This heat and moisture will often cause an overgrowth of bacteria or yeast. Dogs with long, heavily haired ears should be checked regularly for ear infections.

Do not try to diagnose and treat an ear infection by yourself. It's very difficult to tell a bacterial infection from a yeast infection. Treating the incorrect organisms will result in a worsened condition and longer recovery time. Sometimes it will even lead to a chronic condition. An herbal ear wash such as Halo's Natural Herbal Ear Wash works well to help keep the ear canal healthy and is especially useful when ear infections are chronic.

What does an ear infection look like? When infected, the ear is usually red and uncomfortable. Constant scratching at the affected ear is the most common symptom. The ear may be sensitive to touch, so be careful when examining your dog's ears. Sometimes there is a discharge; it can be white, yellow, or brown, depending on the organism causing it. Ear infections rarely go away on their own, so get treatment as soon as possible to control the infection.

Symptoms

- Scratching in or under the ear
- Reddened area inside the ear

Recommendations

For an Existing Ear Infection

- Wash the ear with Halo's Natural Herbal Ear Wash or an ear wash from your veterinarian
- Take to the veterinarian if the condition does not improve after using an herbal ear wash

Preventing Ear Infections

If your dog is prone to ear infections, here are a few steps to help prevent them:

- Put a cotton ball in each ear before bathing to prevent moisture from entering.
- Fix your dog's ears on top of his head with masking tape or a hair clip once daily for at least an hour to allow for ventilation. Be sure the ears are not clipped too tightly, or circula-

tion could be cut off. Although most dogs object to this at first, in time they get used to it.

- When your dog gets wet, fix his ears up over his head as previously described to allow the canals to dry after you've dried the ears themselves.
- *Do not* apply ear medication unless the ear is infected and the veterinarian has prescribed it. Some owners administer medication "for good measure," not realizing that this can upset the balance of the organisms and cause an infection.

EAR MITES

These mites are common inhabitants of the environment and regularly infect both ears. The dog will scratch at his ears, sometimes causing bald areas. The ear canal has a black waxy buildup that will continue to accumulate as long as ear mites are infecting the ear.

Because the mites are in the environment it's best to check the dog's ears regularly. Holistic treatments for ear mites are just beginning to be experimented with and are not yet in wide distribution.

Symptoms

- Black debris in the outer ear and ear canal

Recommendations

- Ear-mite medication prescribed by your veterinarian

FLY STRIKES

Fly strikes are areas of the ear that have been repeatedly bitten by flies. This occurs when flies congregate on the tips of the dog's ears; it usually afflicts outside dogs and breeds whose ears stand upright such as German shepherds. A bloody hairless area on the ear can result. This, in turn, attracts more flies, further aggravating the problem. This is a painful and irritating condition that causes the dog to scratch at the ears.

Symptoms

- Bald, hairless areas on the tips of the ears

Recommendations

- Use petroleum jelly to coat the ears and protect them from flies landing on the ears.
- A sunscreen can be used to protect the damaged ear from sunburn.
- If necessary, commercial products are available that have an insect repellent in a sticky petroleum jelly–type base to keep the flies away, so further damage can be avoided.
- Apply calendula ointment on wounded area.

Eclampsia

(see Pregnancy, Birth, and Reproductive Problems)

Emergencies

(see Injuries)

Eye Problems

The eyes are one of the most important areas to assess in a veterinary exam. Eyes are an interesting combination of resilience and delicacy—as some structures in the eye are incredibly tough, whereas other areas are rather fragile. The outer covering of the eye, the cornea, consists of layers that are relatively strong and dense. The internal areas are more susceptible to injury and more difficult to treat and repair due to their location. A certain pressure is always maintained inside the eye to enable it to work properly. If this pressure is decreased or increased, damage can result. Time can be a critical factor when treating eye injuries, so when your dog has an eye problem, get it checked as soon as possible.

If your dog receives a severe blow to the head, the eyes should be checked. An eye that has received a direct blow will often swell, resulting in an increased pressure. Medication can help to relieve this pressure and prevent damage. However, even if there is no noticeable external damage, internal eye injuries may have occurred. The back part of the eye has a large blood supply that can hemorrhage when severe concussion occurs, altering the pressure and causing injury to other areas.

Let's look at the common problems that affect the eye: allergy-related eye problems, eye infections, corneal abrasions and ulcers, glaucoma, and cataracts:

ALLERGY-RELATED EYE PROBLEMS

Problems such as red, watery eyes can be the result of allergies—much like those experienced by humans. This problem is noticed most often in the spring and fall when many plants are blooming and breezes are blowing the pollen around. Medication can reduce the symptoms and cold laser seems to afford some relief of symptoms. Occasionally injections similar to those used for hay fever are used to decrease the dog's sensitivity to the allergens; however, I have seen only marginal results from this type of treatment. Upgraded diet, acupuncture, and chiropractic can be used to help activate the immune system.

Symptoms

- Red, watery, itchy eyes

Recommendations

- The herb eyebright (euphrasia) is used to treat eye inflammations and other problems. Purchase a ready-made eyebright solution or make a tea by boiling 1 teaspoon of the dried herb in 1 cup of distilled or spring water for five minutes. When it cools, wet a cotton ball in the solution and then squeeze a few drops into the affected eye. You can repeat this treatment several times a day if necessary.
- Your veterinarian may treat with cold laser.

- Acupuncture and chiropractic treatments can help to activate the immune system.

EYE INFECTIONS

One of the most common eye problems, an infection can go unnoticed and cause damage to the eye. The eye may appear red and watery and may be painful, itchy, and sensitive to light. An infection can occur from bacteria or viruses that can be spread by touch or by air. Bacterial infections are generally more responsive to treatment than viruses; however viruses are not as common in dogs. Cold laser will help to stimulate the energy and circulation to the eye, hastening the healing process. Be careful when treating your dog's infected eye, because the bacteria might be contagious to your eyes. This is very rare, however, but it's best to use common sense and wash your hands thoroughly when finished. A variety of antibiotic ointments and drops are available to treat infected eyes. Most dogs respond well to these treatments.

Symptoms

- Red, watery eyes; may be painful, itchy, and sensitive to light

Recommendations

- The herb eyebright (euphrasia) is used to treat eye inflammations and other problems. Make a tea by boiling 1 teaspoon of the dried herb in 1 cup of distilled or spring water for five minutes. When it cools, wet a cotton ball in the solution and then squeeze a few drops into the affected eye. You can repeat this treatment several times a day if necessary.
- Homeopathic euphrasia eyedrops can be used two to three times a day.
- Your veterinarian may prescribe antibiotic ointment or drops.
- Treatment with cold laser can be helpful in combatting an eye infection.

CORNEAL ABRASIONS AND ULCERS

A scratch to the outer surface of the eye is called a corneal abrasion. It usually results in extreme sensitivity, redness, and sometimes a cloudy area. This condition is painful, making the eye sensitive to light, and your dog may guard the eye or try to protect it. Some abrasions are not visible and are stained with a fluorescent dye when examined by your veterinarian. The dye collects in the scratched area, enabling the injured area to be seen. Once diagnosed, the eye is treated with an antibiotic for possible infection. Cold laser treatment will help increase the rate of healing and aid in preventing infection. Eye medications containing steroids should not be used in treating corneal abrasions.

Corneal ulcers are sometimes caused by an untreated abrasion. In this case the ulcer is an unhealed area, usually circular in shape, that affects several layers of the cornea. Generally there is a cloudy area surrounding the ulcer, which can spread across the cornea, giving the eye a bluish-white appearance. Although the ulcer can be difficult to heal, there are many new medications that can assist healing, even those of long-standing. Often an antibiotic is used to protect against infection. Cold laser is very helpful in stimulating healing. One of the successful medications now being used for corneal ulcers is cyclosporin, which is dropped in the eye several times a day. Eye medications containing steroids should not be used.

Symptoms

- Red, watery, painful eyes. Dogs may try to rub eyes.
- Sometimes a cloudy, bluish appearance around the abrasion.

Recommendations

- The herb eyebright (euphrasia) is used to treat eye inflammations and other problems. Make a tea by boiling 1 teaspoon of the dried herb in 1 cup of distilled or spring water for five minutes. When it cools, wet a cotton ball in the solution and squeeze a few drops into the affected eye. You can repeat this treatment several times a day if necessary.

- Homeopathic euphrasia eyedrops can be used two to three times a day.
- Your veterinarian may prescribe antibiotic ointment or drops, or treat the eye with a cold laser. If the injury is severe, minor surgery is sometimes done to keep the eye closed temporarily and allow healing.

GLAUCOMA

Glaucoma is a condition caused by increased pressure inside the eye. It is most common in small dogs with protruding eyes, but is also found in many other breeds. When the pressure inside the eye is increased, damage can occur to the delicate internal structures. Often this damage is irreversible. If you notice your dog's eyes protruding further than normal, the pressure should be checked immediately by your veterinarian. There are excellent medications that can control this problem and save your dog's eyesight.

Symptoms

- Protruding eye, occasionally painful

Recommendations

- The herb eyebright (euphrasia) is used to treat eye inflammations and other problems. Make a tea by boiling 1 teaspoon of the dried herb in 1 cup of distilled or spring water for five minutes. When it cools, wet a cotton ball in the solution and then squeeze a few drops into the affected eye. You can repeat this treatment several times a day if necessary.
- Your veterinarian may treat with cold laser or eyedrops. Philocarpine is a common eyedrop medication used for glaucoma.

CATARACTS

Cataracts affect your dog's ability to see clearly. This condition often occurs with old age and involves a cloudy or bluish coloration to the lens of the eye. Although cataracts are difficult to treat with medications, surgery is now available to remove them from the eyes. This surgery is fairly successful and is most effective when performed early in the development of the cataracts. This surgery requires general anesthesia, however, so many older dogs with other health problems may not be candidates. There are few medications that can help cataracts, but vitamin C–zinc drops seem to give some aid in slowing or even stopping the progression of cataracts. In some cases vitamin C–zinc drops even diminish the cataracts. If left untreated, cataracts will eventually lead to blindness.

Symptoms

- Cloudy, bluish, or hazy appearance in the eye

Recommendations

- Give vitamin C–zinc eye drops
- Confer with your veterinarian about possible surgery to remove the cataracts

Fleas and Ticks

Dealing with fleas and ticks is one of a dog owner's biggest problems. Although fleas are found in both the city and the country, ticks are particularly abundant in the country. Ticks can spread diseases that afflict humans as well as animals, such as Lyme disease and Rocky Mountain spotted fever. An owner must be ever aware of both fleas and ticks and take concerted steps to avoid and control them. Most flea-control measures are also designed to combat ticks, so I will speak specifically to fleas in this section since they are a more common problem.

For those who live in colder climates, at least there is a break in the season. But for those of us in the South, the problem seems unending. Fleas can live inside as easily as outside, so controlling these pesky parasites is challenging. Here are a few facts you should know:

- Fleas can survive in carpeting for up to one year.
- Fleas can live and reproduce in vacuum cleaner bags.
- Dogs and cats share the same type of fleas.
- Some fleas carry tapeworms and infect your dog if eaten.

Most owners become resigned to the fact that ridding their dog's environment of fleas is an ongoing effort. Fleas can easily reinfest both the house and the yard. Also, your dog can easily pick them up on a walk. So it's better to think of this issue as "flea control" rather than thinking of totally eliminating them.

Flea-control options include flea bombs, sprays, powders, dips, collars, tags, flea combs, food additives, and skin patches. Let's look at each type:

- *Flea Bombs:* In cases of severe infestation, flea bombs have been the traditional method to combat fleas. However, the toxic residue makes this method undesirable. A nontoxic system used by the company Fleabusters gives the same overall answer without the problems.
- *Sprays and Powders:* Flea sprays and powders are designed to be "quick kill." Only a small residual amount of the spray is left on the dog's body. This includes both herbal and chemical sprays. Most chemical sprays today are pyrethrin-based; although they are effective, they have little residual or long-lasting effect. (Pyrethrin is actually a natural ingredient, because it is derived from chrysanthemums.) Although some herbal sprays can help in flea control, they vary in effectiveness, and some dogs have allergic reactions to ingredients such as pennyroyal and eucalyptus. When you buy a new herbal flea spray, try it on one paw first. If your dog is allergic to the ingredients in a particular product, you will see reactions such as red and itchy skin, which the dog will bite and scratch at. Flea powders are sprinkled on the dog; they are messy and require reapplication every few days.
- *Flea Dips:* Applied after a bath, flea dips are designed to stay on the hair and skin to repel fleas. Commercial flea dips contain strong pesticides that are effective in repelling fleas, but they are also toxic.

- *Flea Collars and Tags:* I don't recommend flea collars and tags, because I don't find either chemical or herbal types to be effective. The collars and tags that use chemical pesticides emit toxic fumes that are supposed to get rid of fleas but, unfortunately, both the dog and the owner have to inhale these fumes too. Many dogs react with severe cases of dermatitis, ranging from hair loss and scaly skin to open lesions. Many of the herbal collars and tags contain pennyroyal and eucalyptus, which dogs often are allergic to. The bottom line with both herbal and chemical collars and tags is that I don't find that either type gets rid of fleas.

  Tags that repel fleas using sound frequencies have gained some popularity, but I find them to be inconsistent in getting rid of fleas. I don't recommend them because we don't know how the sound frequencies being used will affect the dog's health over a long period of time.
- *Use of a Flea Comb:* This specially designed comb with teeth that are very close together allows you to literally capture the fleas as you comb your dog. When you do this, have a glass of water nearby with a couple drops of dish detergent in it to dunk the combed-out hair and captured fleas into immediately so the fleas will drown.
- *Food Additives to Prevent Fleas:* Food additives have been gaining popularity as an easier way to deal with fleas. But how effective are these additives? The main ones used are yeast, garlic, and a tablet called Proban. Proban's action is similar to a systemic insecticide, because it is dispersed throughout the body. When a flea bites the dog, the insecticide kills the flea. Since the flea must first bite the dog to be affected by the Proban, this product will only kill fleas *after* they have bitten the dog. Some dogs are allergic to the bite of the flea; this product won't be helpful if that's the case. Also, feeding your dog an insecticide can result in toxic problems in the future as well as put additional stress on the dog's entire body.

  Yeast has not been as effective as many holistic veterinary professionals had hoped it would be. Recent studies have found no conclusive evidence that yeast assisted in repelling fleas, and I have known only a few dogs that benefitted from yeast in this way.

Garlic has long been used to repel fleas and I have found it helpful, but it must be fed in large quantities or in condensed, high-potency forms such as Kyolic.

- *Skin Patch:* A newer item available to fight fleas is a spot-on product that is placed in one area of the dog's skin. Products like this contain strong pesticides, and I do not recommend them because I have concerns about how they will affect both the dog's and the owner's health.

Some dogs are extremely allergic to flea bites. This syndrome has steadily increased over the last 20 years, and the veterinary profession is trying to understand why. Veterinarians see many cases of flea-bite dermatitis. These dogs often have hair missing from their backs down to their tails. Some dogs are affected by flea allergies more than others, with hair loss extending down their legs and large bumps and infected areas on their backs. Each case is a little different and each must be treated individually when seeking to improve the condition.

The question that must be answered in order to be successful in treating a flea allergy is: Why is this problem occurring in this dog? Once this is determined, treatment can be initiated. Obviously, there is an immune system problem and we have to play detective to find the underlying cause. The possibilities include vaccine reactions, food allergies, environmental reactions, and genetic predisposition. Often just the signs of symptoms (such as itching and infection) are addressed without trying to treat the cause of the immune system dysfunction. A holistic veterinarian will look at the possibilities and try to find a treatment that will address the immediate symptoms as well as the root cause.

Symptoms

- Scratching and biting at areas of the body
- Pepperlike flea debris in the hair that you comb out during grooming
- Loss of hair over back, extending down to the tail

Recommendations

- Put garlic in the food. Give one clove of crushed raw garlic daily for each 10 pounds of body weight or two tablets or capsules of condensed, high-potency garlic capsules (such as Kyolic) for each 10 pounds of body weight. A higher dose can be used, but start out with this to make sure your dog tolerates garlic. Kyolic is also available in a liquid form that is easy to squirt into the food.
- Use a flea repellent. You may have to use chemical control for an extremely serious infestation of fleas. If so, use a pyrethrin-based product that contains Pre-Cor. This will ensure that fleas in all stages of the life cycle are killed. However, first try natural methods such as the following homemade spray that uses Avon's Skin-So-Soft as an ingredient:

Homemade Flea Spray

In a 16 oz. spray bottle, mix the following:

2 tablespoons cider vinegar
1 cup Avon's Skin-So-Soft
1 cup water
⅛ teaspoon oil of citronella (optional)

Rub into the coat to repel fleas and mosquitoes.

- Bathe the dog with a flea shampoo that is pythrethrin based, or use a regular detergent shampoo and leave it on for 10 minutes before rinsing off. (Flea shampoos can dry the skin, so DO NOT use this type of shampoo unless there is a flea problem.)
- Environmental control: When treating your home with any flea repellent, remember that fleas like areas that have a high degree of humidity so give special concentration to shady and damp areas. Always treat around doorways and corners and anywhere your dog or cat lies down the most.

FIGURE 11. Homemade Flea Trap.

—The Williams Flea Trap is a device which combines a small green light to provide heat and light attraction and a sticky pad which captures the fleas. Available in hardware and pet stores or check the Appendix for Product Suppliers.

—Make a homemade "flea trap": You'll need a night-light, a baking pan filled with water, and an electrical outlet in the flea-ridden area of your home. Plug in the night-light and place the pan beneath it. The fleas will be attracted to the light and heat. When they jump at the light, they will fall into the water and drown.

—Change the bag in your vacuum cleaner after every use or vacuum up flea powder into the bag to stop flea breeding.

—Sprinkle 20 Mule Team Borax (from the detergent section of the grocery store) on your carpets and rugs. (Always test a section first to make sure it will not damage the rug.)

—In the yard spray a solution of borax and water in all flea-infested areas. Discontinue use if your dog licks the borax-treated plants. Do not use on grass unless you test an area first.

—Commercial: A company known as Fleabusters operates in many cities in the United States (see Appendix). They will come into your home and use a nonpesticide formula to control fleas.

Fly Strikes

(see Ear Problems)

Foot Problems

(see Nail and Foot Problems)

Fractures

(see Injuries)

Fungal Disease

(Including Ringworm)

Fungal diseases are a chronic problem in warm moist climates and can be very challenging to treat. There are a wide variety of fungal infections that can affect dogs, and some are difficult to diagnose. The most common diagnostic methods are a skin scrape of the affected area or examining the skin under a "woods light" (black light). The skin scraping can be examined directly under the microscope or applied to a growing media to try to grow the fungus. If a fungus is present, there will be a color change as it grows; however, growing fungus is sometimes slow so don't get impatient. The black light can help diagnose those varieties of fungus that flourish, most commonly some forms of ringworm. Though its name makes it sound like a type of parasite, ringworm is actually a fungal infection. As it grows ringworm spreads in a circular shape.

Fungus can appear as a dry, flaky area, as a red, irritated area, or show no signs at all. It can stay in one location or spread to different areas on the skin. Fungal infections can also resemble bacterial skin infections, making diagnosis and treatment difficult. Why would we be concerned about the possibility of a fungal infection if no signs are present? If your dog has a fungal infection even though he exhibits no symptoms, he could be a carrier and pass it to another animal in your house. Some types of fungus are contagious even to humans. When multiple infections or reinfection occurs, a symptomatic carrier probably exists. While it is more common for cats to be carriers than dogs, I have found a few symptomless dogs who turned out to be carriers.

Treatment must be strictly adhered to since a fungus can be very difficult to kill. Sunlight is one of the best factors to assist in treatment, because a fungus thrives in warm moist areas and doesn't like sunlight.

Symptoms

- Hair loss, flaky skin, itching

Recommendations

- Betadyne solution, diluted 75 percent with water. Apply on affected areas.
- Bathe with Betadyne or antifungal shampoo.
- Be sure your dog gets lots of sunlight.
- Acupuncture will help to stimulate the immune system.

Gastric Bloat

Gastric bloat is truly an emergency. If your dog has the symptoms that are discussed in this section, take him to the veterinarian as quickly as possible. *Do not delay.*

This problem is seen predominantly in large or giant breed dogs but can occur in any dog. One of the small breeds that has occasional problems with gastric bloat is the dachshund. Gastric bloat usually occurs when the stomach is full of food and water. The engorged stomach becomes twisted on its long axis where the esophagus attaches to the stomach and where the small intestine allows the stomach to empty. Because it is twisted, nothing can pass out of the stomach and, as digestion continues, gas builds up within the stomach. The blood supply to the stomach has also been stopped and, as time goes on, areas of the stomach begin to die due to lack of circulation. Eventually the stomach can rupture, emptying its digested contents into the abdominal cavity. As the stomach begins to die or when the rupture occurs, the toxins in the dog's system build up and shock may develop.

It is essential to treat this condition as quickly as possible to prevent loss of stomach tissue and shock. Surgery must be performed to correct the torsion (twisting) of the stomach. After the corrections have been made in surgery, the stomach is attached so the torsion cannot reoccur. However, this severe stress on the dog can cause problems even after surgery is performed, so the dog must remain hospitalized following surgery.

As a preventive measure, the owners of some giant breeds such as Great Danes have surgery performed on the stomach so torsion cannot occur. One method to decrease the likelihood of torsion occurring is to give the dog only small amounts of water following meals. Water can be given freely two or three hours following feeding. Although not foolproof, this method is often helpful.

Why does this condition occur in the first place? There are many speculations, but the one that makes the most sense to me is that the ligaments holding the stomach in place are not as tight as they should be. When the stomach is full of food and water, it starts to swing back and forth with the dog's movement. Rolling or excessive exercise can then cause the stomach to twist around, and it is unable to get untwisted. Partial twists do occur occasionally, with the dog exhibiting the same signs as dogs with full twists.

Symptoms

- Occurs right after eating
- Depression
- Swollen abdomen
- Pain and crying
- Trying to vomit and cannot
- Mucous membranes are pale

Recommendations

- Take to the veterinarian immediately. THIS IS AN EMERGENCY!
- Homeopathic remedies: After the dog is home from surgery, give one or both of the following:

  —Carbo vegetabilis 6C or 12C three times a day
  —Calcarea carbonica 6C three times a day

Homeopathics to support the heart may also be helpful.

Gastritis

Gastritis is a medical term meaning inflammation of the stomach. In most cases this refers to the lining of the stomach. The body responds to this inflammation with symptoms that range from vomiting to decreased bowl movements, poor appetite, and lethargy. How would a dog get such an illness? Most dogs are carrion eaters in nature, and therefore they are attracted to any dead, putrefying animals they might find. The bones from these animals have sharp edges that can irritate the stomach lining. In addition, by the time a dog finds the carrion, it is often full of bacteria that can upset the stomach. Normally, when dogs eat food that is not part of their normal diet, their system compensates by producing additional enzymes in the stomach to digest this food.

There can also be other causes of gastritis. Foreign objects, such as balls and rocks, can irritate the stomach as well. One of my dogs got into the trash and ate some aluminum foil used to cook chicken, producing an irritation of the stomach lining. Gastritis can also be a stress-induced illness.

Listed below are a number of suggestions to treat gastritis. However, if symptoms persist for more than a day or two, call the veterinarian for an appointment as soon as possible.

Symptoms

- Decreased appetite
- Lethargy
- Decreased bowel movements or avoidance of bowel movements due to abdominal pain
- Vomiting

Recommendations

Note: If your dog is suffering from symptoms of gastritis, the following recommendations may be affective. If signs persist for more than one or two days, see the veterinarian.

- Feed only white rice or slightly overcooked brown rice. Feed up to 1 cup of rice for every five pounds of body weight.
- Give a stool softener such as psyllium or Metamucil. Mix into the food 1 teaspoon psyllium (or 1½ teaspoons Metamucil) for every 20 pounds of the dog's weight once a day.
- Homeopathic remedies—choose from the following:

  —Nux vomica 6C or 12C three times a day for vomiting
  —Byronia 3C or 6C if movement causes pain

- Herbs—give one of the following:

  —Pill Curing (a Chinese patent medicine). Give small dogs one-half vial; large dogs one vial.
  —Peppermint tea. Give 1 to 2 teaspoons twice daily.
  —Catnip tea. Give 1 teaspoon twice daily.
  —Chamomile tea if the patient is a puppy. Give 1 teaspoon twice daily.

- Aromatherapy—peppermint.
- Acupuncture treatments can decrease inflammation and help the stomach to return to normal functioning.

Heart Problems

Cardiology is being practiced with dogs more than ever before, making treatment for heart conditions commonplace. The development of new drugs to aid in the treatment of heart problems has allowed veterinarians to provide an improved quality of life for many dogs. It is important to have an accurate diagnosis when deciding how to proceed in treating a heart problem. Sometimes the veterinarian can make a diagnosis by listening to the dog's heart with a stethoscope. Other cases may require an electrocardiograph to measure the electrical impulses of the heart to determine the problem. These diagnostic procedures are easily carried out; there is even a service that provides them to veterinary clinics through a phone hookup. More advanced technology is also available if needed, and many diagnostics that are performed on humans are also available for dogs.

Most heart problems can be diagnosed without excessively stressing the dog. Once the diagnosis is made and medication prescribed, most dogs must remain on treatment. *It's important to give heart medication exactly as the directions state so the dog is provided with a constant source of medication. Dosages must be strictly adhered to because some medications such as digoxin can be toxic if overdosed.* I still remember with horror one owner who thought his other dog might also have heart problems and decided to give him the same medication and dosage that was prescribed for the dog with heart problems. In addition to medicating the second dog, he mixed the medication in both dogs' food, adding a little extra for good measure. Both dogs became very ill and required hospitalization. The man's effort to save an office call fee nearly cost him both dogs' lives.

Heart murmurs are the most commonly diagnosed heart problems. Heart murmurs are caused by a heart valve not closing all the way. This allows a little blood to pass through after closing, making the swishing noise that is heard through the stethoscope. Minor heart murmurs do not usually cause problems. As the dog ages, however, these murmurs may become worse, and medication can help the heart continue to beat in an efficient manner.

Homeopathy is a very effective form of treatment for heart problems. Many cases, if caught early enough, can be managed with homeopathics alone. Dogs already on heart medication can also benefit from homeopathics, which will improve the condition of their heart, sometimes allowing the veterinarian to decrease the regular medication. Dogs with very serious heart problems can have homeopathics added to their medication regimens with excellent results.

Symptoms

- Coughing and/or wheezing
- Lethargy and lack of endurance
- Distended abdomen (only in right-sided heart failure)

Recommendations

- Homeopathics—choose from the following:

  —Cactus Grandiflorus 6C. Give twice a day for endocarditis with mitral valve insufficiency. Heart feels constricted.
  —Digitalis 6C. Give twice daily. Use with valvular insufficiency where there is a weak pulse.
  —Spongia tosta 6C. Give twice daily when pulse is rapid, for angina or hypertrophy of the heart.
  —Crataegus tincture. Put 10 drops of tincture into a ½-ounce dropper bottle and fill with distilled water. Give 5 to 10 drops twice daily. This remedy is effective when arrhythmia (irregular beats) are present and causing the dog to cough.

- Aromatherapy: Rosemary.
- Diet: There is some controversy about the appropriate protein level for dogs suffering from heart problems. There are several special heart diets manufactured by pet food companies, but the ones currently available all contain ethoxyquin, a toxic preservative. I recommend a homemade diet with low salt content. See "Fix-It-Yourself Basic Diet" on page 99.
- Exercise: Moderate, regular exercise is important. For the most part, walking exercise is sufficient. It is important that the dog get this exercise and not be allowed to stay quiet all the time.

Heartworms

Heartworms are parasites that actually live in the dog's heart, posing a life-threatening condition. Heartworms are prevalent throughout the United States, and therefore most dogs are given some form of heartworm preventive medication. Because in this case the potential problem is so serious, even the most holistically oriented veterinarian usually prescribes a heartworm preventive. I recommend giving this drug, because I have found none of the natural methods successful. The heartworm preventive is available in forms that are administered daily or monthly. The drug should be prescribed by your veterinarian to coincide with the mosquito season in your area, because heartworms are spread by mosquitoes when they bite your dog. The larvae injected by the mosquito into the dog's skin take about six months to travel to the heart and grow to adult size. Do not assume that your house dog does not need heartworm medication. Mosquitoes get into houses, too, and most house dogs go outside at least occasionally. So even house dogs must be put on heartworm medication.

Each dog should be tested for heartworms before being started on a heartworm preventive. If a dog who actually has heartworms is given the preventive, it may kill them, but it can result in pneumonia and even death of the dog. In most states it is illegal to sell heartworm preventive unless the dog is tested or the owner can prove that a test was performed by another veterinarian. Puppies need not be tested if they are started on the preventive before four months of age.

Once the heartworm is in the heart and growing, great care must be taken to get rid of it. Heartworms prefer the right ventricle (the large lower chamber of the heart) and, if dislodged, will travel into the lungs through the blood vessels. These long worms resemble spaghetti. They are large enough to cause a reaction in the lung when they get stuck there. The result is a type of pneumonia that can endanger the dog's life. Heartworm medication is so toxic that it can kill heartworms; it is also very hard on the dog's liver and kidneys, which is why I so strongly recommend a heartworm preventive. Dogs with heartworms in the stage where they exhibit clinical symptoms such as coughing, lethargy, and abdominal swelling often require hospitalization.

There are three types of heartworm tests:

1. *Direct test:* In this test the blood is smeared on a slide and examined under a microscope for heartworm larvae or filariae. This test is not always accurate because the filariae may not be active or the adults may not have yet had larvae.

2. *Filter test:* The filter test is more accurate than a direct test but has the same drawbacks. In this test a blood sample is passed through filters isolating the larvae, making them easier to see. The blood sample is also examined under a microscope.

3. *Occult test:* This test is for antibodies to the heartworms. It is the most accurate heartworm test available. This method of testing should be used if your dog misses several months of heartworm prevention.

If your dog tests positive for heartworms, treatment should be considered immediately. Although heartworm treatment is very effective, it is also toxic so the general health and condition of the dog are important considerations in determining if the treatment should be undertaken. Precautions should be taken to ensure your dog will do well when treated. Each veterinarian uses a slightly different procedure in treating heartworms. So you will have some idea of what to expect, here's the way I go about it:

1. First, I evaluate the age and condition of the dog. An older dog with severe health problems or a thin, weak dog may not be a good candidate for treatment.

   Example: A 14-year-old English pointer was found to be heartworm positive. At the time of this diagnosis, she was thin and in the beginning stages of kidney failure. Because of her advanced age and degenerative illness, treatment for the heartworms could end her life. At best, the treatment would not make a big difference in her life span so it was decided not to pursue the treatment in this case.

2. Laboratory tests (blood work) are done to determine the health of the rest of the body. Liver, kidneys, and many other functions are checked through these tests to help us evaluate how the dog will withstand the treatment and how the body is

currently handling the heartworm infestation. Sometimes we are able to strengthen a particular area before treating for heartworms.

3. Start the dog on a supplement to support the liver. I use Methocol.

4. Consider acupuncture and homeopathics if liver, heart, or kidney enzymes are elevated.

> *Example:* An eight-year-old poodle was found to be infested with heartworms. The laboratory tests showed an increase in the liver enzymes, indicating that the heartworms may have caused some damage to the dog's heart. The dog was coughing, short of breath, and had a swollen abdomen. These are all signs of congestive heart failure and not very responsive to medication when heartworms are present. After a thorough evaluation the owner decided to try the treatment anyway since the poodle would not live long without it. In this case the dog was given a supplement to help support the liver (common trade name Methocol) and monitored closely. He came through treatment with some pneumonia problems developing a few weeks later. The pneumonia was controlled and eventually the dog recovered and is still alive four years later. The dog was also treated by acupuncture and homeopathics to help bring down the liver enzymes and support the dog through the heartworm treatment. These treatments were effective in reducing the liver enzyme level and the heart enzymes improved as well.

5. Check into different treatment regimens available. Most common is to use the drug Caparsolate, an arsenic derivative. It is given through intravenous injections twice daily over a two- to three-day period. An alternative regimen is being used successfully by Dr. Michelle Tilghman of Stone Mountain, Georgia. Her treatment does not include use of Caparsolate but has proved to be effective in killing heartworms, sometimes without its side effects. The treatment Dr. Tilghman uses was developed by Dr. Norman Ralston of Austin, Texas, and involves the use of antiparasite compounds given over several weeks.

6. Keep your dog as quiet as possible after treatment. The six weeks following treatment is the crucial period. Excessive exercise may push the dying heartworms into the lungs before they have disintegrated, causing a foreign body pneumonia reaction. If this happens it is difficult to control because we can't remove worms from the lungs.

7. At the end of the six-week period your veterinarian will give the dog something to kill the heartworm larvae still in the blood. Several different products are available for this, and each veterinarian uses the one he or she finds works best. When this procedure is done your dog should stay with the veterinarian for a day to be observed. Occasionally a dog has a reaction when large numbers of the larvae die, so the veterinarian must respond quickly.

8. Two weeks later the dog should be brought to the veterinarian again for a follow-up to see how many larvae are still surviving. Another treatment will be administered at this time to kill the larvae.

9. One week later another blood test for larvae is done. If it is negative, the treatment has been successful. At this time heartworm preventive is begun. If larvae are still present, the larvicide is administered again and the dog is rechecked in a week.

Hip Dysplasia

This genetically carried trait has infiltrated many breeds of dogs. Once hip dysplasia was associated mainly with German shepherds, but now many large breed dogs suffer from this condition, including golden retrievers, Irish setters, and rottweilers. This syndrome involves the hip or coxofemoral joint, which is a ball-and-socket type of joint that should fit snugly together. When hip dysplasia occurs, a variety of different syndromes can be present: the socket may be too shallow, the ball part of the femur bone may be flat, or the ball part of the femur may not be set deeply inside the socket. Whatever the syndrome, the effect is too loose a joint, causing excessive movement. The body tries to compensate and does whatever it can to stabilize the area. Over a period of time, extra bone forms around the femur bone, creating the additional problem of arthritis. Both the hip dysplasia and the arthritis are painful conditions.

Treating hip dysplasia is very challenging because it is an anatomical problem. One surgical solution to the problem is to cut the pectineus muscle, located on the inside of the dog's thigh, to decrease the tension on the joint. This surgery may or may not help your dog, depending on the individual case. Sometimes the surgery helps initially but as the arthritis increases, the pain returns.

Another surgery used is total hip replacement. This may seem rather drastic, and certainly should be avoided if possible. However, this surgery is now very successful and can be remarkably effective in extreme cases.

When a dog suffers from hip dysplasia, I review the dog's care, from diet to exercise. When a holistic health regimen is instituted I find that many dogs who suffer from hip dysplasia have a chance to lead a normal life. A combination of a high-quality diet, exercise, massage, acupuncture, and chiropractic is effective for many dogs.

Although there is no 100-percent effective way to avoid hip dysplasia when you get a puppy, I recommend screening for this problem as much as possible as suggested in chapter 1. Also, vitamin C influences cartilage development, and research has supported the benefits of feeding it beginning at an early age.

Symptoms

If you are considering adopting an older dog or trying to assess symptoms of hip dysplasia in your own dog, what should you look for? X rays will give the best diagnosis, but if that's not possible, here are a few telltale signs. Remember that these signs are not 100-percent accurate:

1. The dog will walk with a "wiggle" or sway of the hips.
2. When the dog sits down he will sit all the way over on the side of his hips, instead of straight down in his haunches.
3. The dog limps in the rear legs or has difficulty rising from a lying-down position.

Recommendations

- Feed a well-balanced, high-quality diet free of preservatives. Keep the weight normal. If the dog is overweight, the hips will be further stressed. (See chapter 6.)
- Add vitamin C to the diet. Depending on the size of your dog, dosage ranges from 500 to 3,000 mg a day. If diarrhea develops, lower the dosage.
- Be sure to give a good vitamin and mineral supplement each day.
- Acupuncture is very effective and often decreases or eliminates pain, allowing the dog to move freely again.
- Chiropractic can help to align the spine, allowing for correct movement.
- Massage can help to decrease the muscle spasms that develop when a dog is walking incorrectly and compensating for pain. The pectineus muscle (located on the inside of the leg in the thigh area) can also be massaged and loosened. It feels like a tight band. Ask your veterinarian to show you the location.
- Herbs:

  —Yucca. Give a pinch of pure yucca daily.

- Homeopathics—choose from the following:

  —Rhus toxicodendron 3C. Give two to three times daily; effective with arthritis conditions.
  —Hekla Lava 6C. Give twice daily; helpful when arthritis is generalized.
  —Arnica 6C or 12C. Give three to four times a day for inflammation and pain.
  —BHI Trameel. Give two tablets twice daily for inflammation and pain.

Hookworms
(see Parasites)

Hypoglycemia

Hypoglycemia is a medical term meaning low blood sugar, a condition that occasionally occurs in dogs. Overproduction of insulin or excessive exercise when not in condition are two possible causes of hypoglycemia. Heredity may be a factor in causing hypoglycemia, but an inadequate diet is also implicated.

Hypoglycemia is often first noticed after extensive exercise. Many dogs are in good physical condition, and yet are not able to deal with the exertion of extensive exercise. When a dog with hypoglycemia is exercised beyond the level he is accustomed to, the body uses up the available glucose (sugar) in the blood. It is then difficult for the dog to continue to exercise. He may become weak and even stagger or collapse. If this happens it is essential to administer a source of glucose immediately or as soon as you can get one. Good sources of glucose are honey, Karo syrup, or maple syrup. If none of these are available, other alternatives are candy (avoid chocolate if possible), Coca-Cola (not the diet version), jelly, jam, or a high-sugar-content food. Put a small amount of any of these foods directly into the mouth. It will be quickly absorbed.

Puppies have a very limited amount of glucose in their bodies and if this supply is exhausted, they can die. The toy breeds are very susceptible to stress, which can also bring on hypoglycemia quickly. For this reason, it's best to limit exercise with toy puppies and definitely limit playtime between any puppy and children. To help decrease hypoglycemia in puppies, add ½ teaspoon of honey per 2 cups of water. Use the honey water as the regular water supply until the puppies are four to six months old. It will provide a constant source of glucose and keep glucose supplies in the body high. It's okay for the mother to drink the honey water too.

If your dog experiences an episode of hypoglycemia, make an appointment with your veterinarian immediately as a precautionary measure. A hypoglycemic episode may be a warning that a more complex problem exists, because there are some disease syndromes that can cause hypoglycemia.

Symptoms

- Weakness, staggering, collapsing, or comatose state

Recommendations

For a Hypoglycemic Attack

- Give a source of glucose immediately or as soon as you can get one. Good sources of glucose are honey, Karo syrup, or maple syrup. If none of these choices are available, other alternatives are candy (avoid chocolate if possible), Coca-Cola (not the diet version), jelly, jam, or other high-sugar-content foods. Put a small amount of one of these foods directly into the mouth. It will be quickly absorbed.

Prevention of Hypoglycemia

- A high-quality diet will help to maintain proper blood sugar levels. (See chapter 6.)
- Keep stress to a minimum. Exercise should be moderate until the dog is in good condition.
- For susceptible dogs, especially toy breeds, add honey to the drinking water in a ratio of ½ teaspoon honey to 2 cups of water.
- Puppies should be monitored so they are not exhausted by prolonged playtimes or rough handling by children.

Hypothyroidism

The thyroid is a small gland located in the throat, which secretes the thyroid hormone. Various stresses can lead to undersecretion of the gland, which is called *hypo*thyroidism. (The opposite problem, *hyper*thyroidism, occurs when the thyroid gland produces too much hormone, resulting in an overactive metabolic state. This problem rarely afflicts dogs.)

Although certain breeds are more predisposed to hypothyroidism, including cocker spaniels and Shar-Peis, it can affect other breeds as well. Thyroid deficiencies are often just a part of a problem affecting a dog. When hypothyroidism is suspected, the veterinarian should do a complete checkup to identify any other areas of the body that may not be functioning properly and thereby affecting the thyroid.

A deficient thyroid condition can affect the dog's energy, appetite, skin, and coat. This condition can have some long-range effects, including skin infection and weight gain. Once the thyroid is adjusted to the correct functioning level, it is amazing how quickly the symptoms disappear. Thyroid problems are very responsive to holistic treatments. In particular, the diet should be assessed. Home-cooked diets are best for dogs with thyroid problems. By making the food yourself you are assured that all by-products and preservatives are eliminated from the diet. Additionally, you can supply a lot of *chi* or energy in the food by adding raw ingredients. Acupuncture is also effective because it balances the dog's energy and treats the thyroid. Chiropractic adjustments, particularly in the cervical area, are an effective complement to the acupuncture.

Symptoms

- Lethargy
- Weight gain; unable to lose weight
- Skin problems
- Dull, dry coat

Recommendations

- Upgrade diet; home cooked is best. (See chapter 6.)
- Give nutritional supplements as suggested in chapter 6.
- Acupuncture can be very effective because it stimulates the thyroid and rebalances the energy.
- Chiropractic adjustments will realign the spine and complement the acupuncture.
- Homeopathics:

  —Thyroid 4C or 9C; give twice daily.
  —Adrenal 6C; give twice daily.

—Your homeopathic veterinarian may find other glandulars to be effective, depending on the individual case.

Injuries

In this section, I'll discuss some of the common injuries dog owners deal with: animal bites, insect bites, snake bites, cuts and abrasions, and fractures.

ANIMAL BITES

When your dog is bitten by another animal, certain precautions must be taken. First, be sure that the animal that inflicted the bite has had a rabies vaccination. This is for your protection as well as your dog's, because rabies virus is communicable to humans. If a wild animal has bitten your dog, consult with your veterinarian immediately. Raccoons, skunks, and foxes are the leading carriers of rabies—although other wild animals could be carriers also.

Clean the bite wound immediately with soap and water. A detergent soap is the best because it will kill many viruses and bacteria. Once cleansed, examine the wound and determine how serious and extensive it is. If the area is badly torn or extremely deep, a veterinarian should be consulted. If your dog has been bitten in the chest area, there is always a possibility of a puncture wound through the chest wall—requiring an immediate trip to the veterinarian. If this type of wound is left unattended, blood can fill the chest cavity, and there is also danger of a collapsed lung.

Most bite wounds, unless they are very extensive, are not sutured because of infection problems. These wounds usually contain a great deal of bacterial contamination from the teeth of the animal who inflicted the wound. It's almost impossible to clean all the bacteria out of deep wounds, so unless extensive repair is required, most bite wounds are left open for more effective treatment.

Medications are given to prevent infections. The allopathic choice is antibiotics, although your holistic veterinarian may prescribe homeopathics and other natural medications. Also, to prevent infection, your veterinarian may treat the wound with a cold laser for several days.

Symptoms

- Puncture wounds appear like small holes
- Bites can look like lacerations

Recommendations

- Clean the wound with a detergent-type soap and water.
- Bach flowers: Use Rescue Remedy for traumatic injuries and when the dog is very upset. See page 160 for directions.
- Apply calendula ointment (available from most natural food stores) on the wound twice daily.
- Homeopathy. Choose from the following according to the type of wound:

  —Ledum palustre 6C. Give twice daily for small puncture wounds
  —Hypericum 6C. Give twice daily for tender, sensitive areas that have been bitten
  —Arnica 6C. Give three to four times daily if swelling and pain are present

- Your veterinarian may choose to use a cold laser over the affected area daily for at least three days.

INSECT BITES

Insect bites can be serious if your dog happens to be allergic to them. Unfortunately there is no way to predict that your dog will have an allergic reaction to a bite until it happens. If a dog has a close relative who has had allergic reactions to insect bites, there is a higher probability that the dog will react.

When an allergic reaction occurs, the dog may seem lethargic at first or begin to stagger as he walks. The area surrounding the bite may swell and the skin may turn red. Occasionally a dog may develop hives, but this may be difficult to detect because of the dog's coat.

If an allergic reaction is suspected, take your dog to the veterinarian immediately. Time is of the essence, because some dogs can die from a severe reaction to an insect bite.

Symptoms

- An area of skin may swell and turn red. (Because of the thick coat on many dogs, you may not be able to see this evidence of an insect bite.)
- Lethargy and/or staggering

Recommendations

- If you suspect an allergic reaction to an insect bite, take your dog to the veterinarian immediately.
- Homeopathy: Apis mellifica 6C. Give one dose, then follow up 15 minutes later with a second dose. A third dose may be given 30 minutes later.

SNAKE BITES

The condition of a dog who has been bitten by a poisonous snake will depend on when the dog was bitten, where the bite occurred on the dog's body, and how much venom was injected. For instance, if a large amount of venom was injected and the dog is small, the dog will have a hard time surviving without an antivenom injection from the veterinarian. Because you have no way of knowing how much venom was injected with each bite, it's best to take your dog to the veterinarian as soon as possible after a snake bite.

Do not rely on identifying the fang marks to make sure that a snake has bitten the dog. Most fang marks appear as tiny puncture wounds; often one is more noticeable than the other, or one fang struck one part of the dog's anatomy and another fang struck elsewhere. An example would be one fang mark on the nose or side of the face and another fang mark on the ear. This can occur with large rattlesnakes.

If one dog has been bitten, be sure to check the other dogs in your household. I know of several tragic cases in which one dog was rushed in for treatment and, when the owners returned home, their other dog was dead. It also helps to identify the snake so the correct treatment can be used. However, do not risk a bite yourself to make this identification. It is best to become familiar with the various types of venomous snakes in your area so you can recognize the species of snake. The veterinarian will also benefit from knowing the type of snake; this will aid in both treatment and in giving a more accurate prognosis.

Symptoms

Note: Symptoms are variable depending on how much time has elapsed since the bite and may include:

- The dog may appear weak, collapse, or go off and hide.

Recommendations

- If a snake bite is suspected, take your dog to the veterinarian immediately.
- Move or excite as little as possible.
- Do not use a tourniquet on a leg unless you do so immediately after the bite has occurred. If a tourniquet is used, loosen it every 10 to 15 minutes for at least one minute and then retighten it.
- *Do not* cut over the bite marks as seen in old cowboy movies.
- *Do not* try to suck out the venom. Venom can be absorbed into your body through any gum problems or cuts in your mouth.

CUTS AND ABRASIONS

Abrasions

An abrasion is an area that has been scraped but not seriously cut. The skin may be broken (but not deeply), and debris may be present in the wound.

Recommendations

- Follow these steps to clean and treat an abrasion:

1. Clean the area using water or a mild disinfectant.
2. Carefully remove any debris such as gravel or thorns. Try not to damage the surrounding skin tissue when removing debris.
3. Try to find out how the abrasion was made. If you can determine the source of the cut, it is easier to know whether there is a likelihood of infection.
4. If the abrasion was extremely dirty, there is a chance of infection. Watch for possible development of pus or redness with swelling and discharge. If it doesn't clear up within a day or so, there is a possibility the infection is going deeper and requires veterinary care.
5. Treat with calendula ointment (from your natural foods store). Arnica lotion or ointment can also be applied.
6. Your veterinarian can use a cold laser around the affected area to stimulate healing and decrease chance of infection.
7. Don't bandage the area unless you have to. Most bandages won't stay on, usually because the dog won't allow it.

Cuts

Cuts can vary in severity from deep to shallow and short to long. The main concerns about cuts are the possibility of excessive bleeding and deciding if sutures (stitches) are required to close it. If a cut area is bleeding excessively, the best technique to stop it is to apply pressure. For small cuts a finger will work. If the cut is large, use a clean cloth to help. Place the finger or the cloth directly over the cut and push down, applying steady pressure. If an artery or vein has been cut, apply pressure over the area for at least five minutes, then check to see if the bleeding has stopped. Sometimes a bandage must be applied over the cloth to keep the pressure constant. *Do not* make the bandage so tight that circulation is cut off. Check the area below the bandage to make sure it does not swell or become cold, indicating a loss of circulation.

To decide if a cut requires sutures, check the depth of the cut. A cut that is over a half inch deep usually requires closing, particularly if the cut gapes open and won't stay closed. Take your dog to the veterinarian as soon as possible so the cut can be properly sutured. If the cut is more than six hours old, the healing will be slower and chances of infection are greater. Infected cuts cannot be sutured, because this would seal the infection inside and create a more extensive infection, possibly an abscess. Your veterinarian will decide if bandaging is required.

Recommendations

- Choose from the following homeopathic remedies:

  —Arnica 6C. Give three to four times daily for pain, inflammation, and bruising.
  —BHI Trameel. Give one tablet four times daily. This remedy contains arnica as well as other ingredients for treatment of acute injuries.
  —Phosphorus 6C. Give as needed for excessive bleeding.

- Topical treatments:

  —Calendula ointment on the wound.
  —Arnica lotion on the area surrounding the wound.
  —Use of a cold laser can help to increase circulation and help to prevent infection.

FRACTURES

A fracture is any type of broken bone. Most fractures require identification and management. Do not assume that your dog will require a cast or surgery just because a fracture has occurred. Some fractures are best set with splints; others require a different type of fixation. The most important thing is to set the fracture and fix it in place so movement cannot occur. If movement occurs, healing is slowed or not possible.

If you suspect your dog has fractured a bone, move the area as little as possible while taking the dog to the veterinarian. If a back injury is suspected, put the dog on a board or hard surface so you can transport her with as little movement as possible. If bones have broken through the skin, cover the area loosely with a clean cloth while transporting. Keep the dog calm with Bach Flower Rescue Remedy. I also recommend Linda Tellington-Jones' T.E.A.M. touch methods, which are used on the tissue surrounding the fracture to help reduce swelling. This technique is described in her book, *The Tellington T-Touch: A Breakthrough Technique to Train and Care for Your Favorite Animal* (Viking Penguin, 1992).

Symptoms

- Not all fractures are easily noticed. Smaller or hairline fractures can have variable signs.

Recommendations

- If you suspect a fracture, take your dog to the veterinarian immediately.
- Give Bach Flower Rescue Remedy for trauma.
- Homeopathics. Choose from the following:

  —Arnica 6C or 12C. Give up to every 30 minutes to decrease inflammation and help with pain
  —Magnesium phosphorica 6C or 12C. Give three or four times daily to reduce muscle spasms

- Apply a topical arnica lotion (available at most natural food stores) on the area surrounding the fracture. Massage lightly into skin, particularly on bruised areas.

Insect Bites
(see Injuries)

Kennel Cough
(see Respiratory Problems)

Kidney Disease

Kidney disease is common in older dogs. It progresses slowly, with no outward signs until the kidney dysfunction becomes serious. Sometimes the signs of kidney problems don't appear until the kidneys are going into failure. At that point, the disease is very difficult to treat. This is yet another reason that yearly exams are vital for older dogs. While laboratory tests are the normal method of diagnosing kidney disease, a holistic veterinarian can check the acupuncture points or test with kinesiology to see if there are any developing kidney problems. Sometimes the acupuncture points will be sensitive before the blood enzyme values have changed significantly, giving an edge to this diagnostic method.

When clinical signs are present, the disease has progressed to an advanced state. Occasionally, however, a kidney problem is due to another factor and may be responsive to treatment if it is begun immediately. An example of this is ingestion of ethylene glycol (antifreeze). For some reason dogs are attracted to the taste of antifreeze and will lap it up if a small pool has leaked from a car onto the driveway. When caught right away and treated appropriately, the damage to the kidneys can sometimes be prevented. If too much time has passed, however, crystals form that are filtered by the kidneys, creating a blockage. Once these crystals are formed, they cannot be reversed, and the dog will die.

One of my own dogs, a miniature poodle named Coco, showed a rise in kidney enzymes on his blood work when he was 14 years of age. A combination of acupuncture, chiropractic, and homeopathy kept Coco's kidney enzymes under control and, with diligent care, he lived another three years.

To detect kidney dysfunction early, have your dog checked yearly for kidney problems. Blood work can confirm the results. In addition, monitor the water consumption and food intake. If an older dog's water intake increases or food intake diminishes, you should suspect kidney problems. Also, if your dog suddenly begins urinating in the house, kidney disease is one of the possible causes.

Symptoms

- Excessive urination
- Increased water consumption; finicky eater
- Decreased food intake; becomes very finicky about food
- Lethargic; staggering in later stages
- Vomiting

Recommendations

- Feed a high-quality diet with a good source of protein and high-quality carbohydrates. A homemade food such as the Restricted Protein Diet on page 118 is best. Do not feed organ meat more often than once a week. See chapter 6 for diet information.
- Homeopathics. Give Berberis vulgaris 6C three times daily.
- Acupuncture can also be very beneficial for kidney disease patients.

Liver Disease

This is one of the most common diseases affecting older dogs, and is difficult and challenging to treat. Liver disease can also result from other medical problems or diseases. When liver disease is suspected, blood work is done to determine what areas of the liver are involved and how serious the disease is. Without blood work it is difficult to evaluate the liver and thus decide how to treat the problem. In addition, other organ systems in the body may be affected, and the blood work will allow this to be evaluated at the same time. Kidneys are commonly involved with liver disease as well as heart problems. Once a total evaluation has been made, treatment can be decided upon.

Treatment for liver disease is challenging because there is very little to offer with allopathic medicine. However, holistic medicine can assist greatly with treatment of this condition. A variety of alternatives are used to treat liver disease, depending on what factors are involved. A complete diagnosis is necessary to decide what type of treatment or combination of treatments would be most effective.

Among the holistic treatments that are effective in treating liver disease are acupuncture, chiropractic, homeopathics, and herbs. Because liver disease often accompanies other diseases, treatment may need to be tailored to treat all of the problems, or a plan made to address the other problems as well as the liver disease.

Liver disease is a serious illness and rarely disappears on its own. The illness is often painful, causing irritability and depression. Appetite may decrease as the disease worsens. When liver disease accompanies advanced heart problems, the abdomen will swell. When it is very advanced, vomiting and jaundice can occur. Jaundice is indicated when areas that are white (such as eyes) become yellow in color because of serious liver malfunction. Stool can be loose with a greatly increased volume, or constipation can result.

Diet is also an important factor in liver disease. The diet needs to be low in protein, but the protein must be high quality. Cottage cheese is an excellent example of one type of protein to use. Many dogs with liver problems do not want to eat and cottage cheese often appeals to them. The fat content of the diet should be decreased as well.

It is advisable to get dogs affected with liver problems out into the sunshine for at least a half hour a day. If jaundice is present, the sunshine is vital, because it initiates chemical reactions in the body that help decrease the jaundice and stimulate the liver in a positive manner. Do not allow your dog to become overheated or sunburned when out in direct sunlight. If it's very hot, put your dog out in the early morning or late afternoon. If sunburn or rapid overheating is a problem, take your dog out for short periods throughout the day.

Symptoms

- Decreased appetite
- Irritability and depression caused by pain
- Vomiting and jaundice
- Swollen abdomen

Recommendations

- Acupuncture is very effective in decreasing liver enzymes and helping the liver to function in a normal manner.

- Chiropractic adjustments can help your dog feel more comfortable and ensure that no vital nerves that are involved in the liver's function are being compromised.
- Homeopathy is extremely effective. Choose from:

  —Nux vomica 6C or 30C twice daily. This works well in most cases involving the liver. Vomiting in the morning, particularly after eating, suggests nux vomica as the appropriate remedy.
  —Byronia 6C or 12C twice daily. This remedy is indicated when dogs are extremely thirsty, vomit first thing in the morning or immediately after eating, and may be constipated.
  —Natrum sulphicum 3C or 6C three to four times daily. This remedy is indicated in cases of jaundice; when diarrhea or watery stools are present; when vomiting occurs; and when the abdomen is sore, particularly around the liver.

- Diet should be low protein and low fat. Decrease the oil in the diet.

Mange
(see Parasites)

Mastitis
(see Pregnancy, Birth, and Reproductive Problems)

Metritis
(see Pregnancy, Birth, and Reproductive Problems)

Mites
(see Parasites; for Ear Mites see Ear Problems)

Nail and Foot Problems

All too often I see dogs with nail or foot problems that could have been avoided if the owner understood how to correct the problem. Many times just clipping the nails can help a dog immensely. Since we don't walk on our toes, and humans' nails don't grow long enough to interfere with the way we walk, dogs' nails often go unnoticed. A great many stifle (your dog's knee) injuries and carpal (front ankle) injuries could have been avoided if correct nail trimming had been done. Overlong nails interfere with correct walking, thus creating a problem.

Nails should not touch the ground when the dog is standing. If your dog's nails are too long, do not try to trim them back all at once. Gradually trim the nails back once a week to avoid cutting the quick and causing soreness and bleeding. If the nails are rough after trimming, use an emery board to smooth the edges. (Also see "Nail Trimming" in chapter 5.)

Dewclaws are the nails on the inside of the leg, slightly above the other nails. On most purebred dogs they are removed at birth because the attachment is loose and could be easily torn. Dewclaws tend to grow to long lengths because there is no wear on them. Check dewclaws often to ensure they are not overgrown. The dewclaws can curl as they grow and penetrate the foot. I once removed a dewclaw that had grown an inch and a half into a large dog's foot, an extremely painful condition.

Feet should be checked often for thorns, infected nails, cuts, or infections. Trim the excessive hair between the pad, both on top and under the pads. This will prevent excessive mud from building up, prevent infections, and allow your dog to walk properly.

If a pad is cut, it's difficult to stop the bleeding. Apply pressure over the pad. If necessary, cover the foot with a pressure bandage. (See "Cuts and Abrasions" on page 285.)

Pancreatitis

Pancreatitis, an inflammation of the pancreas, is a very painful condition that often accompanies liver disease. This inflammation can be caused by many foods, emotional upsets, or other disease in the body. Nausea or refusing to eat are some of the first signs. The abdomen is painful when palpated. If the pancreas is inflamed to the point of a decrease in digestive enzyme availability, digestion is also a problem. The feces might be gray or pale, soft, and smell like rancid fat due to the lack of enzymes.

Pancreatitis can escalate very quickly. Often there is another cause or more severe disease process that is resulting in pancreatitis. If you suspect pancreatitis, it's advisable to take your dog to the veterinarian as soon as possible. Blood work can be performed to confirm the diagnosis.

Symptoms

- Nausea or refusing to eat
- Abdomen painful when palpated
- Stool is gray or pale, soft, and might smell like rancid fat

Recommendations

- Dietary changes: Do not feed foods high in fat or oils; they can irritate the pancreas. To decrease the strain on digestion, divide the dog's meals into several small portions throughout the day.
- Give additional vitamin C (with bioflavinoids) two to three times a day. Dosage is variable but should be around 250 to 500 mg for small dogs and 500 to 2,000 mg for large dogs.
- Give additional vitamin E. Dosage should be 25 to 100 I.U. daily.
- Add digestive enzymes to all meals. Use a digestive enzyme supplement for dogs that contains lipase, protease, and amylase.
- Homeopathics: Choose from the following:

  —Iris versicolor 3C. Give three times daily. If symptoms are severe, give six times daily.
  —Iodum 3C or 6C. Give three times daily. This remedy works well when liver or heart disease is also present.
  —Pancreatinum (a nosode). Prepared homeopathically

from pancreatic extract. Can be used in conjunction with trypsinum.
—Trypsinum (a nosode). Prepared homeopathically and used to treat pancreatitis, particularly in cases where the feces contain undigested food.

- Aromatherapy: Choose one of the following:

—Geranium: works well when loose, frequent stools are present and hemorrhage has occurred.
—Rosemary: works well when the stomach is upset and liver disease is present.

Parasites

Dogs can suffer from internal or external parasites. We'll look first at the common internal parasites. Later in this section I'll review the common external parasites, with the exception of fleas, which appears in its own section.

INTERNAL PARASITES

There are many internal parasites that can infect dogs. We'll discuss the most common ones that your dog might encounter and that you may have to deal with—roundworms, hookworms, whipworms, and tapeworms. These parasites are readily detectable and treatable. Dogs should be checked twice yearly for parasites. If they go undetected, they can cause a great deal of damage to the intestinal tract and the body. Some parasites migrate through the body and various organs causing damage and scar tissue. Other parasites drain blood and nourishment from the dog. Excessive infestations can result in death, although this happens most often with puppies.

How can you get rid of the parasites that infect your dog? At a recent annual meeting of the American Holistic Veterinary Medical Association in Maui, Hawaii, I was one of a panel of veterinarians who discussed that very topic. The effects of worming dogs with holistic methods versus allopathic methods were compared. The allopathic methods were greatly favored by the veterinarians present because these treatments are highly effective, had few to no side effects, and caused the dogs no harm. The holistic methods involving herbs and homeopathics were not highly effective and frequently produced distress from side effects such as abdominal pain and diarrhea. Also, because parasites can cause extensive internal damage, it is important to get rid of all the parasites in the body as quickly as possible. This is another good reason to use the allopathic treatments, since the holistic methods require much longer treatments. I hope we will one day have natural treatments that are effective, but until that day comes I recommend the allopathic ones.

I do *not* advise that you buy worm treatments sold in the supermarket. Most of them are not very effective and they can result in severe side effects. I have seen animals die as a result of being given supermarket wormers. The wormers I'll mention here are available in pet stores and from livestock suppliers.

Roundworms

Although there are several species of roundworms that can affect dogs, we'll talk about roundworms in general. Dog roundworms can infect people; however, they do not come from the dog. People pick them up from infected soil the same way dogs get them, and they migrate within the body. Because the human is not the parasite's normal host, however, it often affects areas of the human body that it doesn't afflict in the dog. The eyes are one of the areas it can infest in humans, causing vision problems. In the South, parents must be ever watchful of their children. I know a number of rural families who have the entire family treated for roundworms regularly.

Dogs can be infected with roundworms through their mother before birth, swallow the roundworm eggs, or eat another infected wild carnivore. Since mothers can infect the puppies while still in the fetal stage, the mother should be wormed on a regular basis prior to breeding. Puppies that are infected at young ages may have worms that are too immature to pass eggs out through the feces. Therefore I do not rely on fecal checks in very young puppies to determine whether worming is necessary. Puppies can die from an infestation of roundworms that is left untreated. In the South, where infestations are heavy, puppies have their first worming at three weeks of age.

Hookworms

Hookworms are tiny worms that inhabit the digestive tract where they suck blood and leave bleeding ulcerations. Infestations can be severe enough to cause anemia and death in puppies. These parasites migrate through the lungs where they can cause further damage. Hookworms can infect puppies through their mother's milk, through ingestion of hookworm eggs, or through skin penetration. As with roundworms, do not depend on fecal examination for parasite eggs—the worms may not be passing eggs when the exam is done. In areas where hookworms are prevalent, worming starts at three weeks of age.

The larvae of hookworms can penetrate a person's skin and crawl under the skin, where they eventually die. This usually results in just a local irritation and is not a serious condition.

Whipworms

Whipworms can cause inflammation in the lower part of the digestive tract, specifically the cecum. Hemorrhage, weight loss, and diarrhea (sometimes with blood in it) can result. A severe infestation of whipworms can lead to weight loss and a general debilitated condition, sometimes opening the door to other diseases.

Tapeworms

Tapeworms are spread several ways in dogs, most commonly through fleas. When a dog eats an infected flea, a tapeworm develops in the body. We rarely see symptoms of tapeworms; however, some dogs lose weight, have diarrhea, and chew their feet or forelegs. Most often we see the larvae that are shed in the feces. The larvae appear as flat, white worms about one-half inch long. A fecal exam may occasionally show tapeworm eggs, but it is not common to find them during fecal checks.

Two commercially available drugs are used to treat tapeworm—Cestex or Droncit. I get good results from Cestex tablets, though both medications work well. Droncit is available in both tablets and injectable form. If it is being used, I don't recommend the injectable form.

When tapeworms persist after repeated wormings, I advise using a strong dose of garlic. Before giving strong doses, give your dog one clove to make sure he tolerates garlic well. One clove of garlic for each five pounds of body weight usually takes care of the remaining tapeworms. A high-potency garlic product such as Kyolic can be used in place of raw garlic. It's available in tablet, capsule, and liquid form. Give this strong dose of garlic daily for three days.

To avoid future tapeworm infestations, take appropriate flea control measures. (See "Fleas and Ticks," p. 260.)

Recommendations

Note: When giving a wormer, be sure to repeat the dosage as directed.

- Strongid T (pyrantel pamoate): Give 1 ml for each five pounds of body weight. Repeat treatment in two weeks. Nemix is a small-animal version of the same product. This wormer is safe for small puppies. Follow directions on the label.
- Rintal (febantel): Give 1 cc for each 15 pounds of body weight for three days in a row. In three weeks repeat the three-day treatment.
- Panacur (mebendazoli): Dosage is the same as Rintal, above.

EXTERNAL PARASITES

Fleas and Ticks

—See "Fleas and Ticks" on page 260.

Mange Mites

There are two types of mites that commonly infect dogs—sarcoptic mange mite and demodectic mange mite. They are not usually found together.

Sarcoptic Mange: This type of mange causes severe irritation of the skin and is sometimes called red mange. These mites prefer areas on the head, around the eyes, ears, muzzle, chest, and tail head, causing hair loss with dry, wrinkled skin. Affected dogs can lose weight and become debilitated. This is the most common type of mange seen in dogs because it is very contagious.

There is a variety of sarcoptic mange mite that is contagious to people. If your dog has a confirmed diagnosis of sarcoptic mange and you suspect you have it too, see your physician as soon as possible for diagnosis and treatment, if necessary.

Recommendations

- Treat with a dip. A commonly used dip is a carbaryl-based product called Paramite. However, your veterinarian may suggest another type that works well. Excessive hair or long hair should be clipped off before bathing so the treatment will be effective. The dip will be most effective if the dog is shampooed first. There is also an oral treatment that your veterinarian may use together with the dip. (See "The Bath" in chapter 5.)
- Aromatherapy: Use peppermint to help relieve itching.

Demodectic Mange: This form of mange can be transmitted from dog to dog. However, it generally affects dogs who are susceptible to it. Dogs can have a generalized form of demodectic mange if their immune system is deficient. This form is very difficult to treat successfully. There is also a form of demodex that occurs in small hairless patches that are located on the face or forelegs. This localized type can be treated with topical medication specifically formulated for demodectic mange or treated with amitraz, which is a dip for demodectic mange. Most localized forms heal without treatment in four to eight weeks.

Generalized demodex requires a combination of diet, immune system support, and other treatments so it will not recur. Demodex cases should be under a veterinarian's care since the dogs are susceptible to bacterial infections and abscesses that can escalate quickly due to the debilitated condition.

I have dealt with cases where the prescribed treatment did not work and the dog was unable to be freed of the demodex mites. Scotties seem to be especially prone to this condition. By using a combination of supplements to build the immune system, a healthy diet, acupuncture, and a variety of other modalities depending on the individual dog, the demodex can be kept to a minimum.

Symptoms

- Hairless patchy areas over the head and forelegs
- Generalized hair loss over the body

Recommendations

- Bathe the dog and use amitraz dip, which is available from your veterinarian.
- *If localized:*

  —Upgrade the diet and give supplements suggested in chapter 6 to build the immune system.
  —Use a topical medicated ointment prescribed by your veterinarian

- *If generalized:*

  —Upgrade the diet and give supplements suggested in chapter 6 to build the immune system.
  —Your veterinarian may use acupuncture and other holistic modalities as well.

Parvovirus
(see Viruses)

Pneumonia
(see Respiratory Problems)

Poisoning

It is often difficult to diagnose ingestion of poison as the cause of illness unless you have caught your dog eating a toxic substance. With many poisonous substances, time is not on your side; poisons can lead to death in hours.

Salt and chocolate are two common household products that can be fatal if ingested in too large a quantity by your dog. Salt can be overingested in the form of heavily salted foods such as potato chips, nuts, or popcorn. Dogs who do not normally eat people foods can be particularly at risk as their digestive systems are not accustomed to strange foods. It's best to keep your dog away from parties where bits of rich and heavily salted foods might be accidentally dropped on the floor by guests and eaten by your dog. Smaller dogs are especially susceptible to this kind of toxicity.

Pesticides can be dangerous if they are applied too strongly to lawns and gardens or if your dog chews a plant which has been sprayed. Most people are aware that pesticides made of toxic chemicals can be dangerous. However, even natural products such as pyrethrins and borax can be toxic if ingested by your pet. Symptoms vary depending on the type of chemical. An overdose of pyrethrins can cause excitement, convulsions, paralysis, or staggering (a reaction often seen in puppies). Borax can cause diarrhea, rapid prostration, or convulsions. Organophosphates may cause the dog to show a variety of signs depending on the type of chemical. Some of the most common signs are excessive salivation, pupils that have constricted to the size of a pinpoint, lack of coordination, nervousness, vomiting, or diarrhea. Many pesticide poisonings are treatable if the dog is taken to the veterinarian quickly.

Snail bait poisoning is often fatal. This poison is usually made of a chemical called metaldehyde. Convulsions, excessive salvation, and muscle tremors are a few of the signs. Many cases respond well to treatment only to have the animal succumb to liver failure a few weeks later.

Ingestion of rat poison can also be fatal. Usually there are no initial signs that a dog has eaten this poison. Bleeding from the mouth or the anus or noticeable bruising will occur after the poison has been digested by the body. (This poison kills the rat by causing internal bleeding.) If you suspect ingestion of rat poison, your dog can be safely treated by a veterinarian with injections of vitamin K if you catch it in time.

Other toxins that can be fatal to dogs include antifreeze, lead (from chewing on fences or walls painted with lead-based paint as well as other sources of lead such as buckshot), and toxic plants in the yard.

(Also see chapter 3, pp. 39–42.)

Symptoms

- Abrupt change in behavior (often the first sign of poisoning)
- Refusal to eat
- Staggering
- Seizures or convulsions
- Vomiting
- Excessive salivation
- Tremors
- Bleeding from the mouth or anus or bruising (if rat poison has been ingested)

Recommendations

Note: POISONING IS ALWAYS AN EMERGENCY SITUATION! If you suspect that your dog has eaten poison, an *immediate* trip to the veterinarian is necessary—*even if it's the middle of the night.* If you can, take a sample of the poison and the vomitus with you. This will guide the veterinarian in treatment.

Before going to the veterinarian: If the poison is not a caustic substance such as some cleaning solutions (which may do more harm if vomited back up) and no seizures or convulsions are present, induce vomiting as soon as possible. Give an oral dose of one of the following and vomiting should occur within minutes:

- Choose from

  —Hydrogen peroxide—1 to 3 teaspoons
  —Syrup of ipecac—2 to 4 teaspoons

—Table salt—1 to 2 teaspoons mixed in one cup of warm water

After emergency veterinary care, the following treatments should be instituted:

- *Homeopathy:* Give nux vomica 6X or 12X twice a day for two weeks. This is particularly important where liver problems might be involved.
- *Herbs:*

  —Milk thistle: potency varies by product so give according to label directions, adjusting for your dog's weight.
  —Dandelion: give 1 to 3 capsules per day depending on your dog's weight.

- *Acupuncture* can be extremely helpful in healing the liver and balancing the body.
- *Bach flowers remedies:* Use Rescue Remedy as long as a traumatic situation exists; choose other Bach flower remedies as appropriate. (See page 160.)

Pregnancy, Birth, and Reproductive Problems

To help assure a smooth pregnancy and birth, a high-quality natural diet is important. The homemade diet for puppies on page 119 is also good for a pregnant or lactating bitch. If you are choosing a commercially available natural dog food, look for one that is specifically designed for pregnant and lactating bitches or a puppy formula.

Sometimes pregnancy and birth problems are related to anatomical problems such as the size of the pelvis versus the size of the puppy's head. This is the case with many English bulldogs. Your veterinarian may be able to determine if a cesarean section birth is required because of this type of problem.

Other common problems related to birth and the reproductive system are as follows.

ECLAMPSIA

Eclampsia is a very serious and potentially life-threatening condition that afflicts new mothers within a few days to a few weeks after birth. It causes vomiting and weakens the dog so she is eventually unable to stand. Breathing is also difficult. It is caused by a severe drop in the body's calcium level. If it is not possible to get the dog to the veterinarian immediately, give Gatorade or electrolytes for infants (called Pedialytes), which are available in the supermarket. Then take the dog to the veterinarian as soon as possible.

Symptoms

- Vomiting, weakened condition, difficulty breathing.

Recommendations

- Give a half cup of Gatorade or electrolytes for infants (Pedialytes) every hour until the symptoms subside. Then give it twice a day for a couple of weeks thereafter.
- Homeopathic remedies: Give magnesium phosphate 6C once an hour until the symptoms subside.

MASTITIS

Mastitis, an infection of the mammary glands, is usually noticed a day or two after whelping. The infection may involve one or more glands, causing them to be swollen, hot, and sore. The milk excreted may be yellow or green in color. If you suspect mastitis, take the mother and the puppies to the veterinarian right away. The puppies should be taken off the mother's milk and be fed a milk substitute until the mother is over the infection. Some bacterial mastitis infections can cause serious illness in both the mother and the puppies. Usually antibiotics are prescribed.

Symptoms

- Mammary glands may be swollen, hot, or sore
- Milk excreted may be yellow or green in color

Recommendations

- Take mother and puppies to veterinarian immediately.
- The homeopathic remedy phytolacca 3C or 6C can be given four times daily until the breasts are no longer hard and inflamed (usually four to seven days).
- Your veterinarian will probably prescribe antibiotics.

METRITIS

This infection of the uterus may occur right after whelping or occasionally after repeated breedings. Most dogs experience a vaginal discharge for about six weeks after the puppies are delivered. A normal discharge is clear to light pink in color. However, if there is an excessive amount of green- to brown-colored discharge, a bad odor, or if the bitch is not feeling well, take her to your veterinarian immediately. An infected uterus can be very serious and life-threatening if not treated right away.

Symptoms

- An excessive amount of foul-smelling vaginal discharge that is brown to green in color
- Depression
- Unwillingness to take care of puppies

Recommendations

To prevent metritis:

- Give *one* of the following homeopathics:

  —Echinacea 3X. Give two to three times a day, starting right after the puppies are born
  —Aconitum Napellus 6C. Give two to three times daily, starting right after the puppies are born

To treat metritis:

- Consult your veterinarian

PYOMETRA

Pyometra, an infection of the uterus, is most often seen in older dogs. The progress of pyometra is often slow and symptoms are usually not seen until the condition is very advanced. Early symptoms are irregular heat cycles, vaginal discharge when not in heat, and depression. As the uterus fills with pus, bacteria invade the body and the dog can become seriously ill very quickly. Surgery to remove the uterus is usually necessary to save the dog, even in the face of severe illness.

Symptoms

- Irregular heat cycles
- Vaginal discharge when not in heat
- Depression

Recommendations

- Consult the veterinarian immediately.

Rabies
(see Viruses)

Respiratory Problems

The most common respiratory problems that afflict dogs are pneumonia and kennel cough.

PNEUMONIA

Pneumonia can be caused by a viral or bacterial source, though bacterial pneumonia is more common in dogs. A dog suffering from pneumonia will seem depressed and lethargic; usually there is a fever. Breathing may be difficult; instead of the chest moving as it does in normal breathing, the abdomen may be doing all the work. In severe cases, you may hear a wheezing sound when the dog breathes. It's best to seek treatment quickly if you suspect pneumonia, particularly with an older dog, since it can be fatal. An antibiotic is usually prescribed.

Symptoms

- Difficulty breathing; breathing from abdomen rather than chest area.
- Wheezing sound with breathing.
- Depression and lethargy; high temperature. A dog's normal temperature ranges from 101 to 102.5 degrees. A high temperature is above 103 degrees.

Recommendations

- Take to veterinarian immediately if pneumonia is suspected.

To assist with healing:

- Choose from the following homeopathic remedies:

  —Sulfur 6C. Give four to six times daily until breathing is better; then give twice daily for five to seven more days. Choose this remedy if a lot of mucus is present.
  —Byronia alba 6C. Give four times daily until symptoms decrease, then give twice daily. Choose this remedy when a dry cough is present and there is difficulty breathing.
  —Phosphorus 6C. Give four times daily until symptoms decrease; then give twice daily. Use when there is a cough, difficult breathing, and a dark red mucus is coughed up.

- Aromatherapy: Eucalyptus

KENNEL COUGH
(Canine Infectious Tracheobronchitis)

This disease is also called bordetella bronchiseptica after the most common bacterial cause. Kennel cough is most contagious when animals are housed together in closed areas, such as kennels or animal hospitals. Usually the disease causes a dry, harsh cough accompanied by gagging and retching. The coughing can persist for weeks. Though it is not a serious disease for most dogs, it can be debilitating for older dogs and serious for young puppies where bronchopneumonia can develop. Most often, though, the dogs become tired of coughing and the owners get tired of hearing them cough.

There are several vaccines that help prevent kennel cough and seem fairly effective. Most boarding kennels require kennel cough vaccination before allowing your dog to stay. The intranasal vaccine is best, with a quick, strong protection. (See the section on "Vaccinations and Nosodes" in chapter 10, p. 183, for more information.)

Because this syndrome does not respond well to treatment, it's best to support your dog, try to suppress the cough, and wait for three weeks or so until it runs its course. Avoid stressing your dog so recovery can be complete. I once continued traveling with one of my dogs while he had kennel cough, and the extra stress caused the disease to recur only four weeks after the first episode was over.

Symptoms

- Dry, harsh, persistent cough, sometimes accompanied by gagging and retching.

Recommendations

- Give a liquid cough suppressant from a natural food store. Most stores carry a wide variety. Dogs prefer slippery elm and horehound flavors.
- Feed a high-quality natural diet.
- Increase the vitamin C in the diet. For small dogs, give 250 to 500 mg daily. For large dogs, give 500 to 2,000 mg daily.
- Give 1 clove of raw minced garlic or a high potency garlic

such as Kyolic (2 capsules or 1 teaspoon liquid garlic) for each 20 pounds of body weight.

- Increase the vitamin E in the diet. Give 25 to 100 I.U. daily.
- Give peppermint tea to reduce coughing.
- Aromatherapy: Use peppermint to suppress the cough.

Ringworm

(see Fungal Disease)

Roundworms

(see Parasites)

Skin Problems

There are many conditions that can affect the health of your dog's skin, including parasites, bacterial and fungal infections, metabolic imbalances, poor diet, and genetic makeup. The difficulty in treating skin problems is to decide which influence or combination of influences is the culprit. This section will help you narrow down the possible cause for a skin problem and list steps you can take to improve the condition.

DIETARY DEFICIENCIES

Sometimes the basic diet does not supply the correct nutrients, but there are also cases where the dog is being fed a balanced diet but does not absorb the correct nutrients, thus creating a deficiency. If the basic diet is the problem, it's best to do a complete review of the diet: What is the protein source of the food? Are the minerals in a form that is being absorbed? Is there is a possible allergy to any ingredients in the food?

As discussed in chapter 6, the best protein sources are from human-food-quality protein, preferably poultry and lamb. Soy proteins are not well digested by dogs and therefore not fully utilized by the body. In addition, some dogs do not do well on soy proteins due to a food allergy. When a dog has skin problems, it's best to feed a high-quality diet that does not contain soy protein, uses a less reactive form of protein such as lamb or venison, and contains a readily available source of carbohydrates such as rice, barley, or corn.

The mineral availability is a more difficult problem because sources of minerals are not usually listed on the label of commercial dog foods. The most important minerals in a dog's diet are zinc, magnesium, calcium, and phosphorus. The other minerals are important also, but a deficiency of one or more of these four minerals can affect the condition of the skin.

Of these minerals zinc is especially important because it has a great influence on skin condition. Dogs deficient in zinc have sparse hair, a moist feel to their coat, and varying degrees of skin irritation. Some dogs respond well to supplemental zinc in their diets, whereas others may have a problem that prohibits them from absorbing and utilizing zinc. Dogs rarely have a zinc deficiency alone so if a zinc deficiency is evident, the metabolism should be evaluated to make sure there are no other diseases present.

I suggest supplementing the minerals in the form of a multiple vitamin and mineral supplement or with specific isolated minerals. However, a vitamin and mineral supplement is usually the best choice, because it will help ensure that all the vitamins and minerals that are lacking or deficient in your dog's diet will be supplied.

There are a variety of supplements on the market especially formulated to maintain the health of your dog's skin. Some of the newest ones, such as Pro-Tec's Body Guard, contain sulfur as well. Sulfur works well when a dog has a constant source of bacterial infection such as a chronic teeth problem, which keeps the dog's system bombarded with bacteria. Feeding a supplement that contains sulfur can help to keep this bacteria reduced. Although there are other reasons that the sulfur might help your dog, feeding sulfur on a constant basis might not be advisable. The sulfur influences many other parts of the body besides the skin, particularly the digestion. I like to give the dog's system a break every four weeks by eliminating the sulfur for a five-day period.

I also frequently prescribe digestive enzymes when a dog has skin problems. These enzymes aid in the proper digestion of the food, allowing the body to fully utilize all of the nutrients in the diet.

Many dogs, particularly older ones, have pancreatic deficiencies of the digestive enzymes.

Protein and mineral deficiencies are often seen after whelping. Because the new mother has a great demand on her system to provide milk for the puppies, her body draws on its own resources if her diet is lacking. Most mothers lose some weight during the nursing process, but this should not be extreme and the coat should stay in good condition. If you notice a mother has begun to lose her hair and has lost considerable weight, there is a good chance that her diet is deficient in protein and possibly carbohydrates.

MEDICAL INFLUENCES

There are many health problems that can affect a dog's skin. Some of the main ones include fungus, bacterial infections, Cushing's syndrome, and parasites.

Fungus is a common problem, particularly in hot, moist climates. The most common signs are patchy hair loss, itching, and flaky skin. There are a variety of fungi that can infect dogs, including fungi from cats, horses, and cattle. Each area of the country has slightly different fungi that flourish, so check with your veterinarian if you suspect a fungus. (See also "Fungal Disease," p. 266.)

Bacterial infections are commonly found on dogs and can accompany another disease. One of the bacteria that most often causes infections is the family called staphylococcal. This bacterium normally inhabits the skin so it is already on the scene if an opportunity should arise to support further growth. This is how "hot spots" occur. The dog licks or chews an area and the saliva acts as an excellent growth medium for the bacteria to flourish. The result is a red, infected area that causes further discomfort to the dog. This problem often occurs in the spring and early summer when the undercoat is shedding and there are areas where a dark, moist environment is available for the unchecked bacteria to grow.

Another form of skin infection is a more generalized type that extends over larger parts of the dog's body. The rear legs and abdomen are often afflicted with red, itchy skin with small pustules (a pimple or blister that contains pus). The causes for the more generalized type of skin infection are variable, ranging from infected anal glands to a deficient immune system. Because of the difficulty in diagnosing a cause, this type of infection is more difficult to treat. The traditional treatment is to put the dog on antibiotics, which will kill the bacterial infection. If the underlying cause of the infection is not dealt with, however, the infection is likely to return. If the immune system is involved, the treatment must include some steps to help support and stimulate it. Acupuncture, nutritional supplements, and herbs are just a few of the treatments that are used. If steroids have been given in the past, the treatment may be more challenging, because steroids suppress the immune system even further. Each case must be treated individually, and all the controllable alternatives should be addressed. There are no easy answers when dealing with chronic bacterial infections.

An example of a disease that affects the skin is Cushing's syndrome, which is caused by excessive levels of cortisol in the body. This disease can be caused by an internal problem affecting the adrenal gland (or one of the other glands that controls the adrenal gland) or by excess levels of steroids that were prescribed in the past. Symptoms of Cushing's syndrome include thin, wrinkled skin that is rough and dry and fragile hair that breaks easily. There may also be areas where there is no hair at all; usually this hair loss is on the neck and the body. Also common are mineralized areas that appear as hardened spots. These are just a few of the main symptoms that demonstrate how a glandular dysfunction can affect the skin. Treatment for Cushing's syndrome is complex and often unrewarding. Even if the problem has been induced by excessive steroid levels, taking away the steroid medication usually does not correct the imbalance.

When considering the cause of a hair loss, always look carefully at where it has occurred. This may be the main clue as to the reason for the hair loss. Ear mites often cause intense itching, and therefore, scratching, of the ears, resulting in hairless areas around them. Ear mites are readily treatable, making this cause of hair loss something that can be corrected or avoided completely.

Another example of a local problem with hair loss are lick granulomas. These are areas where the hair loss begins when the dog bites one area on the leg, usually the front, and continues until the hair is gone and a chronic open lesion is present. These areas continue to be a source of irritation for the dog and they stay open, refusing to heal. First the source of the problem must be found. Lick granulomas may be caused by tapeworm infection (fairly easy to resolve) or a more complex problem. I have sometimes found the answer by comparing the area licked with the corresponding acupuncture point, which guides me to the affected area. Even if the answer cannot be found, the granuloma can be treated with a combination of acupuncture, homeopathy, and herbs. Most are successfully healed.

PARASITES

The most common parasites that affect the skin are fleas, mites, and hookworms. Fleas are discussed on page 260; mites and hookworms are discussed in the section on parasites (p. 295).

Always keep in mind that fleas are responsible for a large majority of the skin problems seen in dogs. A continuing program of flea control is the best way to fight the flea problem. Do not think you can treat the dog or your yard once and achieve complete control throughout the flea season. Fleas can be the culprit that cause the dog to start itching and result in a "hot spot" or generalized skin infection. Mites and hookworms can also result in skin problems, so be sure to check for them too if your dog has an undiagnosed skin problem.

SKIN CARE

Proper skin care includes bathing, frequent brushing, and inspection of your dog's skin. Inspection can be the most important step in controlling skin problems before they become serious, or to prevent them from developing in the first place. For instance, many dogs have a lot of hair that grows between their toes. This excessive hair can act as a wick for moisture, drawing saliva or water deeper in between the pads. The moisture acts as a medium for bacteria to grow, resulting in a bacterial dermatitis. By keeping the hair inside the pads trimmed and by checking regularly for any signs of irritation, a full-scale infection can be avoided. These inspections are particularly important for older dogs or dogs already compromised by health problems. Avoiding a skin problem could save the dog a great deal of stress on the immune system.

Refer to the section on bathing in chapter 5 for directions. Bathing a dog with skin problems can be confusing with all the shampoos and rinses on the market. Here is a guide to help you:

Skin Condition	*Shampoo*	*Rinse*
Moist, itchy, red, infected	Benzyl peroxide	Oatmeal-type rinse
Fungal infection	Betadyne shampoo	¼ Betadyne solution with ¾ water. Leave on the skin.
Dry skin	Coal tar shampoo	Oatmeal- or cream-type rinse
Infected skin	Betadyne or sulfur shampoo	Betadyne solution

Cider vinegar is another type of rinse that is effective for irritated skin, diluted 50 percent with water. This rinse can affect the pH balance of the skin, resulting in a less desirable environment for bacteria.

Snake Bites

(see Injuries)

Tapeworms

(see Parasites)

Thyroid Problems

(see Hypothyroidism)

Tooth and Gum Problems

Tooth problems are often overlooked until they are severe and require immediate attention. Regular checkups to prevent advanced periodontal disease and gingivitis (infected gums) are an important part of your dog's health care.

Severe tartar buildup on the teeth can push against the gums, creating pockets that become infected. The gums will gradually recede, creating open areas where food and debris can collect, resulting in further problems. This condition can take years to develop so it's important to check your dog's teeth regularly to catch it before it worsens.

One of my poodles, Lily, has constant problems with her teeth no matter what I do to prevent tartar. The best solution I have found is to brush her teeth daily. This may be an option for your dog. (For more on cleaning teeth, see chapter 5.)

If the teeth aren't kept clean and bacterial infections develop, the rest of the body can be affected because the bacteria are shed directly into the bloodstream. It can take years to see the total effects of the bacteria that have infected the body. Heart valve disease is one example. Traveling bacteria can grow on the heart valve, leading to a heart murmur years later. There is speculation that other bacteria found in the body also originate from the teeth, causing bladder infections, uterine infections, and arthritis.

Dental cleaning usually needs to be performed at the veterinary hospital. Although anesthesia is frequently required, many dogs are cooperative and can have their teeth cleaned without it. If the procedure can be done without anesthesia, its side effects can be avoided, which is especially important for older dogs and those that are debilitated by illnesses.

If you notice that your puppy's teeth are not coming in straight or the baby teeth (deciduous teeth) have not fallen out when the permanent teeth came in, the puppy needs to be evaluated to determine the best course of treatment. Often an extraction is required to correct the problem. Your regular veterinarian will probably be able to handle this problem, but if not, there are also specialists in veterinary dentistry in most larger cities.

Symptoms

- Tartar buildup on the teeth, which is yellowish to brownish in color
- Bleeding gums

- Loss of appetite due to painful gums

Recommendations

- Increase vitamin C in the diet. While the dosage is variable, give 250 to 500 mg daily for small dogs and 500 to 2,000 mg for large dogs.
- Rinse the dog's mouth with small amount of a mixture of one-quarter hydrogen peroxide (from the drugstore) and three-quarters water once a day.

Urinary Tract Problems

The most frequent urinary tract problems seen in dogs are bladder stones, cystitis, and urinary leakage.

BLADDER STONES

Bladder stones can occur in both males and females, with symptoms often more exaggerated in males. The male anatomy is such that it's difficult for stones to pass through the urethra and out, so if a stone travels out of the bladder it can become lodged in the urethra. The dog will try to urinate frequently, passing urine in small spurts or not at all. There may be blood in the urine due to the stone rubbing the urethra. Usually surgery is required when bladder stones reach this stage. Occasionally homeopathics can help; however, if results are not forthcoming in one hour take the dog to the veterinarian immediately, because this is an emergency situation.

Large bladder stones cause a syndrome similar to cystitis or bladder infection, with frequent urination. Sometimes blood is found in the urine. These large stones can be removed surgically but often recur. There is a special diet designed to help prevent bladder stones, which is effective in some cases. I have found it helpful to add vitamin C to the diet to acidify the urine. Additional supplementation of vitamins A and B and magnesium can also help.

Symptoms

- Frequent urination of small amounts or no urination at all
- Blood in the urine

Recommendations

If your dog has the preceding symptoms:

- Give one or both of the following homeopathics:

  Note: After the first dose, watch the dog's condition closely. If he improves within one hour, continue watching him and give the additional doses. If he does not improve within one hour, an emergency visit to the veterinarian is imperative.

  —Cantharis 6C. Give three times daily.
  —Magnesia phosphorica 6C. Give three times daily or every 30 minutes if the dog is having difficulty urinating.

To prevent bladder stones:

- Give additional vitamin C. Dosage is variable but ranges from 250 to 500 mg daily for small dogs and 500 to 2,000 mg daily for large dogs.
- Be sure to feed a vitamin and mineral supplement so your dog gets sufficient vitamins A and B and the mineral magnesium.
- Give the homeopathic remedy cantharis 6C three times daily when you notice a tendency toward frequent urination.
- Herbal: Give Akebia 14 (Chinese herbal formula) from Animal Health Options (see Appendix, p. 327). Dosage should be ¼ to 1 tablet once a day for small dogs; 1 to 2 tablets once a day for large dogs.

CYSTITIS

Cystitis is an inflammation or infection of the bladder, which causes increased urination or straining without being able to urinate.

It is uncomfortable and often quite painful. If the episodes recur after treatment, suspect an underlying cause such as bladder stones. If your dog has these symptoms, you can try homeopathic and herbal remedies as outlined above under Bladder Stones. If there are no results within six to eight hours, consult your veterinarian immediately.

Symptoms

- Frequent urination or straining without being able to urinate
- Pain that can result in a dog crying out

Recommendations

Same as Bladder Stones above.

INAPPROPRIATE URINATION

Leakage of urine occurs in young dogs as well as old, males as well as females. This complaint is often heard with older spayed females. Young and old spayed females can suffer from lack of hormonal balance, usually due to estrogen deficiency. Males can have a testosterone deficiency or develop a gradual weakness of the muscle that controls the sphincter of the bladder. (This occasionally occurs with females as well.)

For females an estrogen supplement is usually prescribed for this problem. However, in a young female it is best to avoid supplementation with estrogen if possible, because other side effects can result. Homeopathics and acupuncture can stimulate the dog's system and help in the natural production of the hormone by the adrenal gland. If these other treatments do not work, estrogen can then be prescribed.

In older females it is also best to try to stimulate the hormone production and balance the body rather than prescribing estrogen. Then if estrogen supplementation is still necessary it can be used, but perhaps in lower amounts. If your dog is given estrogen, watch her carefully, because side effects such as simulated heat and low thyroid can result.

Males with hormonal deficiency can respond well to acupuncture, homeopathy, and supplementation. I advise using testosterone supplementation only as a last resort. If the problem is related to control of the sphincter, it is difficult to treat. However, there is an enzyme that your veterinarian can prescribe which may help.

(For incontinence problems related to aging, see p. 225.)

Symptoms

- Urinary incontinence

Recommendations

- Homeopathic remedies. The following can be used together:

  —Adrenal 6C. Give twice daily.
  —Thyroid 4C. Give twice daily.

- Feed a high-quality diet with the supplements recommended in chapter 6. A vitamin and mineral supplement is especially important.
- Glandular supplements in tablet form are helpful. Give adrenal, thyroid, and pituitary. The dosage varies with the size of the dog, but you can use the human dosage as a guideline.

Viruses

RABIES

Although uncommon in the United States, rabies occasionally increases in the wildlife population, thus infecting some pets who are exposed to the infected wildlife. Because it can be spread to humans, this disease is always of great concern.

There are two forms of rabies—the "furious" and "dumb" forms. The furious form refers to animals that are exhibiting the excitable phase often associated with aggressive, irrational behavior. These dogs are excited by noise and frequently eat objects like rocks and sticks. The furious form of rabies results in death in about 10 days.

The dumb or paralytic form of rabies causes paralysis of the throat and jaw. The dog cannot swallow and salivates profusely. The paralysis continues in the rest of the body, resulting in death in a few hours.

Just because there is a vaccine for rabies is no reason to become complacent about this dangerous disease. Do not approach any animal—either wild or domesticated—who is exhibiting unusual behavior. Remember that animals with rabies lose their fear, so a wild animal may suddenly seem very friendly or allow you to approach it. Often rabid wild animals wander out into roads or into housing subdivisions, exposing many people to rabies if they are handled. The most common carriers of rabies are foxes, skunks, raccoons, and bats. So exercise caution if you see any of these animals and keep your dog away from them.

DISTEMPER

A contagious airborne disease that once destroyed many dogs, distemper is now somewhat controlled by vaccination. It is a disease that seemed to become more prevalent in dogs as they were fed more commercial food and less raw, natural diets. An infected dog could have distemper for some time before it is diagnosed. During that time the dog can shed the virus, passing it to other dogs.

Distemper is often fatal, gradually progressing deeper into the dog's body. There are three basic stages: First, an elevated temperature occurs, lasting only a few days and often going unnoticed. Second, the eyes and nose have a thick discharge, and the eyes may be red and sensitive to light. The dog is usually depressed in this stage of the disease. Hyperkeratosis, or thickening of the foot pads and nose, commonly called hard pad, can develop. The dog will seem to recover from these symptoms, except for the hard pad. The third stage involves neurological signs, because the virus has entered the nervous system. Muscle twitching, paralysis, and seizures may occur. The length of each of these stages is variable; they can last from 10 days to several weeks.

For the best chance of recovery, treatment must be started in the early stages. Remember that it is contagious to other animals.

Symptoms

- See descriptions of the three stages of distemper above.

Recommendations

- Take the temperature. If it exceeds 102.5°F and the dog has the other symptoms, take immediately for a veterinary examination.
- Begin treatment with a fast:

1. Offer only water, vegetable broth, and honey water (1 teaspoon honey per cup of water) until the temperature has been normal for one day.
2. Gradually begin to feed solid food. Give goat milk with honey, thickened with cooked oatmeal or flaked barley.
3. Add protein back into the diet sparingly, starting with fish or poultry in small amounts.

- Homeopathic remedy: Give Pulsatilla 6C four times daily.
- Herbs:

—Skullcap tea: Put ¼ cup of skullcap into 1 cup of boiling water and brew like tea. Give 2 tablespoons of the strained and cooled tea three times daily. Give as a liquid medication; see page 201.
—Goldenseal: This herb can be purchased in a homeopathic form or given in capsule form. Goldenseal is indicated when there is mucus discharge from the nose and eyes. Do not give goldenseal for longer than two weeks at a time.
—Valerian: Give one capsule three times a day. (Or give a valerian/skullcap mixture.)

- Increase vitamin C supplementation throughout the illness. Give 250 to 500 mg daily for small dogs and 500 to 2,000 mg for large dogs.
- Give raw, crushed garlic: two cloves daily for small dogs or

four cloves for large dogs. Or give concentrated high-potency garlic in capsule, tablet, or liquid form (such as Kyolic).

PARVOVIRUS

This virus is more recent than the others; it was first discovered in 1978. It is theorized that parvovirus is closely related to the cat virus panleukopenia. Parvovirus is spread by ingestion of fecal material from infected animals. This virus is capable of surviving outside the dog for several years. Your dog may walk in the infected feces and later lick her paws, thereby becoming infected. There are several different strains of parvovirus that cause varying symptoms. Generally, however, the signs of parvovirus are diarrhea, vomiting, and refusal of food. The diarrhea may have streaks of blood and is usually watery. The temperature may be elevated, particularly during the early stages.

Another form of parvovirus affects puppies, though it is not commonly seen. This form results in a heart disease called myocarditis, which often causes sudden death.

Because it is so serious, vaccinations are necessary to prevent it. If your dog gets parvovirus, rapid treatment is required to replace the fluids that are lost from the vomiting and diarrhea. Aggressive veterinary treatment can often combat parvovirus, although it is sometimes fatal.

Symptoms

- Diarrhea, usually watery and sometimes with streaks of blood
- Vomiting
- Refusal of food
- Elevated temperature (particularly during early stages)

Recommendations

- If you suspect parvovirus, immediate veterinary care is imperative.

- Homeopathic remedy: Give Ipecacuanha 3C or 6C six times daily.
- Increase vitamin C supplementation. Best if given intravenously by the veterinarian.

Vomiting

When your dog is vomiting, you should keep track of how often he vomits and what the vomited matter consists of. Note if it contains fluid or food. If a trip to the veterinarian is necessary, this information will help in diagnosing the problem. There are many causes of vomiting, from a simple upset stomach to serious diseases. If the vomiting is due to gastritis or mild digestive upsets, it can be treated with homeopathy and herbs. However, if your dog does not respond to treatment and the vomiting continues, call your veterinarian. Do not delay, because a lot of liquid is lost when vomiting occurs and dehydration can result. (Also see "Gastritis," p. 269.)

Symptoms

- Vomiting of food, water, or foamy liquid

Recommendations

- Homeopathic remedies: Choose one of the following:

  —Nux vomica 6C. Give three to four times a day until vomiting has stopped.
  —Ipecacuanha 3C or 6C. Give once an hour until vomiting has stopped or three times a day. Use when vomitus is yellow in color and repetitive.

- Herbs: Make parsley tea from ½ cup of fresh minced parsley leaves and 1 cup of water. Boil softly for a few minutes. Strain and cool. Add 1 teaspoon honey per cup. Let the dog drink as much as he will from the cup of parsley tea or feed by the spoon. (See "Giving Liquid Medications" on page 201.)

Weight Problems

A dog who is overweight could be suffering from a metabolic disorder or an illness—or she might just be eating too much food and getting too little exercise. On the other hand, an underweight dog must be carefully monitored. If your dog is suddenly losing weight, a visit to the veterinarian is necessary, because any number of health problems could be causing rapid weight loss.

If your dog is overweight, you should carefully consider the ramifications of this extra weight. Excessive weight places a stress on the body; it makes the heart work harder, puts additional stress on the muscles, and makes the liver and kidneys work harder when they detoxify the blood. What can you do if your dog is overweight? Most dogs are overweight because of a problem with the daily regimen: What does her diet consist of? How much exercise is she getting? And—let's be honest—are frequent snacks a daily habit?

If your dog gained weight after her spay or his neuter, you can be reassured that this reaction to a spay or neuter often responds to treatment. Do not despair. Refer to chapter 7 for further guidance. Although most weight problems are due to these controllable factors, sometimes a weight gain is due to a disease that is influencing the dog's metabolism. If your dog has gradually picked up a few pounds and she has consistently gotten the same amount of exercise, ask your veterinarian to do some laboratory work to make sure everything is okay. The thyroid should definitely be checked. (Also see "Hypothyroidism," p. 280.)

A dog who just eats too much or is an "easy keeper" who is fed very little and still gains weight is one whose weight needs to be carefully managed. If your dog is not on a healthy, digestible diet, review chapter 6. When a dog is very obese I suggest the homemade Reducing Diet on page 118 or a senior or older dog diet from a natural pet manufacturer. These diets contain few calories and a better balance of nutrients than most commercial diet dog foods.

When starting your dog on the new diet, weigh the dog so you can keep track of her progress. Weigh her every few days and write it down. Begin by decreasing the amount you feed by one-quarter. Gradually reduce the amount to one-half of the normal ration. One of my own dogs, Kelly, gained a lot of weight when I got another dog to live with her. She ate her dinner and part of his, so I had to change the eating arrangements and decrease her food. In Kelly's case she was such an easy keeper that I ended up feeding her one-quarter of the amount she was normally fed. Do not allow your dog to lose weight too quickly. About one-quarter to one-half pound every week is okay. Too fast a weight loss can be harmful to the liver, so it's best to have controlled, slow weight loss.

Exercise is an important factor in weight loss. Be sure your dog gets at least an hour of walking every day if there is a weight problem. Many dogs enjoy playing ball or jogging, so you may be able to include your dog in your own exercise program. Start the exercise slowly because your dog may not be accustomed to a lot of exercise. Do not overdo it; dogs can get sore muscles and suffer from exhaustion just like humans.

Whipworms

(see Parasites)

Worms

(see Parasites; for Ringworm see Fungal Disease)

Appendix

Product Suppliers

PLEASE NOTE: At the time of this writing, the companies listed supply one or more products that are acceptable within the guidelines of this book. This does not necessarily mean that the authors recommend *all* products made by or sold by these companies.

Product quality can change from year to year; companies can change management or policies or standards. We urge you to keep this in mind, to be continuously alert, and to *read labels* and product brochures carefully, even for products you have been using for a long time.

There may be other fine suppliers or new companies not listed here. Our not listing certain suppliers does not necessarily mean that we wouldn't recommend them if we knew about them.

Mail-Order Catalogs for Natural Products

Jerry Teplitz Enterprises, Inc., 219 53rd Street, Virginia Beach, VA 23451. Phone 800-77-RELAX. Carries books, tapes, and music on stress reduction.

L & H Vitamins, 37–10 Crescent Street, Long Island City, NY 11101. Phone 800-221-1152. Carries natural pet supplements, vitamins, herbs, homeopathics, and Bach flower remedies at discounted prices.

Morrill's New Directions, P.O. Box 30, Orient, ME 04471. Phone 800-368-5057; in Maine, call 800-649-0744. Carries a number of products we recommend. Free catalog available on request.

The Natural Pet Care Company, 8050 Lake City Way, N.E., Seattle, WA 98115. Phone 800-962-8266 or 206-329-1417; fax 206-524-0191. Carries several brands of pet foods we recommend as well as numerous other health-care products. Free catalog available on request.

The Vitamin Shoppe, 4700 Westside Avenue, North Bergen, NJ 07047. Phone 800-223-1216. Carries natural vitamins, herbs, homeopathics, and Bach flower remedies at discounted prices.

Suppliers of Natural Dog Foods

Nature's Recipe, 341 Bonnie Circle, Corona, CA 91720. Phone 800-843-4008.

PetGuard, Inc., P.O. Box 728, Orange Park, FL 32073. Phone 800-874-3221. (In Florida, call 904-264-8500.)

Precise Pet Products, P.O. Box 630009, Nacogdoches, TX 75963. Phone 800-446-7148.

Wysong Medical Corporation, 1880 N. Eastman, Midland, MI 48640. Phone 517-631-0009.

Suppliers of Nutritional Supplements and Other Dog Care Products

All the Best, 2713 E. Madison Street, Seattle, WA 98112. Phone 800-962-8266. Manufacturers of Enzymes Plus (enzyme supplement).

Animal Health Options, Inc., 1724 Yardley-Langhorne Road, Yardley, PA 19067. Phone 215-493-2343. Manufacturers of Chinese herbal food supplements.

Anitra's Natural Pet Products, Ltd., Halo, Purely for Pets, 3438 East Lake Road, Suite 14, Palm Harbor, FL 34685. Phone 800-426-4256 or 813-787-4256. Manufacturers of Anitra's Vita-Mineral Mix (food supplement for dogs and cats).

Aubrey Organics, 4419 N. Manhattan Avenue, Tampa, FL 33614. Phone

813-876-4879. Manufacturers of shampoos, conditioner, grooming spray for pets.

Avena Botanicals, P.O. Box 365, West Rockport, ME 04865. Phone 207-594-0694. Manufacturers of Herbal Animal Supplement, Heal-All Salve (herbal salve), and other natural products.

Bio/Chem Research, Lakeport, CA. Phone 707-263-1475. Makers of Citricidal brand of products for disinfection and control of intestinal parasites.

Bioguard for Pets and *Bioguard Plus for Pets,* Biogenetics Food Corporation, 3427 Exchange Avenue, Suite 8, Naples, FL 33942. Phone 800-477-7688. Manufacturers of antioxidant supplements for pets and Vitality, a chewable nutritional treat which contains antioxidant supplements.

Derma Pet, P.O. Box 59713, Potomac, MD 20859. Phone 800-755-4738. Manufacturers of Derma Pet Conditioner for Pets (a spray-on product) and Derma Pet Conditioning Shampoo for Pets.

Dr. Don's Formulas, Ardea Enterprises, Inc., P.O. Box 1426, Snohomish, WA 98290. Phone 206-838-3878. Manufacturers of homeopathic products: Stop Fleas, Stop Stress, Stop Arthritis.

Fleabusters, Inc., 6555 N.W. Ninth Avenue, #411, Ft. Lauderdale, FL 33309. Phone 800-666-3532. This company will come to your home and treat it with a nonpesticide flea product.

Halo, Purely for Pets, 3438 East Lake Road, Suite 14, Palm Harbor, FL 34685. Phone 800-426-4256 or 813-787-4256 (HALO). Manufacturer of Dream Coat (oil supplement for pets), Natural Herbal Ear Wash, and other natural pet care products.

Kelp Products International, 150 Connie Crescent, Unit 4, Concord, Ontario, Canada L4K 1L9. Phone 800-237-5357. Manufacturers of Kelp Mate (nutritional supplement for pets).

Kyolic Garlic, Wakunaga of America Company, Ltd., 23501 Madero, Mission Viejo, CA 92691. Phone 714-855-2776; (in USA) 800-421-2998; (in California) 800-544-5800. Manufacturers of high-potency garlic in capsule, tablet, and liquid form.

Lip Smackers, Inc., P.O. Box 5385, Culver City, CA 90231-5385. Phone 310-641-0578. Manufacturers of Lip Smackers (natural dog biscuits) and Saucy Dog (appetite enhancer). Also publishers of *The No Barking at the Table Cookbook.*

Love Your Pets, 15443 S. Latourette Rd., Oregon City, OR 97045. Phone

800-258-8589 or 503-631-7389. Manufacturer of Love Your Pet Calmer and other health supplements.

Mr. Cristal's, Inc., 1100 Glendon Avenue, Suite 1250, Los Angeles, CA 90024. Phone 800-426-0108. Manufacturers of Mr. Christal's Luxury Shampoo for Dogs.

Natural Animal, Echo Safe Products, P.O. Box 1177, St. Augustine, FL 32085. Phone 800-274-7387. Manufacturers of Natural Animal Coat Enhancer, Ester C (vitamin C supplement for dogs), and other natural pet care products.

Nature's Recipe (see address & phone listed in foods section). Manufacturers of Enzyme Added Formula (trace minerals and enzyme supplement for pets) and Trace Minerals.

N.E.S.S. (Nutritional Enzyme Support Systems), P.O. Box 249, Forsyth, MO 65653. Phone 800-637-7893. Manufacturers of Vet-Zimes (digestive enzymes for pets).

Norfields, 632¾ N. Doheny Drive, Los Angeles, CA 90069. Phone 800-344-8400. Manufacturers of health care magnetic products.

PetGuard, Inc. (see address & phone listed in foods section). Manufacturers of PetGuard Shampoo and Conditioner and other natural pet products.

Probiotics, 55 S. Main, Suite 122, Cottonwood, AZ 86326. Phone 800-741-4137. Manufacturers of Flora Source (acidophilus supplement).

Pro-Tec Pet Health, P.O. Box 23676, Pleasant Hill, CA 94523. Phone 510-676-9600 or 800-44-FLEAS. Manufacturers of Body Guard (nutritional supplement), Vita Guard (amino acid supplement), Coat Guard (natural shampoo), Derma Guard (spray-on topical lotion for hot spots), and other natural pet products.

St. John Pet Care Products, 1656 W. 240th Street, Harbor City, CA 90710. Phone 800-969-7387. Manufacturers of Petrodex Dental Kit for Dogs.

Michelle Tilghman, D.V.M., Loving Touch Animal Center, 5398 E. Mountain Street, Stone Mountain, GA 30083. Phone 404-498-5956. Manufacturer of Homeopathic Animal First Aid Kit.

Williams Industries, P.O. Box 7203, Rocky Mount, NC 27804. Phone 919-442-3160. In Canada, contact Phero Tech, 7572 Progress Way, Delta, B.C. V4G 1E9. Phone 604-940-9944. Manufacturers of Williams Flea Trap.

Wysong Medical Corporation (see address & phone listed in foods section). Manufacturers of natural pet care products.

Zand Professional Formulas, P.O. Box 5312, Santa Monica, CA 90409. Phone 310-822-0500. Manufacturers of herbal formulas for pets and people.

Suppliers of Bach Flower Remedies

Ellon Bach, U.S.A., P.O. Box 320, Woodmere, NY 11598. Phone 800-433-7523. (In NY call 516-593-2206.) Suppliers of Bach flower remedies and books on the subject. (Also see L & H Vitamins on page 326.)

Suppliers of Homeopathic Remedies

Boericke & Tafel, Inc., 2381 Circadian Way, Santa Rosa, CA 95407. Phone 707-571-8202.

Boiron-Borneman, 1208 Amosland Road, Norwood, PA 19074. Phone 800-258-8823.

Dolisos America, 3014 Rigel Avenue, Las Vegas, NV 89102. Phone 702-871-7153.

Longevity Pure Medicine, 9595 Wilshire Blvd., Suite 706, Beverly Hills, CA 90212. Phone 213-273-7423.

Nu Age Laboratories, 4200 Laclede Avenue, St. Louis, MO 63108. Phone 314-533-9600.

Standard Homeopathic, P.O. Box 61067, Los Angeles, CA 90061. Phone 213-321-4284.

Suggested Reading

The books recommended here specifically address the topics raised in this book. With one or two exceptions, books on breeds, grooming, or training are not listed, although there are many good books available on those subjects. I suggest that you scout the pet store for books that will help you get to know your dog better—or help you select the dog that's right for you.

Animal Communication & Dog Training

The Chosen Puppy: How to Select and Raise a Great Puppy from an Animal Shelter by Carol Lea Benjamin, 1990, Howell Book House.

Dog Training My Way by Barbara Woodhouse, 1970, Stein and Day.

Kinship With All Life by J. Allen Boone, 1954, 1976, Harper & Row.

No Bad Dogs: The Woodhouse Way by Barbara Woodhouse, 1978, Summit Books.

Stories Animals Tell Me by Beatrice Lydecker, 1988, Harper & Row.

What the Animals Tell Me by Beatrice Lydecker, 1979, Harper & Row.

Holistic Pet Care

Dr. Pitcairn's Complete Guide to Natural Health for Dogs and Cats by Richard H. Pitcairn, D.V.M., Ph.D., and Susan Hubble Pitcairn, 1982, Rodale Press.

It's a Cat's Life by Anitra Frazier with Norma Eckroate, revised edition, 1990, Berkley Books.

Keep Your Pet Healthy the Natural Way by Pat Lazarus, 1983, Bobbs-Merrill.

The New Natural Cat: A Complete Guide for Finicky Owners by Anitra Frazier with Norma Eckroate, revised edition, 1990, Plume/NAL Books.

The No Barking at the Table Cookbook by Wendy Boyd-Smith, 1991, Lip Smackers.

Pet Allergies: Remedies for an Epidemic by Alfred J. Plechner, D.V.M., and Martin Zucker, 1986, J.P. Enterprises.

The Tellington T-Touch: A Breakthrough Technique to Train and Care for Your Favorite Animal by Linda Tellington-Jones with Sybil Taylor, 1992, Viking Penguin.

Dog Breeds and Breeding Practices

Harper's Illustrated Handbook of Dogs, Robert W. Kirk, D.V.M., and Roger Caras, 1985, Harper & Row.

The Puppy Report: How Reckless Breeding Threatens to Ruin Pure-Bred Dogs by Larry Shook, 1992, Lyons & Burford.

Holistic Health and Natural Living

Alternatives in Healing by Simon Mills, M.S., and Steven J. Finando, Ph.D., 1988, Plume/NAL books.

Alternatives for the Health Conscious Individual (newsletter), Mountain Home Publishing, P.O. Box 829, Ingram, TX 78025; phone 512-367-4492.

A Cancer Battle Plan by Anne E. Frähm with David J. Frähm, 1992, Pinion Press.

Common-Sense Pest Control: Least Toxic Solutions for Your Home, Garden, Pets, and Community by William Olkowski, Ph.D., Sheila Daar, and Helga Olkowski, 1991, Taunton Press.

Health and Healing by Andrew Weil, M.D., 1983, 1988, Houghton Mifflin.

How to Heal the Earth in Your Spare Time by Andy Lopez, published by The Invisible Gardener, 29169 Heathercliff Road, Suite 216-408, Malibu, CA 90265; phone 302-457-6658.

Natural Health, Natural Medicine by Andrew Weil, M.D., 1990, Houghton Mifflin.

Nontoxic, Natural and Earthwise by Debra Lynn Dadd, 1990, Jeremy P. Tarcher.

Perfect Health: The Complete Mind/Body Guide by Deepak Chopra, M.D., 1991, Harmony Books.

Prescription for Nutritional Healing by James F. Balch, M.D., and Phyllis A. Balch, C.N.C., 1990, Avery Publishing Group.

A Quick Guide to Food Additives by Robert Goodman, 1981, 1990, Silvercat Publications.

Vibrational Healing by Richard Gerber, M.D., 1988, Bear & Co.

Your Body Doesn't Lie by John Diamond, M.D., 1980, Warner Books (also published under the title *BK: Behavioral Kinesiology*, 1979, Harper & Row).

Antioxidants, Enzymes, and Oxygen Therapy

Echo, Inc. (Educational Concern for Hydrogen Peroxide) (newsletter), P.O. Box 126, Delano, MN 55328.

Enzyme Nutrition: The Food Enzyme Concept by Dr. Edward Howell, 1985, Avery Publishing Group.

The Family News (quarterly newsletter on Oxygen Therapies), 9845

N.E. Second Avenue, Miami Shores, FL 33138; phone 800-284-6263.

Food Enzymes: The Missing Link to Radiant Health by Humbart Santillo, B.S., M.H., 1987, Hohm Press.

Free Radicals, Stress and Antioxidant Enzymes—A Guide to Cellular Health by Peter R. Rothschild, M.D., Ph.D., and William J. Fahey, 1991, University Labs Press, Honolulu, HI (booklet).

Bach Flower Remedies, Herbs, and Homeopathy

Bach Flower Remedies by Edward Bach, M.D., and F. J. Wheeler, M.D., 1952, 1979, Keats Publishing.

Bach Flower Therapy: Theory and Practice by Mechthild Scheffer, 1981, 1984, Thorsons Publishers.

The Complete Herbal Handbook for the Dog and Cat by Juliette deBairacli-Levy, sixth edition, 1991, Faber and Faber.

Discovering Homeopathy: Medicine for the 21st Century by Dana Ullman, M.P.H., 1991, North Atlantic Books.

Everybody's Guide to Homeopathic Medicines by Stephen Cummings, M.D., and Dana Ullman, M.P.H., 1991, Jeremy P. Tarcher.

The Herb Book by John Lust, 1974, Bantam Books.

Herbal Handbook for Farm and Stable by Juliette deBairacli-Levy, 1976, Rodale Press.

The Homeopathic Treatment of Dogs by G. Macleod, 1983, The C. W. Daniel Company, Ltd., England.

Rodale's Illustrated Encyclopedia of Herbs, by Claire Kowalchik and William H. Hylton, Editors, 1987, Rodale Press.

Legal Issues

Dog Law by Mary Randolph, 1988, Nolo Press. Phone 800-445-6656 or 415-549-1976.

Dealing with Death and Dying

Death: The Final Stage of Growth by Elisabeth Kübler-Ross, 1976, Prentice-Hall.

The Fall of Freddie the Leaf by Leo Buscaglia, 1982, Slack Incorporated.

On Death and Dying by Elisabeth Kübler-Ross, 1969, Macmillan.

Associations and Organizations

Holistic Veterinary

American Holistic Veterinary Medical Association, 2214 Old Emmorton Road, Bel Air, MD 21015. Phone 410-569-0795; fax 410-515-7774. Professional organization that serves as a forum to explore alternative veterinary health care. Publishes a quarterly journal for members. Send self-addressed stamped envelope for list of holistic veterinarians in your area.

International Veterinary Acupuncture Society, 2140 Conestoga Road, Chester Springs, PA 19425. Phone 215-827-7245. Professional organization fosters research on acupuncture in veterinary medicine. Call or write for information and lists of veterinary acupuncturists in the United States and other countries.

National Center for Homeopathy, 801 N. Fairfax, #306, Alexandria, VA 22314. Phone 703-548-7790. Directory of homeopaths, including veterinarians. Offers a catalog of books and annual courses.

Environmental and Holistic Health Organizations

Bio-Integral Resource Center, P.O. Box 7414, Berkeley, CA 94707. Phone 510-524-2567. A nonprofit organization that researches and promotes information on the least toxic methods of pest management.

International Bio-Oxidative Medicine Foundation, P.O. Box 619767, Dallas/Ft. Worth, TX 75261. Phone 817-481-9772. Promotes the use of intravenous hydrogen peroxide infusion.

Price-Pottenger Nutrition Foundation, P.O. Box 2614, La Mesa, CA 91943-2614. Phone 619-582-4168. Educational organization dedicated to promotion of enhanced health. Call or write for catalog of books, pamphlets, and tapes.

INDEX

INDEX

B

INDEX

INDEX

INDEX

INDEX

I

J

K

Q

R

V

W